Theology After
Christendom

AFTER CHRISTENDOM *Series*

Christendom was a historical era, a geographical region, a political arrangement, a sacral culture, and an ideology. For many centuries Europeans have lived in a society that was nominally Christian. Church and state have been the pillars of a remarkable civilization that can be traced back to the decision of the emperor Constantine I early in the fourth century to replace paganism with Christianity as the imperial religion.

Christendom, a brilliant but brutal culture, flourished in the Middle Ages, fragmented in the Reformation of the sixteenth century, but persisted despite the onslaught of modernity. While exporting its values and practices to other parts of the world, however, it has been slowly declining during the past three centuries. In the twenty-first century Christendom is unravelling.

What will emerge from the demise of Christendom is not yet clear, but we can now describe much of Western culture as "post-Christendom." *Post-Christendom is the culture that emerges as the Christian faith loses coherence within a society that has been definitively shaped by the Christian story and as the institutions that have been developed to express Christian convictions decline in influence.*

This definition, proposed and unpacked in *Post-Christendom*, the first book in the After Christendom series, has gained widespread acceptance. *Post-Christendom* investigated the Christendom legacy and raised numerous issues that are explored in the rest of the series. The authors of this series, who write from within the Anabaptist tradition, see the current challenges facing the church not as the loss of a golden age but as opportunities to recover a more biblical and more Christian way of being God's people in God's world.

The series addresses a wide range of issues, including theology, social and political engagement, how we read Scripture, youth work, mission, worship, relationships, and the shape and ethos of the church after Christendom.

Eleven books were published by Paternoster between 2004 and 2016:

Stuart Murray, *Post-Christendom*

Stuart Murray, *Church after Christendom*

Jonathan Bartley, *Faith and Politics after Christendom*

Jo Pimlott and Nigel Pimlott, *Youth Work after Christendom*

Alan Kreider and Eleanor Kreider, *Worship and Mission after Christendom*

Lloyd Pietersen, *Reading the Bible after Christendom*

Andrew Francis, *Hospitality and Community after Christendom*

Fran Porter, *Women and Men after Christendom*

Simon Perry, *Atheism after Christendom*

Brian Haymes and Kyle Gingerich Hiebert, *God after Christendom*

Jeremy Thomson, *Relationships and Emotions after Christendom*

Two of these (*Worship and Mission after Christendom* and *Reading the Bible after Christendom*) were also published by Herald Press.

The series is now in the hands of Wipf and Stock, who are republishing some of the existing titles, including *Post-Christendom*, and commissioning further titles, including:

Joshua Searle, *Theology after Christendom*

Andy Hardy and Dan Yarnell, *Missional Discipleship after Christendom*

John Heathershaw, *Security after Christendom*

Jeremy Thomson, *Interpreting the Old Testament after Christendom*

These books are not intended to be the last word on the subjects they address, but an invitation to discussion and further exploration. Additional material, including extracts from published books and information about future volumes, can be found at www.anabaptistnetwork.com/AfterChristendom.

Stuart Murray

Theology After Christendom

Forming Prophets
for a Post-Christian World

Joshua T. Searle

FOREWORD BY
Rev. Canon Steve Chalke MBE

CASCADE *Books* · Eugene, Oregon

THEOLOGY AFTER CHRISTENDOM
Forming Prophets for a Post-Christian World

After Christendom Series

Cascade Books
An Imprint of Wipf and Stock Publishers
199 W. 8th Ave., Suite 3
Eugene, OR 97401

www.wipfandstock.com

PAPERBACK ISBN: 978-1-5326-1730-0
HARDCOVER ISBN: 978-1-4982-4195-3
EBOOK ISBN: 978-1-4982-4194-6

Cataloguing-in-Publication data:

Names: Searle, Joshua T. | Chalke, Steve, foreword writer
Title: Theology after Christendom : forming prophets for a post-Christendom world / Joshua T. Searle.
Description: Eugene, OR: Cascade Books, 2018 | Series: After Christendom | Includes bibliographical references.
Identifiers: ISBN 978-1-5326-1730-0 (paperback) | ISBN 978-1-4982-4195-3 (hardcover) | ISBN 978-1-4982-4194-6 (ebook)
Subjects: LCSH: Theology | Discipling (Christianity) | Mission of the church | Spiritual formation
Classification: BT65 S437 2018 (print) | BT65 (ebook)

Manufactured in the U.S.A.   FEBRUARY 6, 2018

DEDICATION

To the memory of

Nathan John (1992–2014)
Minister-in-Training at Spurgeon's College, 2013–2014

"He will wipe away every tear from their eyes, and death shall be no more, neither shall there be mourning, nor crying, nor pain anymore"

and

Tom Pelham (1981–2017)
Minister-in-Training at Spurgeon's College, 2008–2011

"Well done, you good and faithful servant . . . enter into the joy of your Lord"

"The human race in the course of time has taken the liberty of softening and softening Christianity until at last we have contrived to make it exactly the opposite of what it is in the New Testament."[1]

SØREN A. KIERKEGAARD (1813–1855)

1. Kierkegaard, *Attack upon Christendom*, 39.

Contents

Foreword

Rev. Canon Steve Chalke MBE

I am not an academic theologian. I have spent my life as a local church pastor. And, since my late twenties, I have also served as the founder and leader of a Christian charity which now works to provide housing, education, healthcare, and various other community initiatives both in the UK and in various other countries around the world. In other words, I spend my time in the ongoing challenge—sometimes the exhausting struggle—of hammering out with friends, critics, and colleagues what it means to do good, Christ-centered theology in ever-changing and diverse social settings.

My job requires the use of a variety of professional disciplines from pastoral empathy at an individual level to mass public communication skills; from team management to strategic and structural planning; from financial analysis and inter-agency negotiation to good governance and succession planning. It is vital, however, that each of these is underpinned by biblical, culturally engaged, and grounded theology. Such theology is not just another tool in the tool bag for successful Christian leadership. Rather, it is the lens through which all else must be viewed; the foundation on which the whole house must be built if it is to stand.

Some years ago, I was asked to become a contributor to a weekly political commentary for one of the UK's national broadsheet newspapers. I was duly appointed as their "Diary Vicar." I remember the day, a year or so on, when the editor—who, by then, I had gotten to know well—rang to ask my opinion about a visit he had made the night before to a very well-known evangelical church in central London.

"It was extraordinary," he commented. He then explained how the meeting began when the well-known leader appeared on stage and welcomed the audience. "He led a prayer and assured us that God was with us, before a band launched into a long selection of very happy and excited songs about how much God loved us all." "But then, just as the leader headed back onto the stage to announce the next component of the evening, a middle-class man in one of the front rows suddenly stood up and shouted, "I am the Lord your God. And you, my children, are like trees planted by a river; you will grow strong and thrive for your roots are secure and well-watered." My editor friend joked about God's physical presence and appearance being a bit of a shock to him. "But, that's not really the point," he continued. "It's what happened next that confused me."

He went on to explain that as the well-spoken gentleman finished speaking, but before the church leader could intervene, another member of the audience, this time a woman, popped up at the back of the hall and in a booming voice exploded, "My children, my children, I am your God. You are like eagles, my chosen ones. Celebrate, rise up, fly, soar, and excel." And that was just the start, he said. From then on, throughout the evening, "God just kept addressing that group of gathered followers, through the medium of various audience members, so intent was he to reassure them of their divine acceptance. Your God really wanted them to get his message, loud and clear."

I began to wonder where all this was going. I knew well just how incisive my friend's thinking was and that there was bound to be both a point and question for me at its end. I also knew that any comment I made would end up in print even if that comment was "no comment."

"So what's your point?" I asked, aware that the story even thus far had raised numerous difficult issues. "It's simply this," he replied without hesitation. "After the meeting ended I travelled home. I left the building and headed to the tube station. As I did, I passed a homeless man begging for food. I listened for God, who had been so vocal just a few minutes before, but I heard nothing. As I boarded the train, two young girls sat opposite to me, on their way to a nightclub, already drunk, provocatively dressed and, from their conversation, looking for love which they had mistaken for sex. I listened for God, but I heard nothing. In the far corner of the carriage sat a very poorly dressed old woman, with a face lined by pain, poverty and loneliness. I listened for God, but I heard nothing. Completing my journey, as I walked to my flat, on the corner stood a group of hooded young men, oozing menace and the smell of Marijuana, though actually huddled together in a shared despair of the future. I listened for God, but I heard nothing."

"So, the question is this. Why is it that your God can't seem to stop talking in private, yet has lost his voice in public? Why has he gone silent on the streets? Why has he so much to say behind shut doors to his chosen flock, but so little to bring to the complexity of civil society's conversation about community? When did your God lose his confidence?"

Where have all the prophets gone? How do we form prophets for a post-Christian world? How do we develop Christ-centered prophetic communities in a multi-faith, multi-ethnic globalized society? How do we construct healthy theology after Christendom?

I am convinced that the questions Joshua Searle raises in this book are the ones that we must address in response to these issues. The conversation that he seeks to spark is not only long overdue, but one that we now must engage in together, nationally and globally, in the lecture theatres and senior common rooms of our theology departments as well as in the leadership teams and home groups of our churches. To do anything less is to neglect our responsibility. For, whether we consider ourselves to be based within the academy or the local church, it is only this urgent, joined-up conversation that will equip us for the momentous task and the astonishing opportunity of the road ahead.

Rev. Canon Steve Chalke MBE
Founder and Leader of Oasis Global

Preface

What does theology have to say to the "crucified people"[1] who represent the suffering of Christ in the world today? What does theology mean to "the wretched of the earth"[2], to those "non-persons"[3] without status, wealth, or power? How does theology connect with the lived experience of the "poor in spirit" (Matt 5:3), of those who are "sat upon, spat upon, ratted on"?[4] How does theology speak into the plight of the starving, the refugee, the Alzheimer's patient, the cancer sufferer, or the traumatized child caught up in a genocide? What does theology have to say to the homeless people on the streets of our cities who die in solitude, unknown and unpitied without anyone even to mourn their loss?

This book is the product of a long-term endeavor to discover a vision for the renewal of theology that can address these questions and speak prophetically into these situations. The main aim is to envision a rejuvenated theology that can stimulate the emergence of a renewed Christianity in a post-Christian age. My key contention is that theology has a role akin to that of a midwife[5] bringing to birth a dynamic Christianity that is attuned to the signs of the times and orientated towards the Kingdom of God. This emerging theology will put compassion, creativity and freedom at the heart of Christian life and will be more concerned with the transfiguration of the world than with the revival of the church. My upbringing, temperament, and training have instilled in me the conviction that theology must engage with the basic questions of life in the world in order to elucidate and, if possible, to overcome the urgent problems of concrete existence. The emer-

1. This term is taken from Ellacuría, "Crucified People," 580–603.

2. Gutierrez, *Power of the Poor,* 186.

3. Ibid., 57.

4. These words are taken from Simon and Garfunkel's song, "Blessed" (1966), quoted in Willard, *Divine Conspiracy,* 111.

5. This metaphor recalls Socrates's depiction of the philosopher as a midwife, guiding the soul as it gives birth to true knowledge. See Plato, *Theaetetus,* 148e7–151d7.

gence of post-Christendom offers an auspicious occasion to reflect on these problems and to navigate a new course for theology.

In the present "Secular Age"[6] a deep crisis has engulfed theology. I have a presentiment that the judgement of God is upon Christian theology. The stifling rationalism of systematic theology and the dubious endeavor to establish Christian doctrine on a dogmatic foundation have enfeebled Christian witness and enervated the spiritual vitality of theological reflection. Theology has been marginalized or ignored altogether, as theologians have been slow to grasp the magnitude of unprecedented developments in biotechnology, the emergence and expansion of international terrorism and the so-called "clash of civilizations,"[7] the rise of religious fundamentalism, the appearance of lethal and incurable diseases, a major global financial crisis and a sudden resurgence of fascism and nationalism throughout the world.[8]

The term "Christendom" describes "a social order in which, regardless of individual belief, Christian language, rites, moral teachings, and personnel were part of the taken-for-granted environment."[9] The signs of the times indicate that this social order is fading as society transitions into a new era of post-Christendom. The terminology of post-Christendom is finding resonance among a growing number of theologians and Christian leaders.[10] Post-Christendom can be understood as an emerging cultural and spiritual condition. The world is on the brink of a radical, revolutionary change. The consequences of these changes for Christian faith in the world are, as yet, unknowable. What is clear is that spiritual values are disintegrating under the constant assault of powerful dehumanizing forces in today's society. In this new authoritarian age, a new world is coming into being – a world that is moved not by the Christian values of love, compassion and solidarity, but by power, by the racial politics of blood and soil, and the demonic power of collective national identity and the media-fabricated "will of the people."

---

6. This term is expounded at length in Taylor's significant work, *Secular Age*.

7. Huntington, *Clash of Civilizations*.

8. Searle, Joshua, "Future of Millennial Studies and the Hermeneutics of Hope," 132.

9. McLeod, *Religious Crisis of the 1960s*, 265.

10. Notable contributions have been made to the post-Christendom debate and the validity of its application to the contemporary world. It does not fall within the scope of this book to consider these contributions in detail, particularly concerning the different manifestations of post-Christendom in Europe and North America and further variations within these regions. Readers wishing to understand the post-Christendom phenomenon in detail should first consult Murray, *Post-Christendom*. Other important contributions with a more American focus include: Hauerwas, *After Christendom*; Carter, *Rethinking Christ and Culture*; Bolger, *Gospel after Christendom*.

All these and an innumerable host of other contemporary phenomena indicate that, in the words of one prominent commentator, "humanity is approaching a zero-point of radical transmutation."[11] The world is living through a dangerous era of dehumanization and God-forsakenness. Human dignity is degraded in a consumer society in which "relations between people assume the guise of relations among things."[12] The present "moral apocalypse"[13] is expressed in the increasing mechanization and digitization of life through the technological revolution and the renunciation of spiritual values. The world in this new age is dominated by information and communication.[14] The global telecommunications revolution and the powerful forces of globalization and the mechanization and exploitation of the natural world have brought humanity to the edge of an apocalyptic precipice. According to Jürgen Moltmann, the social and ecological convulsions in our age betoken "nothing less than a crisis in human beings themselves. It is a crisis of life on this planet, a crisis so comprehensive and irreversible that it can justly be described as "apocalyptic."[15]

Critical questions must be asked about why theology seems to have contributed so little towards the elucidation and resolution of the spiritual crisis of our times. This crisis has engendered a passionate thirst for deep and authentic spiritual life. This spiritual thirst follows a long period of relentless exposure in the parched desert of secular materialism, which has left the world virtually bereft of spiritual values of love, truth, and freedom. We are now living in a time of creative forces, in which foundations are being shaken, old certainties are disintegrating and new solutions to the great issues of our times are being sought. The world is being convulsed by elemental powers, the heavens are being shaken, and people's hearts are failing them for fear of what is coming to the world. The world is passing through a painful period of "ontological insecurity."[16] "Everything solid evaporates, all things sacred are desecrated"[17] and the beleaguered people of the earth are reduced to "the semblance of broken puppets"[18] or of "bits of paper, whirled by the cold wind."[19]

---

11. Žižek, *Living in the End Times*, 336.

12. Marx, quoted in Žižek, *Less Than Nothing*, 1004.

13. Žižek, *Living in the End Times*, 322.

14. Boff, *Global Civilization*, 43.

15. Moltmann, *God in Creation*, xiii.

16. Laing, *Divided Self*, 40.

17. Marx and Engels, *Manifest der Kommunistischen Partei*, 23.

18. Berdyaev, *Self-Knowledge*, 170.

19. Eliot, "Burnt Norton," 174.

The signs of the times betoken a crisis of compassion and the commencement of a new faithless age in which people have lost reliable criteria for distinguishing between love and hate, freedom and slavery, and truth and falsehood. Christians must now face up fearlessly to the challenges of living in a "post-truth" age in which deceitful politicians present their media-spun fabrications as "alternative facts." The followers of Christ must be prepared morally and intellectually for an enduring spiritual struggle in defense of gospel values. Any attempt to evade these challenges by clinging to sugary optimistic dreams about imminent revival amounts to a hypocritical collusion in the decline and degradation of the world. This book is an attempt to enact a transformative theology for these changing times that will equip, empower and encourage the global Christian community to take a stand for the gospel in an age of cultural decline and despair. The overriding aim is to envision theology in terms of prophetic redress of urgent and pressing issues in the world today.[20]

If it appears that Christianity is passing through its twilight period and entering the darkness of night, it should be remembered, in the words of Berdyaev, that "the night is no less resplendent than the day, no less divine. The night is illuminated by the stars and brings to light that which is invisible during the day."[21] Accordingly, amid these crises a new movement of the Holy Spirit can be discerned. This movement defies the dehumanizing tendencies in contemporary society. It aims for the rediscovery of the true meaning of Christianity in terms of the creation of a global community of solidarity. This community radiates the gospel values of kindness, compassion, truth, solidarity and justice. Within this global Christian community, the gospel is emerging as a transformative and world-shattering message of the good news concerning the resurrection of Jesus Christ.

In these times of transition from Christendom to post-Christendom, the gospel can become a powerful "historical force for the humanization of the world."[22] This gospel message, purified from deadening legalism and degrading notions of substitutionary propitiation for divine wrath, has a new basis not in judgement and retribution, but in divine-human creativity, compassion and the indestructible power of resurrection life. The gospel is a message not only of individual salvation, but of the transfiguration of the world in the power of the resurrection.

The cultural tide has now turned and the church, unfortunately, has found itself stranded on a sandbank of social and political irrelevance.

---

20. Berdyaev, *Istoki i Smysl*, 222.

21. Berdyaev, *Smysl Tvorchestva*, 545.

22. Boff, *Church*, 19.

"Institutional sclerosis" has set in, leading to a lack of vigor in the church's witness to the gospel.[23] The church is losing its prophetic spirit. Many of the inert and moribund churches of Christendom are incapable of alleviating the spiritual thirst of the world in this new religious age. The churches of Christendom, enthralled by the snares of wealth, power and social status, cannot answer the spiritual longings for authentic Christian consciousness. The value of the post-Christendom shift consists in the opportunities it creates for the Christian movement to respond to these yearnings and thereby to exert a leavening effect on society beyond the walls of the church. Post-Christendom allows for the rediscovery of the gospel's power for the salvation of the whole world.

Sharing the conviction of Kierkegaard that "Christianity was abolished in Christendom,"[24] I believe that, despite its numerous challenges, the post-Christendom era signifies a transition to a new cultural context, which will prove to be more authentically Christian than a secular humanist or even nominal Christian past. Under Christendom, Christianity lost its vivacity and creative dynamism. Churches and religious subcultures sometimes became human institutions that sheltered people from the scandalous truth of Christ and the radical demands of the gospel. Christianity was compromised by nominal religiosity and disfigured by a rigid dogmatism that prioritized doctrine over life in the Spirit. Post-Christendom signifies a creative revelation of a new era and even a momentous movement of the Holy Spirit in our times. The emerging post-Christendom reality signifies an age of the Spirit, an era in which Christianity has come of age and expresses itself in ways that connect with the spiritual crisis of our times. Like other authors in this series, I thus regard post-Christendom not as a misfortune to lament, but as an opportunity to grasp.

Therefore, rather than lamenting the passing of the "good old days" when the church used to wield power and theology was "queen of the sciences," this book seeks to encourage the Christian community in post-Christendom to demonstrate both a gracious acceptance of the new circumstances and an ability to discern in them the activity of the Holy Spirit.

---

23. The term "institutional sclerosis" is taken from Olson, *Rise and Decline of Nations*.

24. Kierkegaard, *Training in Christianity by Anti-Climacus*, 222.

Acknowledgements

On my way towards completion of this work, I have been encouraged and inspired by many friends. Among my many gifted and dedicated colleagues at Spurgeon's College, Stephen Wright and Debra Reid, who have been a constant source of wisdom and encouragement to me over the past few years, deserve special appreciation. My thinking has been stimulated by conversations with Sonya Alexanyan, Liliya Melkonyan, Mariam Melkonyan, Misha Melkonyan, Knara Oganesyan, Diana Schonert, Alexander Boyko, Klaus John, David Reid, Steve Chalke, Simon Jones, Peter Morden, Dotha Blackwood, Pieter and Hetty Lalleman, Tony Rich, Jason Ferenczi, Steve Reed MP, Andy Byers, David McLachlan, David McMillan, Hayley Gowen, Rob May, Ian Stackhouse, Igor Bandura, David Kerrigan, Andrew Pierce, Gladys Ganiel, and Crawford Gribben. It is a pleasure to express my deepest thanks to the following people who read and commented on drafts of this work, offering perceptive feedback: Jeremy Thomson, Graham Watts, Zoltán Schwáb, Stuart Murray Williams, Nancy Lively, Jessica Richmond, Kate Coleman, and David Coffey, though I take full responsibility for any errors that remain in the text.

Greatest thanks are due to my family, particularly to Varduyi and to my mum and dad, Roy and Shirley Searle, who read various drafts and offered support at key moments of wavering when I doubted that I would ever be able to finish this book. Their example of patience, courage and compassion has reminded me time and again that theology should envision the world through the optic of faith, hope and love.

It has been said that, "every Christian theology is written from and for a community."[1] This book is no exception. I offer this work in gratitude to the Northumbria Community, based in the northeast of England, which now has thousands of Companions and Friends dispersed throughout the world. Although I have spent many years working abroad and now find myself living in a "foreign land" (Ps 137:4) of Croydon in South London, I am

---

1. McClendon, *Doctrine*, 9.

a Northumbrian by birth and temperament. The Northumbria Community is where I grew up, came to faith and where I feel most at home spiritually. I hope that this book might assist and encourage my fellow Community Companions in our common task of bringing renewal to the church and transformation to the wider society through our commitment to the monastic imperative of "uncompromising allegiance to the Sermon on the Mount."[2]

My other "community of reference"[3] is Spurgeon's College, where I teach Theology and Public Thought. Spurgeon's is a remarkable community, whose students continue to amaze and inspire me through their devotion to the gospel and commitment to their studies. I have found conversations with several students particularly helpful. Deji Ayorinde, Jonathan Findlater, Abiola Durosinmi-Etti, Nat Moody, Richard Asante, Tolleiv Oseland, Novlette Smith, Alan Donaldson, Gum Soon Back, Azar Ajaj, and Matt Hebditch deserve special mention. I am grateful to God for giving me the privilege of knowing two outstanding young Christian leaders, Nathan John and Tom Pelham, who both trained for ministry at Spurgeon's College. Nathan died of a seizure in 2014. He was only twenty-one years old. Tom, aged thirty-five, finally succumbed in 2017 after a brave battle with cancer. The courage, compassion, and pioneering spirit of both Nathan and Tom have been a constant inspiration. I dedicate this book to them in the blessed hope of Christ's unfailing welcome.

Dominus dedit, Dominus abstulit . . . sit nomen Domini benedictum
(Job 1:21).

Joshua T. Searle
Spurgeon's College, London

---

2. Bonhoeffer, *Testament to Freedom*, 424. The full quotation is, "The renewal of the church will come about through a new type of monasticism which only has in common with the old an uncompromising allegiance to the Sermon on the Mount." This quotation has been foundational to the Northumbria Community's understanding of its identity and vision.

3. McClendon, *Ethics*, 215.

Introduction

Thinking outside the Box

The basic argument of this work is that the emerging post-Christendom context demands a wholesale reenvisioning of theological formation and even of theology itself. Theology needs to be shaken to the foundations in light of the new reality of post-Christendom. This book is not a compendium of practical suggestions about how to produce more effective teaching environments and successful learning outcomes. The aim, rather, is to imagine and envision, rather than merely to describe and explain, a way of forming people for mission in today's post-Christendom context. This book, in other words, is more concerned with the first-order question concerning the truth that theology aspires to elucidate than with the methods, models and techniques of learning and teaching theology.[1] The book aims to make visible the powerful currents of philosophical and cultural change that surge beneath the froth of here today, gone tomorrow education policies and church initiatives.

The reenvisioning of theological formation in post-Christendom requires a reimagining of the nature, scope and aim of theology in general. There is now a broad consensus that "our theological convictions should influence our approach to education and spiritual formation."[2] As Elizabeth Schüssler Fiorenza remarks, "The crucial issue for theological education is: what constitutes good theology?" and she maintains that, "the reform of theology is the condition for the reform of theological education."[3] This

---

1. For a discussion of the difference between "first-order" and "second-order" questions in theology, see Davies, *Theology of Transformation*, 87–88.

2. Estep, "Role of Developmental Theories."

3. Fiorenza, "Thinking Theologically," 318–19.

book thus considers the nature, aim and scope of theology with the aim of formulating an account of Christian formation that can elucidate and transform the contemporary world, which is transitioning into a spiritual condition to which some have applied the label, "post-Christendom." The following study will be concerned with fundamental questions concerning how theology can be reconstructed in light of the changes associated with this new phenomenon.

The post-Christendom shift involves not only social and political changes, but a deep, tectonic metamorphosis in thinking, culture and relationships which impinge upon the pressing spiritual issues of our times.

Adjustment to the new configuration is difficult because it requires the kind of clear-sighted vision and bold, prophetic leadership that Christendom churches have singularly failed to produce. Christendom churches have thus tended to respond slowly or half-heartedly to these momentous changes. As John Douglas Hall laments, "Why is there such a reluctance to recognize this great transition through which the Christian movement is passing? Why do Christians in our context so consistently resist the opportunities for genuine discipleship that historical providence has opened up to us just at this point?"[4]

Part of the answer to this question can be found in the failure of Christendom to imagine an appropriate and attainable vision of theological formation that can connect transformatively with the deep issues of life in the world today. The formation deficit, in turn, can be attributed to a feeble and compromised theology that has subordinated life in the spirit to systems of required dogma. If theological formation is to be reenvisioned for a post-Christendom age, theology itself must undergo a radical transformation, corresponding to what one philosopher called a "transvaluation of values."[5]

It is sometimes difficult to envision what the future might hold for theology and Christian formation. This is because we are sometimes so assimilated into systems of administration and acculturated within set paradigms of academic theory and practice that it is difficult even to think without the aid of familiar categories and concepts. As the existentialist philosopher, Jose Ortega y Gasset (1883–1955), lamented: "How shall I talk of the sea to the frog, if he has never left his pond? . . . How shall I talk of life with the sage, if he is the prisoner of his doctrine?"[6] Often the very proximity implied by immersion conceals important aspects of one's ethos and practice and

---

4. Hall, *End of Christendom*, 20.
5. Nietzsche, *Thus Spoke Zarathustra*.
6. Gasset, *Mission of the University*, 45.

the invisible layers of tradition that lie behind them.[7] The deep-rootedness of established patterns of thinking and behavior can stifle creative thinking about how to break out of the current impasse. Such habituation runs deep and even if we break out of accustomed ways of thinking, there may be other external hindrances that can limit the horizon of what is possible.

Perhaps this is one of the advantages of being a relative outsider. Although I am a full-time lecturer at a theological college, I am part of a Baptist community that is a minority even within the dwindling Christian community of post-Christendom Britain. Moreover, as a Baptist nurtured by the Anabaptist vision, I am on the margins even of this minority community. I do not see anything particularly virtuous in any of this; it is a simple fact or consequence of various circumstances, rather than any attainment on my part. Since this is in many ways a very personal work, in order to give readers a perspective on how I came to my conclusions, it seems appropriate to begin on a personal note with a brief narration of the circumstances that led me to write this book.

My Confession: A Few Biographical Reflections

My path into theology was presumably not the one usually taken by theology lecturers. I was born in 1985, which means that I belong to the so-called "Millennial Generation" or "Generation Y." As a child, I served as an altar boy in my local village Anglican church in the far north east of England. I was particularly struck by the beauty, depth, and historicity of the liturgy and the hymns that were the mainstay of the Sunday services. During this early period, I had a childlike faith. I prayed to God every day and spoke to him as a friend. My faith was simple and unrefined. I believed presumably because I had been socialized into a faith tradition that gave me a framework to make sense of everything from the meaning of the universe to the cruel behavior of school bullies.

I knew almost nothing about the doctrines of incarnation and atonement and nothing at all about theodicy or the Chalcedonian formula or the theories of Calvin and Arminius concerning divine foreknowledge. Despite my ignorance of the classical theological tradition, I did exhibit a devotion to the Scriptures and was particularly fascinated by the Gospels and the great stories of the Old Testament. At school, taking a keen interest in the natural sciences, especially biology, I was also fascinated by the phenomenon of life and by how astonishing it was simply to be alive and to

---

7. Heidegger referred to this concealment by immersion in terms of the "paradox of proximity" (*das Paradox der Nähe*). See Heidegger, *Being and Time*, 13–15.

inhabit such a wondrous universe of excessive beauty and exuberance. This impression was intensified by the fact that I grew up in the foothills of the magnificent Cheviot Hills of my native Northumberland.

Even when I learned about evolution and the Big Bang Theory, and began to develop a scientific understanding of the laws and principles that govern the operation of forces in the natural world, it never occurred to me to doubt my theological beliefs about the nature of God, sin, salvation, death and suffering. I never seriously considered the question of how a crucified man could be regarded as the Savior of the world. Nor did I seem to question how my image of a God of infinite goodness, wisdom, power and beauty could be reconciled with the immeasurable pain of the world and such ugly, painful and destructive obscenities, such as volcanoes and cholera and malaria. It was as though, in my childhood naivety, I had unthinkingly admitted the existence of an all-powerful God who seemed to watch on as people were stricken with cancer or as children were buried alive under tsunamis of ash and sludge. Although I never seriously doubted the existence of God, I did experience moments of God-forsakenness. I was perplexed by a painful awareness of God's absence from the world and His seeming indifference to the immense suffering of its human (and non-human) inhabitants. In the face of the tragic anguish of the world, any rational attempt to "justify the ways of God to men" (Milton) seemed futile and invalid.

Therefore, although I identify as a "Christian," I am by no means an uncritical exponent of the faith I profess. I have read the sceptical literature, including Sigmund Freud's psychological depiction of Christianity as a neurotic infantile projection, Karl Marx's denunciation of Christianity as the "opium of the people" and Friedrich Nietzsche's vehement tirades against religious truth claims. Yet for all my sympathy with the impulses that inspired these critiques, I have never relinquished my faith. That I have not done so can be explained in quite simple terms, in fact in one word: *Jesus.* I freely proclaim Christ as Lord and Savior and I gladly affirm the saving power of Christ's crucifixion and resurrection. For all the frustrations that I have experienced with organized religious rituals and the institutions and hierarchy of Christendom; despite all the intellectual doubts I might entertain about certain dogmatic claims; notwithstanding all my depressing encounters with other Christians; despite all the moral objections that I have against certain Old Testament passages in which an irascible deity purportedly commands the ethnic cleansing of entire populations—despite all this I still find myself drawn irresistibly to the person of Jesus, particularly as He is depicted in the Johannine writings of the New Testament.

In Jesus, I perceive a God who is very much alive, a God of sacrificial love, a God of irresistible grace and vitality who is active in the world in wondrous and mysterious ways—in a "divine conspiracy," to borrow a term from one of my favorite books by Dallas Willard.[8] I agree with the observation of Dag Hammarskjöld (1905–1961) that, "God does not die on the day when we cease to believe in a personal deity, but we die on the day when our lives cease to be illuminated by the steady radiance, renewed daily, of a wonder, the source of which is beyond all reason."[9] For those who want to retain a sense of childlike wonder at the sheer beauty and absurdity of the world, the person of Christ provides a fulcrum for the imagination as well as a rational framework for critical reflection.

I recognize the God who reveals himself in Christ not as an omnipotent, impassible cosmic dictator, but, as one notable philosopher put it, as "the fellow sufferer who understands" and "the poet of the world, with tender patience leading it by his vision of truth, beauty and goodness."[10] I gradually became convinced that the almighty, omnipotent deity, who demands blood sacrifice as a substitutionary propitiation for his wrath, was a fiction invented by theologians who were still in the thrall of primitive pagan superstitions. The God to whom I have pledged my life and fate is the God revealed in and through Jesus Christ. This is the God whose nature is unfathomable and mysterious, yet all-loving, gratuitously merciful and generous. I understood Jesus as the Lord of life and the one in whom all the treasures of wisdom and knowledge are hidden (Col 2:3).

In the midst of these reflections, I commenced my studies at Oxford University, where I ostensibly read modern history, but also devoted myself to literature, theology, philosophy and the study of modern languages. I cherished the freedom afforded by the Oxford University environment and the opportunity to immerse myself in the intellectual treasures of the historic libraries. It was while I was in Oxford that I was conscious of being claimed by Christ and I became aware of how He began to transform my life. I was, of course, far from perfect, but I felt the liberation of knowing that I was "in Christ" and that His grace was saving me, bringing me to a new awareness of the depth, beauty and mystery of life. I experienced how the Holy Spirit was expanding my horizons of imagination, perception and compassion. For the first time, my faith developed a depth and meaning that surpassed the simple childlike belief of my youth. I experienced this transformation as a kind of "new birth" (John 3:1–21). Verses like Colossians 3:3 ("For you died, and your life is hidden with Christ in God") and Galatians 2:20 ("I have been crucified with Christ and I no longer live, but Christ lives

---

8. Willard, *The Divine Conspiracy*.

9. Hammarskjöld, quoted in Dixon, *Nietzsche and Jung*, 151.

10. Whitehead, *Process and Reality*, 351, 346.

in me") started to make sense to me, not because I had managed to fit them into a doctrinal framework, but because I was experiencing the existential reality of having been crucified and raised with Christ.

In addition to the experience of faith awakening, this was also a formative time in my intellectual development. I remember the tutorials and instruction of my teachers with admiration and gratitude, but my experience of church was less favorable. Although I never seriously questioned the fundamental beliefs of my faith, I did find myself constantly questioning the way these beliefs were presented by institutions and individuals claiming to represent Christ. My instinctive aversion to clericalism resisted the hierarchical order of church life. This conviction was confirmed through my reading of Kierkegaard, who had claimed that "established Christendom . . . might be called the caricature of Christianity"[11] and that the "so-called Church falsifies Christianity by watering it down."[12] I recoiled from the notions of a "Christian country" and an "Established Church" and shared Kierkegaard's conviction that these constituted "an apostasy from the Christianity of the New Testament."[13]

The attempts to assign a sacred or sacramental character to church institutions, which seemed to me to be based on unspoken worldly conventions of dominion and submission, never carried any conviction with me. Sacramentalism seemed not to resemble New Testament Christianity any more than a square resembled a circle.[14] I was similarly unimpressed by the notion of ordained ministry. The whole idea of ordination seemed to have the unfortunate effect of institutionalizing a double standard for Christians. I preferred to think about a single vision of discipleship that was binding on all those who claimed to follow Christ. Similarly, I never felt any affinity for the sacramental elements of church life. I found church rituals and the usual worship songs insufferably dull. With a tinge of nostalgia, I longed to recite again the hymns from my childhood and I felt agitation and even discomfort when I was expected to sing about "*My* Jesus, *My* Savior." I preferred to sing to Jesus as the "High King of Heaven," rather than the romanticized "Beautiful One" or "Darling of Heaven" of contemporary Christian popular music.

I realized that I could only come to God the Father through Jesus the Son. I concurred with Berdyaev when he asserted that, "Only God who has

11. Kierkegaard, quoted in Hyde, *Concepts of Power in Kierkegaard and Nietzsche,* 165.

12. Kierkegaard, *Journals of Søren Kierkegaard,* 1358.

13. Kierkegaard, *Attack upon Christendom,* 19, 31. Kierkegaard asserted that, "A Christian nation is an impossibility."

14. Kierkegaard, *Attack upon Christendom,* 42.

become flesh and has Himself experienced the suffering of human beings and the whole creation can overcome the source of evil which gives rise to suffering."[15] In other words, I could not think about God except in terms of sacrificial love, which drew me instinctively towards Jesus in my search for the divine. Finding so little of this kind of compassion within the church fellowships that I visited, I soon regarded the conventional religiosity of church life repellent. My most significant spiritual experiences and encounters with Christ have always occurred outside of church.

At one time, I even began to regard the institutional church and the organized collective beliefs known as orthodoxy as antithetical to the freedom of the gospel and an obstacle to the fulfilment of the Great Commission. Whereas Nietzsche had applied the epithet, "the coldest of cold monsters," to the state,[16] I began to attach it to the church. Although I later came to nuance these views, this suspicion of orthodoxy and institutional expressions of Christianity left a lasting stamp on my intellectual formation. Around this time, I became aware of a paradox: at the same time when I was growing in my theological understanding and deepening my commitment to Christ, I was becoming more conscious of a painful sense of exile from my childhood faith and from the church institution that had sustained it; the more I devoted myself to Christ, the less religious I became and the more alienated I felt from church life.

Attempting to come to terms with this sense of alienation, I began to look for answers. I read widely in theology and attended several public theological seminars and debates that were held at various colleges in Oxford. In many ways these experiences were mind-broadening and fulfilling, but I soon grew bored of the intricate discussions concerning minute details of textual criticism and the speculative metaphysical fictions that seemed to preoccupy so many theologians. These distinguished dons seemed to resemble the kind of people castigated by Kierkegaard who were training students "in the art of introducing Christianity in such a way that it signifies nothing."[17] Instead of forming prophets to be change agents for God's Kingdom, it seemed that pastor-teachers were being trained in how to unleash what Gasset called "a torrent of drivel and bluff."[18] I could understand and even empathize with the lament of Rousseau's Savoyard Vicar, who complained that, "The chief source of human error is to be found in general and abstract ideas; the jargon of metaphysics has never led to the discovery of

---

15. Berdyaev, *Ekzistentsialnaya Dialektika*, 472.

16. Nietzsche, *Also Sprach Zarathustra*, 57.

17. Kierkegaard, *Journals of Søren Kierkegaard*, 1305.

18. Gasset, *Mission of the University*, 47.

any single truth, and it has filled philosophy with absurdities of which we are ashamed as soon as we strip them of their long words."[19]

In addition to this dislike of speculative metaphysics, I also became weary of tedious debates—for example, between one scholar, who held that the Pentateuch was written solely by Moses, and another, who insisted that these books were transcribed by various Hebrew writers over several generations. I regarded these kinds of questions as nothing but hair-splitting sophistry and sterile speculation. I could not understand what difference these speculations made to life, even if an eminent scholar were able to establish the case irrefutably one way or the other.

These experiences initiated in me an enduring suspicion towards biblical studies. Kierkegaard once quipped that, "Christian scholarship is the Church's prodigious invention to defend itself against the Bible, to ensure that we can continue to be good Christians without the Bible coming too close."[20] Although I respected Scripture as the *"norma normans"*[21] and the first reference point for all theological reflection, I thought that much of what passed for biblical studies was, in reality, a frivolous fetishization of ancient texts or "a series of desperate efforts to domesticate the scandalous character of the [Bible] by way of historicist contextualization."[22] By their preoccupation with the origin and transmission of biblical texts to the neglect of their real-life impact on contemporary readers, some scholars seemed to have become enmired in exegetical quagmires. Instead of understanding the Bible as "a means of approaching its life-transforming truth,"[23] biblical studies sometimes seemed intent on dissecting the minute details of a text from a historical-critical perspective. Biblical studies thus became the *Sitz im Tode* of post-Enlightenment Christian theology. Sometimes, among evangelical and fundamentalist scholarship, the fetishization of authoritative texts is expressed in unbiblical notions of inerrancy, which reduce the life-giving, spirit-filled words of Scripture to a cold and sterile text of factual claims.

During my studies, I began to understand more about the historical influences that had shaped Christian faith throughout the centuries. My sympathies were always with the losers and the rebels of church history. I read with deep fascination about St Francis of Assisi (c.1182–1226), who had

19. Rousseau, *Emile, or On Education*, 283.

20. Kierkegaard, quoted in McLaren, *Secret Message of Jesus*, 216.

21. The "norming norm" or "absolute norm." See Harle, *Outline of Christian Doctrine*, 122. See also Grenz, "Conversing in Christian Style," 88–89.

22. Žižek, *Living in the End Times*, 125.

23. Rollins, *Fidelity of Betrayal*, 62.

humbly revolted against the wealth and power of the institutional church. I also admired the Czech reformer and martyr, Jan Hus (c.1370–1415), and my frequent visits to his statue in the Old Town Square of Prague were always deep and meaningful occasions when I lived in the Czech capital. I was also in awe of Martin Luther's revolt against the moribund and anti-Christian system of ecclesial tyranny that had blasphemously set itself up as the only true "Holy Catholic Church." However, I was disturbed by Luther's vitriolic diatribes against both the Jews and against the Anabaptist communities, who suffered brutal persecution at the hands of Protestants and Catholics alike.

Of all the Christian movements that I read about in church history, it was Anabaptism that made the most lasting impression. The early Anabaptists—Felix Manz, Balthasar Hubmaier, Jakob Hutter, Dirk Willems, and others—seemed to embody a spirit of uncompromising allegiance to the gospel and a faith that emphasized obedience to Christ above all other commitments. Their faith in Christ was a matter of costly discipleship that led, in many cases, to martyrdom. I made a clear distinction in my heart and mind between this kind of sacrificial obedience and the cheap grace of adhering intellectually to a system of doctrine. The Anabaptists confirmed my conviction that Christianity was a matter of *faith*, rather than mere *belief*.[24]

I also derived great encouragement from the spirituality of the new monastic movement. I was drawn towards the *Rule of Life* of the Northumbria Community. The *Rule* consists in a commitment to "Availability" and "Vulnerability," which arose out of the monastic emphasis on the priority of seeking God with singular devotion in every aspect of daily life. Availability entails a commitment to respond to the call of God in the practice of service, mission, prayer and hospitality.[25] Vulnerability, in the words of the *Rule*, is expressed through "being teachable in the discipline of prayer . . . applying the wisdom of the Scriptures and through a mutual accountability in the advocacy of soul friends." Vulnerability also extends to a commitment to value relationships higher than reputation and to live "openly among people as a 'Church without walls.'"[26] This *Rule* gave me a framework of hope within which I could make sense of life from the perspective of my faith in Christ.

Not being able to afford the costs of pursuing further studies immediately, after graduating with a BA in Modern History, I had a brief spell pushing paper around an office in the Civil Service. Thankfully, the boredom of

24. This distinction is explained in greater detail in chapter 3.

25. Northumbria Community, *Way for Living*, 12–17.

26. Miller, *Way for Living*, 10. For a fuller account of the Northumbria Community and its vision of "Church Without Walls," see chapter 8.

form filling and box-ticking did not kill me, and, in hindsight, I am grateful for this experience because it taught me first hand about how the impersonal routines of rational bureaucracy smother human creativity and dehumanize social relations. After having experienced the absurdity and injustice of how bureaucratic systems operate in modern society, I began to read some of my favorite writers, such as Karl Marx, Max Weber and Franz Kafka, with new eyes.

Putting this unhappy yet valuable experience behind me, I was able to resume my studies, this time in Prague, where I graduated with a master's degree in Applied Theology from the International Baptist Theological Seminary. I was grateful to my gifted teachers in Prague, who taught me, among many other things, that theology is about life rather than doctrine and that Christ came not as a lawgiver, but as a liberator. I was also confirmed in my conviction that the petty disputes about the banal details of exegesis that occupy some specialists in the sphere of biblical studies are unworthy of the name, "theology."

For me another result of my experience in Prague was a deep and enduring interest in Eastern Europe. I was—and still am—privileged to count several Ukrainians, Moldovans, Czechs, Lithuanians and Armenians as some of my closest friends. My connections with Eastern Europe offered the opportunity to learn Russian and to become acquainted with the philosophy of Berdyaev and Solovyev, the theology of Bulgakov and Lossky, the poetry of Pushkin and Yevtushenko, and the literature of Dostoevsky and Tolstoy.

After graduating from Prague, I then pursued my studies to doctoral level at Trinity College Dublin. At Trinity I was a member of the School of English and I taught classes on Literary Theory as a graduate teaching assistant. When I read a poem or part of a novel with the students, I tried to encourage them to interpret the text through what Paul Ricoeur called a "hermeneutic of suspicion." I wanted to challenge students to identify the subtle ideological subtexts within diverse literary genres from the plays of Shakespeare to the novels of James Joyce. My classes on Literary Theory also taught me about how the mechanisms of truth and power are dispersed within texts. This training in Literary Theory provided a robust framework within which to understand the task of theology in terms of moral and intellectual formation through the application of the methods of critical thinking.

These experiences nurtured in me the conviction that theology should extend beyond notions of individual formation and should encompass the vital issue of social responsibility. I believed intuitively that theology makes a profound difference not just to the individuals who are formed by it, but also to the broader society in which Christians are called to be salt and light.

The social responsibility of theology has been revealed to me in a particularly poignant way in my teaching work among the deprived, marginalized and underprivileged in the countries of Eastern Europe where I have lived and worked. Ukraine made a powerful impression on me. Although I have enjoyed and learned a great deal from teaching relatively privileged young people in elite Western academic institutions, some of the most liberating and fulfilling teaching experiences that I can recall have occurred in less affluent, primarily Eastern-European contexts.

The way I approach my vocation as a theologian is reflected in the kind of society in which I wish to live and serve. I believe in the fundamental convictions concerning the absolute sanctity and intrinsic value of human life, the freedom of speech and conscience, the democratic and egalitarian principles of civic participation in political power and the fundamental rule of law. In a post-Christendom age these basic humanitarian principles can by no means be taken for granted and need to be defended robustly and proactively. I believe theologians should stand on the front line in the battle for civilization, reason and enlightenment against barbarism, prejudice and ignorance. Theologians should contend for truth, beauty and goodness in a world of falsehood, ugliness and cruelty.

I mention these biographical details only because they provide the backdrop to the ideas and concepts that I set forth in this book and they correspond with the notion of "biography as theology,"[27] which has been instilled in me by my theological training. I believe that theologians in post-Christendom have an important role to play in inculcating the values of universal tolerance and respect for life and the freedom of conscience that constitute free societies. I understand theology as a transformative enterprise that can join with progressive forces in society in order to create a dynamic movement that upholds the gospel values of compassion and social, economic, political and environmental justice. These are some of the convictions that underlie the various arguments and perspectives that will be advanced throughout this book.

Aims and Scope

The aim of this book is to present an overview of some of the challenges and opportunities confronting theology in a post-Christendom context and to offer proposals about how to address the current state of crisis. This book is written in the conviction that theology has reached a crucial phase in its historical development. The great need today is not only for "professional

27. McClendon, *Biography as Theology.*

Christians," but also for "Christian professionals" who are able to be salt and light, bringing transformation to the various spheres in which they work.

The Christian community also needs to raise up a new generation of prophets, apostles and evangelists. The academic curricula and ethos of our institutions of theological education can address this need by moving beyond the training of pastor-teachers, whose vision is circumscribed by the Christendom mentality, which continues to inform the studies of those who are graduating from training colleges and seminaries. This book takes the Kingdom of God as its point of departure to consider how theology can best serve the *missio Dei* in this post-Christendom age.

The aim of this book is not to provide a comprehensive theological method, but to elucidate an account of theological formation that is consistent with the overall vision of the biblical witness and Christian tradition, while being sensitive to the cultural context and responsive to the missional challenges of post-Christendom. Underlying these explorations is a basic question concerning the nature of theology and its meaning and relevance to an emerging culture. This book thus explores the connection between theological formation and prophetic vocation. In a post-Christendom era, the demand for pastor-teacher theologians and ministers is diminishing; the demand is for pioneering, prophetic innovators who can envision new and creative ways of confronting issues affecting the Christian community and its witness to the world.

It is now recognized that "God calls people into the teaching and scholarly professions just as much as he does to any ministerial or missionary profession."[28] However, within Christendom churches, the tendency to exaggerate the importance of church-focused "ordained ministry" persists. For instance, there is much talk these days about "pioneering ministers," but rarely do I hear people talking about "pioneering theologians" as prophets of the gospel or as apostles to culture. Theologians and creative scholars in post-Christendom have a prophetic vocation to speak into cultures of religious complacency and remind people about Christ and His gospel. Theology must retain its prophetic vocation to speak truth to power and to revolt against what is ugly, commonplace and vulgar in contemporary social life. Theology has a prophetic calling to overcome all those degenerate forces that erode the sacred sinews of spiritual solidarity and compassion. Theological education needs to do more than induct students into a system of Christian ideas and doctrines, but should inculcate in people what one philosopher called "an intense awareness of suffering in the world and in

---

28. Henry and Agee (eds.), *Faithful Learning*, xi.

human existence."[29] Moreover, theological formation should train people to think and act in ways that are directed towards the creative transfiguration of such suffering.

Keeping in mind the principle that "good theology should drive our pedagogy,"[30] the primary focus of the book is on theology, rather than on theories of learning. Many scholarly books and articles have been written on theological education and even more on spiritual formation. Several of these studies have made valuable additions to our understanding of teaching techniques, learning processes and curriculum design. Far fewer works, however, have formulated a future-oriented vision of a larger strategy to navigate a course for theological education through the doldrums of postmodernity and the storms of secularization.

Therefore, another aspect of this book is its focus on the future at a time when many studies on this theme are characteristically oriented to times past or which are empirical studies describing the present state of theology. The radical call to envision and embrace the future is muffled amid all the well-intentioned—but, in my judgement, misguided—clamor to "return to the sources" in order to "recover Christianity in all its fullness and purity."[31] Harvey Cox correctly asserts that, "there is no road back to the primitive church some Protestants long for, or to the splendid medieval synthesis many Catholics dream of, or to the "old time religion" American revivalists sing about." Furthermore, he argued, "Much of this attempt to revert to the "way it was" is based on fanciful reconstructions of some previous period."[32] Nostalgic extrapolations from an idealized past will not serve the coming of the Kingdom of God, because the Kingdom belongs not to the past, but to the future and the future may be fundamentally discontinuous with what has gone before. The Kingdom of God is the inbreaking of the future, expressed through a "passion for the possible."[33] This Kingdom comes not through historical fetishization of any alleged past "golden age," but through envisioning the future in the power of the Holy Spirit. In other words, the Kingdom of God is realized and expressed, not in the historical past, but in the eschatological future. As Gasset once remarked, "Life is a series of collisions with the future; it is not the sum of what we have been, but what we yearn to be."[34] The hurdle that we encounter is the natural hu-

29. Berdyaev, *Dream and Reality*, 28.

30. Shaw, *Transforming Theological Education*, 19.

31. De Lubac, *Paradoxes*, 67–69.

32. Cox, *Future of Faith*, 56.

33. Moltmann, *Theologie der Hoffnung*, 15.

34. Gasset, quoted in Sherl, *Future for Curious People*, 32.

man fear of the future. Being afraid of the future, one finds it easier to take refuge in history, as memory and nostalgia supplant vision and creativity. Therefore, the future can be perceived only through an optic of faith and hope; normal sight is inadequate to the task of envisioning the future of theological formation in the new cultural reality of post-Christendom— "Only in hope will we be saved" (Rom 8:24).

Structure of the Argument

The book, in the first chapter, begins with an elucidation of the nature, aims and scope of theology. The second chapter explores the link between theological formation and prophetic vocation. The next chapter builds on this foundation in order to account for the socio-cultural factors that have contributed to the marginalization of academic theology in post-Christendom. Against this backdrop, chapter 4 follows a well-established approach that refuses to consider mission and theological formation as two separate tasks. Once considered practically synonymous with "evangelization," the word, "mission," now has a much wider currency, encompassing not only proclamation (*kerygma*), but also community (*koinonia*) and service (*diakonia*). This chapter discusses the implications of this broadening of mission and the challenges and opportunities presented by post-Christendom in relation to theological formation. This chapter will indicate the need for theology to break out of its captivity to church structures by realigning itself with the Kingdom of God.

Chapter 5, accordingly, reflects theologically on the meaning and significance of the Kingdom of God as the focal point of theological formation. In light of these reflections, the aim of the next chapter is to understand how specific Kingdom imperatives apply to diverse contexts of theological formation. The concepts of freedom, compassion, and creativity are invoked as useful points of departure for thinking about the nature and role of theological formation in post-Christendom. Chapter 7 considers the interrelation of the church, the academy, and the public sphere and discusses the contribution of a post-Christendom perspective to the emerging field of Public Theology. This chapter also examines the broader cultural shifts in the focus of theological research away from knowledge and truth towards interpretation and theory and makes proposals about how the post-Christendom Christian college or theology faculty can reimagine itself as a hub of transformative knowledge. The final chapter illustrates how a transformative vision of theology in post-Christendom can be applied towards the renewal of Christian community in these times of transition. This chapter draws on the experience of the Northumbria Community as an example of how Christian faith can become relevant, credible and compelling even in the seemingly hostile conditions of the post-Christendom shift.

1

What Is Theology?

On Theology

Theology after Christendom will need to be thought of as more than simply the sum of human knowledge of God. Deriving from the terms, *Theos* (God) and *logos* (word), theology has often been understood as "God-talk." However, theology is not just human talk about God, but also denotes "a place where God speaks into human discourse."[1] Moreover, theology is irreducible to discourse; it encompasses a mode of being-in-the-world, an existential orientation towards material reality, a way of relating to issues of "ultimate concern,"[2] and, ultimately, a vision involving the wholesale transformation of the world. As Laurie Green remarks, "Christian theology implies challenge, response and transformation. One cannot do theology without expecting change."[3]

Theology is a transformative enterprise in so far as it envisions the world through the optic of faith, hope and love—the most important of which is love (1 Cor 13:13). The Scottish poet, Kathleen Raine, remarks that, "unless you see a thing in the light of love, you do not see it at all."[4] Similarly, Father Zosima in Dostoevsky's *Brothers Karamazov* declares, "Love all creation, the whole of it and every grain of sand within it. Love every leaf, every ray of God's light. Love the animals, love the plants, love everything. If you

1. Rollins, *How (Not) to Speak of God*, 21.

2. Tillich, *Systematic Theology: Volume 1*, 11–14.

3. Green, *Let's Do Theology*, 13.

4. Raine, quoted in O'Donohue, *Anam Cara*, 65. The German philosopher, Max Scheler (1874–1928), pursued a similar thesis in his great work, *Zur Phänomenologie und Theorie der Sympathiegefühle und von Liebe und Hass*, first published in 1913.

love everything, you will perceive the divine mystery in things."[5] Relating this insight to academic vocation, Gavin D'Costa affirms that "the purpose of the university is to find love at the heart of all things, for love is the cause of the world."[6]

Emphasizing the imperative of love in any theological endeavor, Mary Ingham notes that, "theology is praxis and its goal is not simply a way of doing, but rather a way of being human in the image of the divine trinitarian mystery of personhood and communion. This way of being unites us with God and with one another in a communion of love as an imitation of the love which Christ embodied."[7] This passionate commitment to theological formation through love lies behind James K. A. Smith's "pedagogy of desire," which posits that "to be human is to love, and it is what we love that defines who we are."[8] Theological formation is therefore concerned with the reorientation of desire towards the Kingdom of God. This involves the subordination of erotic desire to the higher passions of wisdom and beauty, expressed in a vision of life in the transfiguring power of divine grace.[9]

Theology, Passion, and Imagination

Under Christendom, theology tended to neglect passionate commitments to such spiritual values of truth and love, and was often in captivity to overly rational and cognitive methods of apprehending life and faith. The kind of "reasonable Christianity" promoted in various forms by Christendom theologians from Thomas Aquinas (1225–1274) to John Locke[10] (1632–1704) and Immanuel Kant[11] (1724–1804) seemed not to realize that "we come to God not because rational thought demands His existence but because the world is bounded by a mystery in which rational thought ends."[12]

The over-emphasis on rational and cognitive expressions of Christian faith was predicated on an incomplete understanding of the human condition, which failed to recognize that, in the words of Cardinal J. H. Newman (1801–1890), "man is not a reasoning animal; he is a seeing, feeling,

---

5. Dostoevsky, *Brothers Karamazov*, 352.

6. D'Costa, *Theology in the Public Square*, 190.

7. Ingham, "John Duns Scotus," 227.

8. Smith, *Desiring the Kingdom*, 51.

9. The classic expression of the creative power of sublimated *eros* is to be found in Plato's *Symposium*.

10. Locke, *Clarendon Edition of the Works of John Locke*.

11. Kant, *Religion Within the Bounds of Bare Reason*.

12. Berdyaev, *Destiny of Man*, 33.

contemplating, acting animal."[13] *Pathos*, as well as *logos*, is a crucial mode of human intentionality that supervenes on Christian faith. Kierkegaard maintained that "passion is the real thing, the real measure of man's powers" and he castigated the stifling rationalism of his age, which he regarded as dismal and enervating because it was "without passion."[14]

Theology, too, was drawn away from life and towards abstraction and objectivization. "It harms Christianity in a high degree and alters its very nature," contended Kierkegaard, "that it is brought into an artistic remoteness from reality, instead of being in the midst of real life."[15] James McClendon rightly insists that, "The only relevant critical examination of Christian beliefs may be one that begins by attending to lived lives."[16] In reaction to the tendency of modern theology towards abstraction and "logocentrism,"[17] some postmodern theologians have asserted the futility and even idolatry of attempting to lay claim to God through fallible human language. Kevin Vanhoozer thus observes that, "Postmodern theology is a resistance movement that seeks to liberate *theos* from its captivity to this or that human *logos*."[18]

Addressing the Missiological Deficit

The abstraction of theology from life was reflected in the compartmentalization of theology as an academic discipline. The subdivision of theology into biblical, historical, systematic, philosophical, liturgical, missiological, pastoral, practical, and applied theology has not served theology well in the long run and has contributed to the marginalization of theology as an esoteric pursuit. This classification also contributed to the marginalization of mission in theological curricula and its virtual exclusion from systematic theology.[19] As a result, missiology, up until the mid-twentieth century functioned as "a discrete and largely marginal discipline within the theological

13. Newman, quoted in Short, *Newman and His Contemporaries*, 369.

14. Kierkegaard, quoted in Attwater (ed.), *Modern Christian Revolutionaries*, 27.

15. Kierkegaard, *Attack upon Christendom*, 2.

16. McClendon, *Biography as Theology*, 22.

17. The term, "logocentrism," refers to the Greek words, *logos*, meaning "word" or "logic," and "centrism," meaning to center on or to focus on. Logocentrism is the term coined by postmodern philosophers (pre-eminently Derrida) to denote a naive assumption that ultimate reality can be expressed in linguistic form and that words refer to stable objects or facts. See Ward, *Barth, Derrida and the Language of Theology*, 5.

18. Vanhoozer, *Drama of Doctrine*, 269.

19. For instance, in Charles Hodge's influential work, *Systematic Theology* (1845), mission does not feature.

canon."[20] Even up to the present day, instead of being the starting point for all theological reflection, mission continues to be regarded by many as synonymous with evangelism or church planting and treated as an appendage to practical theology.

Thankfully, several works have appeared in recent years that have sought to correct the missional deficit that characterizes the heavily Christendom-oriented curricula of many colleges, seminaries and university faculties. In academic theology, it is widely claimed that, "mission is the mother of theology."[21] Applying this insight to the issue of formation, Banks insists that, "theological education is a dimension of mission and has a vital missiological content." He rightly remarks that, "only by maintaining its close links with mission will it [theological education] remain relevant, and hold true to the missionary impulse that gave rise to the church and theology."[22]

These missional impulses have not been confined to Protestant theology. The Orthodox theologian, Vladimir Fedorov, who served as Director of the Orthodox Institute of Missiology and Ecumenism in St Petersburg, added his influential voice to these calls for a new missional paradigm for theological formation: "Theological education today should be mission-minded . . . The word "education" implies not only the academic routine of communicating some knowledge, fostering some skills and training various specialists for various fields of action, but also a strategic task for the whole culture."[23] The late Steve De Gruchy helpfully added that, "missional practice gives to theological education an outward orientation that gives a focus to the world rather than the church or the academy."[24] By maintaining an appropriate posture of critical solidarity with the world, theology can protect itself against clericalizing forces that would seek to compartmentalize theological disciplines according to traditional Christendom-laden categories.

The division of theological studies into the classical categories arose out of a Christendom context, which, in the words of one experienced teacher of theology, "has never been relevant in the non-Western world and is no longer relevant in most of the West."[25] In the new reality of post-Christendom, the subdivision of theology into its biblical, theological, historical and practical aspects, has far outlived its usefulness. It is becoming increasingly

20. Guder, "Theological Formation," 52.
21. Kähler, Schriften zur Christologie und Mission, 190.
22. Banks, Reenvisioning Theological Education, 131–32.
23. Fedorov, quoted in Searle and Cherenkov, Future and a Hope, 132.
24. De Gruchy, "Theological Education," 42.
25. Shaw, Transforming Theological Education, 17.

apparent that the current models of theological education have lost legiti-
macy; the emperor has no clothes. The dismal legacy of Christendom, together with its nominalism and its fatal compromise of gospel values, was
accompanied by an equally dismal theology that prioritized systems over
truth and dogma over life. As Kierkegaard noted rightly, "The object of faith
is not a doctrine, but God's reality in existence as a particular individual."[26]
Christendom caused the dynamic vitality of living faith in Christ to ossify
into a sterile sacramentalism and rigid systems of sound doctrine. Under
Christendom, rather than undermining this enfeebling tendency towards
clericalism, theology became the handmaid of the church institution.

The Poverty of Systematic Theology

The orientation of theological education towards missional practice also
has the salutary effect of reminding theologians that their discipline is not
a systematic scholastic discourse on religious metaphysics. Neither is theology a minute, tedious exegesis of ancient texts; nor is it concerned with
the construction of fragile idolatrous edifices of so-called sound doctrine.
Christendom posited a "prodigious illusion"[27] that the truth of Christ could
be contained within the sinful edifice of all-too-human systems of truth.
God will always resist any attempt to colonize Him with our conscience.[28]
As Brian McLaren remarks, in the same way that medieval Christians built
cathedrals of stone and glass, some modern Christians have attempted to
build "conceptual cathedrals" of systematized beliefs.[29] Within the new
configuration of post-Christendom, Systematic Theology will become less
and less relevant, as its essentially oxymoronic character becomes more and
more apparent. Even the great systematic theologian of the twentieth century, Karl Barth (1886-1968), seemed to realize that the days of Systematic
Theology were numbered:

> My lectures at the University of Basel are on "Systematic Theol-
> ogy." In Basel and elsewhere the juxtaposition of this noun and
> this adjective is based on a tradition which is quite recent and
> highly problematic. Is not the term "Systematic Theology" as
> paradoxical as a "wooden iron"? One day this conception will
> disappear just as suddenly as it has come into being.[30]

26. Kierkegaard, *Concluding Unscientific Postscript*, 290.

27. Kierkegaard, *Attack upon Christendom*, 97.

28. Rollins, *How (Not) to Speak of God*.

29. McLaren, *Generous Orthodoxy*, 168.

30. Barth, quoted in McLaren, *Generous Orthodoxy*, 168.

A vision of theology that is in tune with the new realities of post-Christendom would regard theology not as a systematic academic discipline, but as a transformative enterprise that encompasses theory and practice, the spiritual and the social, tradition and modernity, the rational and the mystical, the tragic and the comic, and the Apollonian and the Dionysian[31] elements of life. Theology is to be experienced not just behind a desk or in an armchair, but in hospitals, care homes, food banks, shops, and football stadia—and even in churches. Theology is to be lived as well as read; it is to be experienced as well as learned.

Reconnecting Theology with Life

Theology seeks answers to such fundamental questions as, "where is God's reign manifest today? What idols oppose it? How should the church respond to injustice?"[32] These questions lead theology away from rational deductions derived from the study of authoritative texts and into the concrete realities of life in the world. Far from being an "erudite discussion of inaccessible nonentities,"[33] theology is inseparably connected to life in all its joy, trauma and pathos. Theology, to use an expression from Kierkegaard, is "drawn from life and expressed again in life."[34] Life expresses itself in the creative struggle of dynamic forces.[35] Dietrich Bonhoeffer, James McClendon and others have claimed that theology is birthed in specific contexts of struggle[36] and that the practice of theology is a dynamic process that is in continual flux as it responds creatively to the existential challenges to human life, which vary from age to age.

Theology aims to comprehend the meaning and significance of life within a frame of reference that encompasses the totality of the cosmos, including its ideals, pathos and spiritual destiny. To this extent, theology is comprehensive; nevertheless, it is always provisional and unsusceptible to conclusive formulation. Only the impulses of hubris and self-deception could ever aspire to construct a "Total Theology" that constitutes a static

31. Nietzsche's analysis of culture posited a dichotomy between the Dionysian, which celebrated ecstasy, passion and vision, and the Apollonian, which emphasized rationality, moderation and scientific method. See Nietzsche, *Birth of Tragedy*.

32. Brackley, "Theology and Solidarity," 12.

33. McClendon, *Witness*, 398.

34. Lowrie, *Kierkegaard*, 214.

35. Bergson, *Creative Evolution*.

36 McClendon, *Ethics*, 17; McClendon, *Witness*, 420. Similarly, Luther claimed that the primary qualification for a theologian was a capacity to suffer. See Haile, *Luther*, 304.

system of divine truth. In the same way that the Lamb of God was the only one who was found to be worthy to *open* the scroll and loose the seven seals (Rev 5:1-10), so is it the case that only God himself could ever *close* the book on theology.

Theology is always concerned with life; theology takes life as its object and point of departure. Nothing that concerns human life in the world is foreign to theology. If "the earth is the Lord's, and everything in it" (Ps 24:1), it follows that there is no aspect of life that should not come under the saving grace of God. Ever since Paul Tillich (1886–1965) formulated his "Theology of Culture," theologians have become increasingly aware that theology cannot be confined to the interpretation of overtly religious materials, such as the scriptures, doctrines, and religious symbols and church rituals.[37] This is even more the case in post-Christendom. In fact, the very concept of post-Christendom is an implicit critique of the validity of the whole concept of "church," as the term is often used in everyday Christian discourse—i.e., as a special or sacramental institution, set apart for a special mission.

The scholarship on theological education is full of appeals for academic theology to become more integrated with the church. I believe that such appeals betray a lingering allegiance to an obsolete Christendom model of theological education. If theological education is too closely tied to church institutions, it will share in the decline and possible eventual disappearance of the churches from public life. As the visible cultural relics of Christendom lose their shine or disappear altogether, theologians will need to search creatively for manifestations of God's activity within the diverse cultural expressions of post-Christendom.

Instead of confining themselves to churches, theologians should search for the religious "substance" that is embedded in cultural phenomenon[38] and think creatively about what God is teaching the Christian community even through those movements which appear to be anti-Christian. In order to discern these signs of the times, Christians need to be formed so that they can respond appropriately to the tectonic shifts in public life. Such responses should be creative, rather than imitative. The demands of responding imaginatively to the challenges of post-Christendom may require theology to assume a posture that is antagonistic to the prevailing culture.

---

37. Tillich, *Theology of Culture*.

38. This approach is similar to Tillich's understanding of the "theology of culture." Tillich wrote that, "Religion as ultimate concern is the meaning-giving substance of culture, and culture is the totality of forms in which the basic concern of religion expresses itself. In abbreviation: religion is the substance of culture; culture is the form of religion." See Tillich, *Theology of Culture*, 42.

For instance, in a post-Christendom society that is materialistic, pragmatic and relativistic, theology can become spiritual, mystical and evangelical.[39]

Amor Quaerens Intellectum: Theology as Love Seeking Understanding

Theology aspires to what the philosopher, Spinoza (1632–1677), called the *amor Dei intellectualis* "intellectual love of God."[40] However, God is to be loved and cherished not only with the intellect. Blumhardt thus offers salutary advice to theologians: "Don't place yourself above God with your intellect. Rather, put yourself beneath him with your heart."[41] Ultimately, theology is about loving God with heart, soul, mind and strength and loving one's neighbor as oneself (Luke 10:27). Any teaching that does not issue from this kind of love, regardless of how pious or doctrinally sound it may appear, falls short of the mark and does not deserve the appellation of "theology." On this point, the words of Dallas Willard are so pertinent that they deserve to be quoted at length:

> The acid test for any theology is this: Is the God presented one that can be loved, heart, soul, mind, and strength? If the thoughtful, honest answer is "Not really," then we need to look elsewhere or deeper. It does not really matter how sophisticated intellectually or doctrinally our approach is. If it fails to set a loveable God—a radiant, happy, friendly, accessible, and totally competent being—before ordinary people, we have gone wrong ... Theologians on both the left and the right, and those on no known scale of comparison, are all loved by God, who has great things in mind for every one of them ... They need to love God. The theologian who does not love God is in great danger, and in danger of doing great harm, for he or she needs to know him and believe with assurance concerning him.[42]

39. Mysticism and evangelicalism are not necessarily mutually exclusive, as Winfried Corduan explains in his book, *Mysticism: Evangelical Option?* Corduan concludes that, "in the final analysis what we find in the New Testament is Trinitarian mysticism," 132.

40. Lloyd, *Routledge Philosophy Guidebook to Spinoza*, 111.

41. Blumhardt, *Gospel of God's Reign*, 2.

42. Willard, *Divine Conspiracy*, 361.

Theology is not only *fides quaerens intellectum* (faith seeking understanding),[43] but also *amor quaerens intellectum* (love seeking understanding).[44] As one Catholic theologian wisely remarked, "the essence of Christianity is the *real* self-communication of God to the world and our acceptance of that gift in love. In Christianity, love—God's love and our response—takes precedence over knowledge, even knowledge of the truths of the faith."[45]

Such a love-centered theology requires a renewed focus on mission. Mission expresses the heart of God for the world and His care for and solidarity with all its inhabitants. Mission is an expression of divine love for the world and therefore deserves a central place in all theological reflection. Mission-shaped theology involves a passionate pursuit of truth that leads to lasting transformation. Under the influence of Christendom, Christians tended to regard theology as an academic discipline, rather than a tool for the transformation of the world in the power of God's love. This is a serious problem because it has left Christian communities ill-equipped to deal with the unique missional challenges posed by post-Christendom. This issue must be addressed in this book. I do not assume that this study will be able to pronounce the last word on these crucial and complex issues, but I hope that it will at least spark a debate and provoke new thought towards the resolution of these major challenges.

Conclusion: The Bitter Fruits of Theological Knowledge

Theology, as "faith seeking understanding,"[46] is a gift of God's prevenient grace. Faith is both a gift from God and a human response to the initiatives of divine grace. Theology is about making creative connections with life and faith in ways that are life-giving and life-enhancing. However, let it not be assumed that theology is all sweetness and light. Theology is hard work and its fruits can be bitter. Often the knowledge yielded by a serious study of theology can be sweet in the mouth, yet bitter in the stomach (Rev 10:9–10).

Theology requires a poise of vulnerable attentiveness to the movement of the Holy Spirit in the world, which can be unsettling and even disturbing. Theology brings into sharp relief not only the glorious heights of divine grace, but also the ugly depths of human sin. Nevertheless, even in the raging

43. Migliore, *Faith Seeking Understanding*.

44. This definition is associated with Sobrino. See Valiente, *Liberation Through Reconciliation*, 110.

45. Brackley, "Theology and Solidarity," 11.

46. This term, "*fides quaerens intellectum*," is one of the earliest definitions of theology. It is attributed to Anselm of Canterbury, c.1033–1109.

abyss of sin into which the theologian is sometimes obliged to stare, there continues to flicker a great light that shines all the more gloriously against the shadowy backdrop. There is a kindness in the heart of God, which perforates into the deepest caverns of human misery. This "kindly light," which penetrates even the most dismal hollows of hell, is none other than the light of Christ that "conquers the world and illuminates all things."[47] The theologian thus discovers that whether she ascend to the heights of heaven or be forced to make her bed in hell, God is right there in her midst (Ps 139:8). "There is no place, no situation," Blumhardt insists, "to which God's love does not have the right of entry."[48]

47. Berdyaev, *Smysl Tvorchestva*, 527.
48. Blumhardt, *Gospel of God's Reign*, 6.

2

Where Have All the Prophets Gone?

Christian Formation in a Disciple-Making Culture

Would that all the Lord's people were prophets, that the Lord would put his Spirit on them!

—NUMBERS 11:29

What is Prophecy?

Prophecy is a term that has been so universally misunderstood by Christians that when a genuinely prophetic word is spoken, most people are unable to perceive it. Prophecy has been cheapened and demeaned by those who associate it with bizarre speculation about the end times. It therefore needs to be said at the outset that true prophecy has nothing to do with speculative ferment that indulges in biblical code-cracking or date-setting for Doomsday. Prophecy has nothing to do with facile speculations that attempt to find specious connections between the apocalyptic Beast and prominent political or religious leaders. Despite all the online ferment and far-fetched conspiracy theories, there's nothing prophetic about trying to identify Antichrist and the False Prophet with Barack Obama, Paul McCartney or the Spice Girls. In fact, prophecy is *not* about trying to set out a mechanical itinerary of future events. Such efforts are even antagonistic to the true meaning of prophecy.

The true goal of biblical prophecy, rather, as Sergei Bulgakov (1871–1944), pointed out, is "to indicate what is possible and to deflect what should not be, by an appeal to repentance and courage."[1] The prophet sees the present in light of eternity and is able to perceive God's redemptive purposes in the world. Prophecy is not a matter of "arbitrary prediction" but "attempts to delineate the underlying pattern to which historical events are likely to conform."[2] Berdyaev concurs that, "is not prediction, it is not a forecasting of events. Rather, it is the vision which apprehends things present in the light of their eternal issues. It is apocalyptic, it is an unveiling."[3] The prophet envisages the future across the boundaries of the present, but he sees only as one looking through a glass darkly.

The truly prophetic figure is thus someone who is aware of the spiritual forces acting in history and knows all the possibilities contained within the infinite sphere of the effective action of God for whom all things are possible. Prophecy is therefore not a matter of passive expectation, but of creative realization of the best possibilities that will maximize the thriving of God's good creation and the flourishing of all its human (and non-human) inhabitants. As Berdyaev maintains, "It is not true that the prophet is merely a passive instrument in the hand of God. In prophetism humanity too is in the highest degree active; prophecy is a divine-human activity, it is divine-human creativeness."[4]

Notwithstanding its human instrumentality, prophecy is wholly dependent on the activity and inspiration of the Holy Spirit, who inspires the prophet's imagination to reenvision reality from an eternal perspective. Since they operate on the level of grace and spirit, whereas most people remain at the level of the mundane reality, prophets can be lonely people. Kierkegaard, himself a prophet for his times, expressed a great truth when he wrote that, "Truth always rests with the minority, and the minority is always stronger than the majority, because the minority is generally formed by those who really have an opinion, while the strength of a majority is illusory, formed by the gangs who have no opinion."[5] Even more provocatively, Berdyaev proposes that, "Truth may be revealed to one person only and be refused by the rest of the world: it may be prophetic and a prophet is always lonely."[6]

1. Bulgakov, *Bride of the Lamb*, 246.
2. Lincoln, *Spiritual History*, 11.
3. Seaver, *Nicolas Berdyaev*, 119.
4. Berdyaev, *Divine and the Human*, 176.
5. Kierkegaard, *Diary of Søren Kierkegaard* (np).
6. Berdyaev, *Truth and Revelation*, quoted in Lowrie, *Christian Existentialism*, 167.

Prophets are generally more interested in what God is doing in the world than in what Christians are doing in churches. Words of prophecy can be found not only in ancient canonical texts, but also in art, poetry, music and even, as one popular song of the 1960s reminds us, "on the subway walls and tenement halls."[7] Prophets are usually antagonistic to the dominant currents of thought that prevail in social life. Prophets fulminate against errors that have become so widespread among Christians that they often feel completely alone and isolated, as if their voice were as one crying in the wilderness.

Despite its original and often unexpected character, prophecy does not always have to be about innovation. Sometimes a prophetic message can be as simple as the injunction to "Stand at the crossroads and look for the ancient paths" (Jer 6:16). Most crucially, the prophet reminds us that God's ways are not our ways and that His thoughts are not our thoughts (Isa 55:8). The prophet warns us that "what is highly esteemed among men is an abomination in the sight of God" (Luke 16:15) and that, conversely, those things and people that we hold in contempt are often glorious in God's eyes. This idea is poignantly expressed in this prayer known as "The Invocation of the Holy Spirit" from *Celtic Daily Prayer* of the Northumbria Community: "Most powerful Holy Spirit, come down upon us and subdue us; from heaven where the ordinary is made glorious; and glory seems but ordinary."[8]

Prophets have diverse social and economic backgrounds. They can be humble shepherds or sycamore fig farmers (Amos) or they can be descended from a distinguished lineage of priests (Ezekiel); they can even be courtiers of the ruling elite (Isaiah). The prophetic message likewise has diverse expressions. Prophecy can involve lamentation,[9] exhortation,[10] and protest.[11] Prophets inveigh against idolatry and religious complacency.[12] The prophet reminds people that God demands mercy and true knowledge of Him more than sacrifice and burnt offerings (Hos 6:6; cf. 1 Sam 15:22; Ps 40:6). The prophet decries the hypocrisy of praising God with one's lips and, at the same time, denying him in one's heart (Isa 29:13; Matt 15:8). The prophet is as unafraid to speak truth to power as she is to weep for the wretched state of the world. The prophet testifies to the truth of Christ that

---

7. Simon and Garfunkel, "Sounds of Silence."

8. Northumbria Community, *Celtic Daily Prayer*, 273.

9. Rah, *Prophetic Lament*.

10. See, for instance, Isa 1:10–14 and Zeph 1:1—3:20.

11. Boesak, *Comfort and Protest*. My thanks to Nick Megoran for bringing this source to my attention.

12. Wright, *Message of Jeremiah*, 98.

opposes the institutional lies that uphold the structural injustice of a society that has taken leave of God.[13]

Prophets say things that people often do not want to hear; they may bring "a word out of season" (2 Tim 4:2). Therefore, prophecy can be dangerous, not only for the powerful people and institutions against whom the prophecy is directed, but also for the prophets themselves. A. W. Tozer (1897–1963) explained that, "The essence of the message of the prophet is truth. Truth is always a double-edged sword. It cuts both ways. There is a cost factor for the prophet to deliver the message, and there is a cost factor for us to receive that message."[14] The Bible provides abundant illustrations of the cost of prophecy. The prophets of ancient Israel were locked up (Jer 37); ignored (Isa 6); persecuted (2 Kgs 17:33); and despised and rejected (Isa 53). Sometimes the truth to which the prophet testifies is "unbearable" for an entire people (Amos 7:10). Therefore, prophets speak a word of truth to their own people, but they are not usually received by their own (John 1:11).

Not only are prophets usually "acquainted with grief" and held in low esteem (Isa 53:3), but history is full of examples of prophetic individuals, from Socrates (c.470–399 BC) to Martin Luther King Jr. (1929–1968), who met a tragic end. One thinks not only of the biblical prophets Zechariah, John the Baptist, St. Paul, St. Peter, St. Stephen, and nearly all of Jesus's disciples, but also of more recent prophets, such as Dietrich Bonhoeffer (1906–1945); Edith Stein (1891–1942); Mahatma Gandhi (1869–1948); Oscar Romero (1917–1980); Alexander Men (1935–1990); Pavel Adelgeim (1938–2013); Brother Roger of Taize (1915–2005); Sister Dorothy Stang (1931–2005); Serhiy Nigoyan (1993–2014); Boris Nemtsov (1959–2015); and Jo Cox (1974–2016), who also all suffered violent deaths because they took a brave stand for truth and justice.

The sacramental interpretation of Christianity, which prevails in Christendom-minded churches, is inimical to the spirit of biblical prophecy. Christendom, for all its magnificent artistic, architectural and literary accomplishments, in its theology tended to be prosaic, literalistic and dogmatic. Prophetic discourse, by contrast, is lively, poetic and often disturbing. Therefore, when prophecy was not actively or violently resisted, the prophet's voice tended to go unheeded or even unheard altogether. The Christendom Church was tone-deaf to prophecy. As theologians have observed, it is hard to bring a prophetic message to a "prosaic world" that cannot comprehend

---

13. The role of the prophet as one who exposes structural injustice is a keynote of Sobrino's transformative theology. See Pope, "On Not Abandoning the Historical," 46.

14. Tozer, *Voice of a Prophet*, 41.

symbolic language.[15] In the words of Hans Urs von Balthasar (1905–1988), "God needs prophets in order to make himself known, and all prophets are necessarily artistic."[16] Likewise, Berdyaev contends that, "God reveals himself to the world in the prophets, in the Son, in the Spirit, in . . . men and women who have attained the summits of spiritual vision and who, while sharing the destiny of the world, do not feel at ease in the world."[17]

Although some prophetic figures did arise within Christendom, they tended to do so in opposition to the established churches, which viewed prophets with suspicion and even hostility. In many cases, they were ostracized as troublemakers or persecuted as blasphemers by the ecclesiastical authorities. Prophets are particularly unpopular among their own people, who can pay them homage only when the prophet is safely dead. As Dostoevsky remarked, "People do not receive their prophets, but kill them, whereas they love their martyrs and honour those they have slain."[18] It has long been acknowledged that, "A prophet is not without honour, but in his own country, and among his own kin, and in his own house" (Mark 6:4).

Therefore, most of the outstanding prophetic figures in Western history have arisen from outside the church, sometimes even in explicit opposition to the established church—e.g. Karl Marx, Fyodor Dostoevsky, Friedrich Nietzsche and James Joyce. Perceiving their own prophets as a threat, the churches of Christendom have not known what to do with them and have tended to downplay their significance or to castigate them as mad, deluded or heretical. The cry of Nietzsche's Zarathustra offers an exemplary instance of prophetic lament in the face of the opposition and misunderstanding to which the prophet is fated: "They understand me not: I am not the mouth for these ears . . . Calm is my soul, and clear, like the mountains in the morning. But they think me cold, and a mocker with terrible jests. And now do they look at me and laugh: and while they laugh they hate me too. There is ice in their laughter."[19]

Prophets can be radically out of step with the march of the prevailing culture. G. K. Chesterton (1874 1936) remarked that, "it is the paradox of history that each generation is converted by the saint who contradicts it most."[20] Prophets can be eccentric and are often stigmatized as oddballs and antisocial misfits. Christendom churches and the wider society are likely to

---

15. Rowan, *Nicene Creed*.

16. Balthasar, quoted in McLaren, *Generous Orthodoxy*, 163.

17. Berdyaev, *Dream and Reality*, 175.

18. Dostoevsky, *Bratya Karamazovy*, 296.

19. Nietzsche, *Thus Spake Zarathustra*, 7.

20. Chesterton, *Collected Works of G. K. Chesterton*, 424.

classify them as insane and perhaps even seek to get them sectioned under the Mental Health Act. Often, they are either politely ignored or openly ridiculed. The biblical prophets certainly did some bizarre things, such as using dung to bake bread and lying on their side for months at a time (Ezek 4:4-12); others spent three years walking around Jerusalem naked and barefoot as a sign against Egypt and Ethiopia (Isa 20:3).

Some prophets were even "mad" enough to believe that evil could be overcome by good, that truth triumphs over falsehood and that the way to deal with one's enemies was to love them all the way through to reconciliation (Luke 23:34; Rom 5:8). Prophets, in the words of Leonardo Boff, are "people moved by the inner fire who have kept alive and held high the human hope that it is not the brutality of the real that has the last word but the power of that which can bring a better future."[21] Prophets remind not only the church, but also the world that, "The last word will not be that of death but of the transfiguration of life in all its fullness."[22] Their whole lives testified against the cycles of deceit and violence that govern the ways of the world. No wonder many them met a violent or undignified end.

The prophet is endowed with faculties of spiritual perception that make visible the savagery of demonic spirits that incarnate themselves within the banality and triviality of everyday existence and the institutions that sustain social life. In an eloquent tribute to Martin Luther King Jr., who was one of the most remarkable prophets of the twentieth century, Max Stackhouse comments on the prophetic vision of the black Baptist pastor from Georgia:

> We were blinded by our racism and our economic advantages. We kept talking of prejudice and demonstrations, of discrimination and civil disorder . . . And he [King] was telling us about sin and salvation, about chaos and community, about justice and redemption. We spoke of urban strife. He told us that the Lord has a controversy with his people. We worried about those we pitied. He spoke of the soul of a nation in sin. We saw modern society in a situation of stress. He saw it to be founded on a metaphysical disease of racism and violence and economic self-interest. We saw problems to be solved. He saw systematic death to be overcome. Our diagnosis was much milder than his. We wrung our hands. He acted in faith.[23]

In other words, the prophet is endowed with a special ability to penetrate beyond the facade of superficial social reality and to bring to light the true

21. Boff, *Christianity*, 67.
22. Ibid., 69.
23. Stackhouse, quoted in Paeth et al. (eds.), *Shaping Public Theology*, 31.

nature of the issues. Martin Luther King Jr. was able to perceive that racism was not merely a social wrong pathology, but a spiritual disorder and a blasphemous distortion of God's intentions. He saw that racism had brought divine judgement upon the nation as a whole. As is well known, this brave and principled prophet was assassinated. For a racist society that was propped up by an ideological crutch of lies and prejudice, the truth to which the prophet testified was too much to bear.

Therefore, when the prophet raises their voice, the world typically responds with the predictable cry of "crucify him, crucify him" (Luke 23:21). The world will always seek to crucify the truth, because truth is deeply disturbing and unsettling.[24] This sad reality lies behind the quip, often attributed to George Bernard Shaw, that, "If you want to tell people the truth, be sure to make them laugh. Otherwise they'll kill you." Martin Luther King Jr.'s "mistake" was that he brought people not to laughter, but to tears and repentance, which is why they killed him.

Despite the danger and disturbance that prophecy invariably evokes, in post-Christendom, it is vital that the Christian community should rediscover its prophetic or revolutionary vocation in a post-Christian world. This calls for a vision of spiritual formation which will enable people to perceive the "signs of the times" (σημεῖα τῶν καιρῶν—Matt 16:3) and to discern the activity of the Holy Spirit in the world. Prophecy, like all the *charismata* of the Holy Spirit, is not a competence that can be acquired from taking a course in theology, but it is a gift that can be nurtured and produced as the fruit of discipleship and spiritual formation into Christlikeness. All people who claim allegiance to Christ should be prophets to the extent that they are learning to perceive the world through the eyes of love and thus to see things in the light of eternity.

The Need for Depth and Authenticity

In the same way that all Christians are prophets, so it is that all Christians are theologians. To be a Christian is to be a theologian to the extent that all Christians express faith convictions in the way they interact with the world.[25] Moreover, it could even be claimed that even those who self-identify as atheists engage with theological questions to the extent that they express

---

24. Berdyaev asserts that, "Christianity is the religion of crucified truth." See Berdyaev, *Tsarstvo Dukha i Tsarstvo Kesarya*, 326.

25. This is a persistent theme of Grenz and Olson, *Who Needs Theology?*

transcendent longings, which are an inherent part of the human condition. As Berdyaev maintained, "the revolt against God and especially the moral revolt, presupposes the existence of God." He thus added that, "In reality no atheists exist; there are only idolaters."[26]

I am convinced that God looks kindlier upon a sincere agnostic than upon a Christian hypocrite. Sincere atheism may even be closer to God than apathetic, nominal Christianity that characterizes so much church life in the diminishing fragments of Christendom. "Even the fight against God may be a service to God and more religious than a lukewarm and apathetic Christianity."[27] Similarly, I am persuaded that an open-minded Muslim who loves her neighbor is closer to the Kingdom of God than a Christian bigot, who upholds sound doctrine, but who expresses fear, suspicion and even hatred towards those who are different. In other words, the compassionate Muslim receives God's grace, whereas the "Christian" racist stands under God's judgement. Blumhardt remarked that, "The world no longer tolerates heartless people who try to pass as pious. To love all people, to love the world, to despise and condemn nothing—this is what is paving the way for God's kingdom in our time."[28]

Christian faith in a post-Christendom key thus prioritizes depth, authenticity and compassion over tribal identities and belief systems. This emphasis facilitates the reengagement of faith and practice. Post-Christendom theology thus offers a critical perspective that facilitates the process through which faith and practice are correlated. To the extent that Christians attempt to live out their faith convictions, they can be said to be engaged in some form of theological reflection. Therefore, every Christian is to some extent a theologian. Dallas Willard explains this point eloquently:

> Theology is a stuffy word, but it should be an everyday one. That's what practical theology does. It makes theology a practical part of life. A theology is only a way of thinking about and understanding—or misunderstanding—God. Practical theology studies the manner in which our actions interact with God to accomplish his ends in human life . . . Practical theology's overall task is, in effect, to develop for practical implementation the methods by which women and men interact with God to fulfil the divine intent for human existence.[29]

---

26. Berdyaev, *Divine and the Human*, 2.

27. Berdyaev, *Ekzistentsialnaya Dialektika*, 511.

28. Blumhardt, *Gospel of God's Reign*, 22.

29. Willard, *Spirit of the Disciplines*, 14–15.

The choice for a Christian is never between either having a theology or not having a theology; the choice is always between having a good theology or having a bad one. A good theology is one that is life-giving, life-enhancing, and faithful to the biblical teaching, whereas a bad theology is one that is shallow, thoughtless, life-denying and which reduces the God to a sterile, one-dimensional caricature. A bad theology can be compared to spiritual junk food. A. W. Tozer even referred to the "toxic food" that is often fed to Christians and which leads to unfortunate symptoms of gospel-denying superficiality and "celebrity Christianity." "This toxic food," Tozer explains, "is a little bit of psychology, a little bit of inspiration, a dash of theology, a touch of Bible and a whole lot of personality."[30]

Theology is therefore not a dry academic discipline, but an inevitable and unavoidable part of the life of every Christian. William C. Placher concurs that, "If Christians pretend not to think about theology, we end up with unexamined theology, sometimes in forms that are silly or even dangerous."[31] Willard maintains that, "Theology is a part of our lives. It's unavoidable. And . . . a thoughtless theology guides our lives with just as much force as a thoughtful or informed one."[32] Among Christians, part of the problem is that most people, as Grenz and Olson observe, "live in the world of popular theology, not of academic theology." In popular theology, "biblical doctrine becomes fused with elements of popular culture to form various expressions of Christian faith." Popular or "folk theology" constitutes a level of Christian conviction which "rejects critical reflection and enthusiastically embraces simplistic acceptance of an informal tradition of beliefs and practices composed mainly of clichés and legends."[33]

In contrast to the superficiality of appearances, sound-bites, and slogans that characterize our present "visually aggressive age,"[34] theology issues an invitation to deep living, to deep questioning, and to abundant life (John 10:10; Ps 42:7). Richard Foster opened his landmark book, *Celebration of Discipline*, with a prophetic statement: "Superficiality is the curse of our age . . . The desperate need today is not for a greater number of intelligent people, or gifted people, but for deep people."[35] Spiritual depth comes not from being inducted into systems of sound doctrine or by attending

---

30. Tozer, *Voice of a Prophet*, 32.

31. Placher, *Essentials of Christian Theology*, 1–2; cf. Hart, *Faith Thinking*.

32. Willard, *Spirit of the Disciplines*, 26.

33. See chapter 2 of Olson and Grenz, *Who Needs Theology?*

34. O'Donohue, *Anam Cara*, 141.

35. Foster, *Celebration of Discipline*, 1.

Christian meetings, but through disciplined, costly commitment to following the Risen Christ.

The tragedy of the contemporary church is that instead of being a movement for the transformation of the world, in many cases the church has become an alternative leisure pursuit, primarily for middle class religious consumers. Many churches have capitulated to the ideologies of consumerism, individualism, careerism, respectability, and security, which resemble more the idols of middle class morality than the radical, self-denying and communitarian values of Christ and His gospel.

Attempting to respond to cultural trends, many churches have ended up mimicking the worst features of consumer culture by packaging Christianity into a marketable bundle of theological propositions that can be distributed and sold to religious consumers. The prevailing assumption has been that once these propositioned have been "accepted," the religious consumer receives the "full package" of benefits, including, most importantly, forgiveness of sins and eternal life. As Dallas Willard rightly argues, this creates the unbiblical notion that "you can have a faith in Christ that brings forgiveness, while in every other respect your life is no different from that of others who have no faith in Christ at all."[36] James McClendon sets out a more integrated vision of how mission and discipleship cohere: "The faithfulness of Christ made it possible for us to be his disciples, citizens of his new kingdom. And our faith, our faithful response to him, is the quality of our lives as disciples, as citizens of the kingdom. To put it in a stylish, but I hope helpful way, Christ's faithfulness is the objective possibility of our salvation."[37]

One of the most urgent tasks of post-Christendom theology is therefore to repair the broken connections between mission, discipleship, life, and salvation. As a result of the Christendom tendency towards nominalism, saving faith has often been cheapened into "mental assent to correct doctrine."[38] Such a conception of cheap faith is as far removed from the teaching of Jesus as the opposite error of assuming that salvation depends on the performance of good deeds. What results from nominal Christianity is the unexamined assumption that progress in the discipleship will "somehow automatically take place through the normal course of life, if only the [believer] holds on to certain beliefs."[39] Such notions of "cheap grace"

---

36. Willard, *Divine Conspiracy*, 44.

37. McClendon, quoted in Freeman's "Introduction," in McClendon, *Witness*, xxvi.

38. Willard, *Spirit of the Disciplines*, 23.

39. Ibid., 111.

constitute little more than a truncated "gospel of sin management,"[40] rather than a transformative vision of life in the Kingdom of God, which was always at the heart of Jesus's proclamation of the gospel. This leads to the unacknowledged assumption of some Christians that "Jesus can 'save' us when we die, but . . . on earth he should leave us in peace."[41]

Therefore, in Christendom, apart from church attendance and mental assent to a system of belief, there is very little that sets Christians apart from the unbelievers among the general population.[42] The faith of Christendom has tended to reduce salvation in Christ to cognitive fidelity to certain doctrines. The assumption has often been that salvation is a matter of passing down the "deposit of faith" (*depositum fidei*)[43] in doctrines that can be affirmed in order to guarantee salvation. As a result of this passive understanding of salvation, the gospel has been deprived of its transforming power. Dallas Willard thus laments, that "More often than not, faith has failed, sadly enough, to transform the human character of the masses, because it is usually unaccompanied by discipleship and by an overall discipline of life such as Christ himself practiced."[44] Remarking on the lack of distinctiveness of a typical "born-again Christian," Tozer notes that, "His life is unchanged; he still lives for his own pleasure, only now he takes delight in singing choruses and watching religious movies instead of singing bawdy songs and drinking hard liquor. The accent is still on enjoyment, though the fun is now on a higher plane morally if not intellectually."[45]

The failure of many Christians to distinguish themselves from the blandness and workaday existence of life in a sinful world has created the impression that it is possible to believe in Christ without aspiring to be conformed either morally or spiritually in His image. As a result, there are many so-called Christians who, as Kierkegaard explains, "instead of following Christ are snugly and comfortably settled, with family and steady promotion, under the guise that their activity is the Christianity of the New

---

40. See Chapter 2 of Willard, *Divine Conspiracy*.

41. Blumhardt, *Gospel of God's Reign*, 1.

42. See, for instance, the findings of the 2006 Barna Group Survey, which showed that among the population of the USA, there are no considerable differences between the lifestyles of those who self-identify as "born-again Christians" and those who did not regard themselves as "Christians." See http://www.christiantoday.com/article/american.study.reveals.indulgent.lifestyle.christians.no.different/9439.htm [accessed 7.1.2016].

43. Hvidt, *Christian Prophecy*, 30.

44. Willard, *Spirit of the Disciplines*, 230.

45. Tozer, quoted in Tomasella, *I Die Daily*, 172.

Testament."[46] In contrast to superficial notions of "conversion" and decadent "bourgeois Christianity," F. W. Robertson (1816–1853) formulated a more profound definition of Christian identity when he claimed that, "A Christian is one who is in the process of restoring God's original likeness to his character."[47]

Post-Christendom offers an opportunity to think of Christian identity in terms of character and convictions, rather than doctrines and beliefs. In Christendom the differences between born-again Christians and the general population tend to be primarily cosmetic, concerning matters of doctrine, worldview and behavior. At the deeper, structural level of consciousness and spiritual formation, many Christians are just as captive to the anti-gospel forces of consumerism and are just as indifferent to the pain of the world as everyone else. Tozer, again, notes that, "Our error today is that we do not expect a converted man [sic] to be a transformed man, and as a result of this error our churches are full of substandard Christians."[48] In the same spirit, Berdyaev lamented that, "Christians, people who believe in God, live and arrange their affairs on earth as if God did not exist, as if there had been no Sermon on the Mount. Christians, like non-Christians, live according to the law of the world and not according to the law of God."[49]

For instance, it has been shown that Christians in the West on average spend just as much time on Facebook and Twitter, send as many text messages and spend as much time watching television and playing video games as those who do not self-identify as Christians. Many Christians have faithfully been attending religious services on Sundays (and perhaps also the midweek fellowship meetings) and have then spent the rest of the week living like everyone else—i.e., according to the predictable patterns and routines that determine the life of the world. Many Christians are just as affected by spiritual fatigue and seem to have lost the capacity to ask ultimate questions.

Consequently, society has remained without a transformative influence as Christians unwittingly relinquish their vocation to be salt and light. Jesus was clear on this point when He said to His disciples: "You are the salt of the earth. But if the salt loses its saltiness, how can it be made salty again? It is no longer good for anything, except to be thrown out and trampled underfoot" (Matt 5:13). Christoph Friedrich Blumhardt (1842–1919) made a similar telling remark concerning the ways that many Christians have

---

46. Kierkegaard, *Attack upon Christendom*, 42.

47. Robertson, quoted in Seaver, *Nicolas Berdyaev*, 32.

48. Tozer, *Evenings with Tozer*, 300.

49. Berdyaev, *Ekzistentsialnaya Dialektika*, 439.

abandoned the prophetic call of Christ to change the world, and have instead been content to found religious clubs:

> Our task is to "put on the new self" (Col 3:9–11). If we strive
> to do this, and if the boredom of our theology and our Chris-
> tianity has not already killed us, we can become people truly
> enthusiastic for Jesus. If Christ alone is our light and life, then
> we can possibly be of some help to those who don't believe. But
> religious talk is useless (Matt 7:21). So is forming some kind of
> religious community where everyone sits together in a corner
> and prays and reads the Bible. No, make an effort to get rid of
> the lies that darken this world. Do this by endeavoring to live
> with an upright heart, in the power of God's truth.[50]

Christians living in the midst of post-Christendom must not be content
with attending services or even professing so-called sound doctrine. Followers of the Risen Christ are called not to be separate from the world, to
retreat into religious shelters and church buildings, but to *dissolve* like salt
(i.e. after the pattern of Matt 5:13) into the wider society and thereby to
be a catalyst for humanizing forces, such as compassion, dignity, respect,
and courtesy. There needs to be a concentrated, focused and coordinated
strategy to overcome the lies, deceit, and inhumanity that characterizes so
much of our public life. Meeting in church buildings on Sunday mornings
and singing escapist songs that make vacuous professions of romantic love
to Jesus will not change the world, but will merely perpetuate a religious
subculture and widen the gulf between faith and life.

Taking a Prophetic Stand for Truth in a World of Lies

In a world in which lies and deceit constitute the default mode of social reality, it is very difficult to live in the truth. Winston Churchill once quipped
that, "A lie gets halfway around the world before the truth has a chance to
get its pants on." Since social reality is saturated in falsehood and superficiality, it takes sustained effort and constant vigilance to live in the depth of
truth. Twentieth century existentialist philosophy has compellingly demonstrated that it is far easier and more comforting to live a lie than to live the
truth.[51] Truth is hard work, but the gospel of truth demands nothing less
than uncompromising allegiance to a life of truth and authenticity.

50. Blumhardt, *Everyone Belongs to God*, 34–35.

51. See, for example, Sartre, *Being and Nothingness*, 462; Heidegger, *Essence of Human Freedom*. For an in-depth discussion of this topic from a Christian existentialist
perspective, see Berdyaev, *O Rabstve i Svobode Cheloveka*.

The gospel presents every human being with a basic choice: either to choose the authentic existence of "walking in the truth" with Christ (3 John 1:4) or to live an inauthentic existence in which we lose ourselves to the trivial distractions of entertainment and superficiality. In other words, the basic human choice, as one notable existentialist theologian put it, is between God and the world: "Will we live life with Christ or without Christ?"[52] Similarly, Berdyaev once remarked that, "There are two fundamentally different types of people: those whose relationship with the world is accommodating and harmonious, and those who are continually at variance with it."[53] This corresponds with the incisive critique of Tozer, who lamented that, "The weakness of so many modern Christians is that they feel too much at home in the world. In their effort to achieve restful adjustment to unregenerate society they have lost their pilgrim character and become an essential part of the very moral order against which they are sent to protest."[54]

The cultural environment of triviality, mass media, sensationalism, and "the doctrine of instant satisfaction"[55] present formidable obstacles to spiritual formation into Christlikeness. Part of the goal of theological formation is to empower people to protest against the blind acceptance of traditions and customs inspired by what Friedrich Nietzsche (1844–1900) called the "herd instinct" (Herdentrieb)[56] that governs the collective consciousness, which is sometimes labelled "public opinion" or the "will of the people." Such protest may put Christians in the difficult and costly position of being a despised minority amid a herd of "people talking without speaking; people hearing without listening."[57] If the default position of society is falsehood and superficiality, then those who pursue the truth and depth will inevitably be in the minority. This is the tragic irony of prophecy, as countless prophets through the ages, from Jesus Christ to Martin Luther King Jr., have demonstrated. The prophet may have been proved right in the end, but this did not prevent them from meeting a violent end.

The world's current penchant for violence is just one indication of such a disregard for truth. Violence testifies to the "poverty and hysteria of the modern consciousness."[58] Violence is one of the many baneful manifestations of the poverty of imagination in a world ruled by technological

---

52. Macquarrie, *Existentialist Theology*, 22.

53. Berdyaev, *Dream and Reality*, 35.

54. Tozer, *Man the Dwelling Place of God*, 98.

55. Foster, *Celebration of Discipline*, 1.

56. Abel, *Nietzsche: die Dynamik der Willen zur Macht*, 54.

57. Simon and Garfunkel, "Sounds of Silence."

58. Tillich, *Courage to Be*, 132.

gadgetry, celebrity culture, junk TV, and various forms of mind-numbing propaganda, including the alluring lies disseminated by the industries of advertising and so-called PR. Under such conditions, people live under the illusion that the violent feelings and extreme xenophobic views that they have adopted as a result of watching and listening to the mass media are their own. They become "victims of the information deluge."[59] "Public opinion" is the product of what social identity theorists have called "group think,"[60] which turns groups into the kind of demonic collectives character-ized by Jesus in Milton's *Paradise Regained* as "a miscellaneous rabble, who extol things vulgar."[61]

Followers of the Risen Christ can be at the spearhead of a new cultural movement that resists the violent tendencies and zoological impulses of contemporary society. In such a world where living in socially-constructed illusions of violence and falsehood is the "default position," formation into the likeness of Christ—who embodies the gospel values of love and truth— is hard work and requires great moral strength and spiritual engagement. In Christendom, many people, including those who profess Christian faith, have become either willfully distracted or have had their compassionate fac-ulties numbed by the constant assaults by the popular media on the values of truth, respect, dignity and humanity. Berdyaev noted prophetically that people are capable of "paralyzing their consciousness through a system of hypnosis, of psychological . . . poisoning."[62] Under a constant barrage, these values are gradually eroded as power, greed, selfishness, image, and violence triumph over freedom, generosity, solidarity, substance, and peace.

Such a condition leads to a distortion of people's moral conscience and induces people to call good that which is evil, and to name as evil that which is good (Isa 5:20; cf. Mark 3:22–30; Matt 12:31–32). For example, the personal sins of egoism, narcissism, self-seeking, careerism, deceit and aggression are baptized and sanctified by the new religions of PR and ce-lebrity worship. The most pernicious falsehoods are disseminated in such a way as to cause maximum offence. Newspaper columnists try to outdo each other in attaining new levels of depravity and inhumanity. Vulgar gossip and obscene xenophobic views are printed in tabloids and posted on blogs, which are eagerly consumed by a credulous public that seeks not truth and enlightenment, but titillation and entertainment. One person's tragedy is another's amusement.

---

59. Bauman and Donskis, *Moral Blindness*, 145.

60. Hogg and Williams, "From I to We," 81–97.

61. Milton, quoted in Hammond, *Milton and the People*, 231.

62. Berdyaev, *Slavery and Freedom*, 156.

Under such conditions, the Holy Spirit is quenched, human dignity is debased and the powers and principalities are unleashed in all their destructive fury. Lies, myths and fabrications are hostile not only to the truth, but to life itself and to the humane, life-affirming values of the gospel. James Alison explains that, "leading us into the whole truth means the active and creative overcoming of the lie which is at the root of human culture."[63] Contemporary post-Christendom society is in revolt against the gospel and thus stands under the judgement of God.

Instead of a culture of compassion and solidarity, we have a celebrity culture that wages an undeclared war against the truth. In an unjust world, justice is hard work and requires perpetual vigilance. The problem today is that many good people have become distracted and apathetic. After all, why should we care about social injustice when we have much more important things to worry about, such as whom to vote for in the latest round of X-Factor, Pop Idol, or Celebrity Big Brother? Why should we care about poverty when we need to attend to far more pressing issues, such as checking our Facebook profiles for the thirtieth time in a single day? And why do we need to bother ourselves with global poverty and disease when there are much more critical demands on our time, such as needing to find out about how celebrity X ended up in bed with celebrity Y?

We, including Christians, are preoccupied with the latest gadgets and gossip, which have distracted us from the plight of other people, particularly those in desperate situations. Many Christians have become too enmired in a swamp of religious practices and materialistic preoccupations to be concerned about the plight of the world. So, I think we can say that we are experiencing a crisis of compassion in contemporary culture and that the retreat of Christians into religious clubs has played its role in fomenting the crisis. The failure of Christians to salt the wider world with gospel values of truth and compassion has even lent some credence to Berdyaev's provocative statement that "the unbelieving humanist has given a better expression of Christianity than the believing Christians who have done nothing for the improvement of society."[64]

The erosion of spiritual values leads to a descent into a hostile social context which is characterized by a chronic deficit of compassion, solidarity and even basic courtesy. Without the necessary foundation of compassion, society degenerates into what Thomas Hobbes (1588–1679) called a "state of nature" in which, according to the proverb, *homo homini lupus est*—"a

---

63. Alison, *Living in the End Times*, 68.
64. Berdyaev, *Russkaya Ideya*, 105–6.

man is a wolf to another man."[65] Theology needs to be able to speak into this crisis, but will never be able to do so as long as the best and most original Christian minds today are distracted by pointless disputes concerning the meaning of church sacraments, apostolic succession or the latest take on the Chalcedonian formula or the eternal pre-existence of the Second Hyposta-sis. Instead, theology should address the urgent issues in the public sphere. In order to promote a social context in which justice and peace can thrive, Christians are called to embody and inculcate humane virtues in society, so that degenerate forces of inhumanity and callous indifference to the suffer-ing of others will not be able to flourish.

Prophecy and Christian Formation

Concerning the issue of theological formation, the question may be stated in the following way: "how can Christians be more proactive in pervading (or "salting") the social sphere with the gospel values of dignity, respect, truth, freedom, solidarity, and compassion?" One of the lessons of church history is that the de-Christianization of society leads inexorably to the dehumanization of society. Writing just before the outbreak of the Second World War, Berdyaev warned about the forces of "depersonalization and dehumanization now menacing the world."[66] He foresaw "not only the de-Christianization but also the de-humanization of man, which were gathering momentum."[67] He thus made the prescient remark that, "The new Christi-anity must re-humanize humankind and society, culture and the world."[68] This is a succinct statement of the task of theology in post-Christendom.

Theology is called to envision "a new kind of Christianity"[69] that connects meaningfully to an emerging generation of spiritual seekers, who are moved not by the propositional postulates of dogmatic theology, but by the spiritual reality of lived experience and transformed humanity. As Harvey Cox put it, "The experience *of* the divine is displacing theories *about* it."[70] Moreover, this kind of Christianity does not reject or condemn the world, but demonstrates its solidarity with people in the world, particularly those who are suffering—whether from sin, illness, personal shortcomings or injustice. In other words, the flourishing of this kind of Christianity is

65. Hobbes, *Leviathan*, 70; see also Gottlieb, *Dilemmas of Reaction*, 175.

66. Berdyaev, quoted in Nicolaus, *C. G. Jung and Nikolai Berdyaev*, 23.

67. Berdyaev, *Dream and Reality*, 290.

68. Berdyaev, *Fate of Man in the Modern World*, 129.

69. McLaren, *New Kind of Christianity*.

70. Cox, *Future of Faith*, 20.

expressed not in the triumph of Christianity over society, but in compassion for and involvement in society.[71]

In order for this new kind of Christianity to come into being, there needs to be a fundamental restructuring of theological education, so that every aspect of the teaching and learning process is directed towards forming students into mature followers of Jesus who can respond appropriately to the post-Christendom context. The answer is not to be sought in any institution, be it the university or the church. Institutionalized expressions of Christian faith are becoming increasingly marginalized. Organized forms of Christianity are declining. In the UK alone, hundreds of church buildings have been sold off and converted into carpet warehouses, apartment blocks, mosques, New Age centers, or even nightclubs. The hierarchical structures of crumbling church institutions and educational establishments are becoming more defective and even dysfunctional in contemporary post-Christendom. Given the increasing irrelevance of churches, theological educators will need to think creatively about how to form students in ways that are not too dependent on church structures.

Post-Christendom and the broader tendencies of post-modernity require a holistic and integrated vision of theological formation that extends far beyond seminaries and church buildings. Theology facilitates a way of being or a mode of apprehension through which to navigate the course of faith through all the specialized forms of life in a post-modern and post-Christian era. Prophets are formed when people are brought to such a level of existential awareness that they are able to make informed valuations concerning truth, goodness and beauty. Nurturing such an awareness is crucial to forming people spiritually into the likeness of Christ.

Spiritual Formation as a Comprehensive Process of Transformation

Pedagogical wisdom begins with the recognition that all education—in so far as it shapes the formation of character and personality—is a spiritual process. "In the very act of educating," notes Parker Palmer, "we are in the process of forming or deforming the human soul."[72] Moreover, spiritual formation is a universal human experience. As the wise Christian philosopher, Dallas Willard, used to remark, everyone from a compassionate saint, such as Mother Teresa to a murderous egomaniac like Adolf Hitler has

71. Searle and Cherenkov, *Future and a Hope*, 116.
72. Palmer, "Toward a Spirituality of Higher Education," 75.

undergone a process of spiritual formation.[73] "Spiritual formation" comes in many shapes and sizes and can happen at home in front of a television screen or a games console just as readily as in a church building when people are praying. One of the many failures of Christendom was the unthinking tendency of many Christians to exaggerate the role of church, particularly church activities, in the process of spiritual formation. By thinking about spiritual formation in terms of fidelity to church teaching, Christians who operated under Christendom assumptions tended to downplay the ways in which formation occurs in subtle ways in the midst of ordinary life.

Furthermore, Christendom tended to subordinate spirituality to doctrine, which lead to an impoverished understanding of formation which, as Smith claims, "fails to honor the fact that we are embodied, material, fundamentally desiring animals who are, whether we recognize it or not (and perhaps most when we don't recognize it), every day being formed by the material liturgies that are forming us every day."[74] If the church is forming our doctrines, but the world is forming our desires then the world has the most important part of us: "For where your treasure is, there will your heart be also" (Matt 6:21). When Jesus speaks about "treasure" in this instance, He has in mind the desires of the heart. This insight lies behind Smith's commendable call for theological education to be reenvisioned in terms of a "pedagogy of desire."[75] Within post-Christendom there is a necessary exposure of the fallacy of assuming that spiritual growth into Christlikeness will simply happen, provided that people attend enough church services, sing enough hymns, listen to enough sermons or say enough prayers.

This is clearly an ungrounded assumption. There is nothing passive about spiritual formation. Formation within the Kingdom of God occurs not through passive waiting, but through active preparation for its coming and realization. Spiritual formation, or growth in Christlikeness, is attainable only by responding actively to the initiatives of divine grace. Such a response is made by applying the "vision, intention and means," which are necessary to make such a transformation possible.[76] This is because the default mode of contemporary culture is fundamentally in conflict with the moral and spiritual values of the Kingdom of God.

The *Zeitgeist* of the world is diametrically opposed to the Holy Spirit and to the gospel. The world is in the grip of dynamic forces, many of which

73. For a fascinating, yet disturbing, account of Hitler's "spiritual formation," see the first volume of Ian Kershaw's definitive biography, *Hitler 1889–1936: Hubris*.

74. Smith, *Desiring the Kingdom*, 33.

75. Ibid., 24–25.

76. Willard, "Living A Transformed Life Adequate To Our Calling."

are demonic in origin (Eph 6:12; cf. 1 John 4:3; 5:19). Even among Christians, spiritual formation is something that happens not primarily during church services, but in the midst of ordinary life. For instance, if a Christian spends three or four hours per day watching television or playing computer games and then spends fifteen minutes reading their Bible, it is obvious that the hours they spent in front of the screen will have a far greater influence on the formation of their spirit.

Christians are therefore living in a disciple-making culture. Our culture tries to form us in other ways that do not correspond to the way of Jesus. Culture is no blank canvas or neutral space, but is shaped by powerful elemental impulses and spiritual forces, the "principalities and powers" (Eph 6:12) that incarnate themselves in the institutions of politics, society and the media.[77] The media works through powerful, mind-forming selectivity in order to colonize the consciousness in ways that lead to impulsive behavior. The culture of marketing and advertising orchestrate well-aimed campaigns that are carefully devised to appeal to the zoological impulses of the human psyche. The modern advertising industry wants us not only to buy certain products, but also to *buy into* media-fabricated identities and lifestyles. These identities confer a sense of belonging and offer people a justification for continuing with their bland, workaday lifestyles that do not glow with the *anima* of spiritual vitality or depth. Martin Heidegger (1889–1976) lamented the dehumanizing tendencies of mass culture in which "everything that is primordial gets glossed over as something that has long been well known . . . Everything secret loses its force."[78]

As a result, many people have lost the capacity to appreciate beauty or to express themselves creatively. George Steiner decries what he calls the "commercialization of the aesthetic," noting reproachfully that citations from Shakespeare and Kant have been used to sell soap powder.[79] Within a consumer culture, most people have only a worm's eye view of the world and the injunction to "seek those things which are above" (Col 3:1–2) is nullified. Consequently, expressions of spiritual creativity are replaced by the trite imitations of fashion and chaotic banality of market trends and patterns of consumer consumption.

In a post-Christian consumer culture people's minds are being formed into the image of a consumerism, which one Christian sociologist referred

---

77. Wink, *Naming the Powers*; Wink, *Unmasking the Powers*; Wink, *Engaging the Powers*.

78. Heidegger, *Being and Time*, 164–65.

79. Steiner, *Grammars of Creation*, 34.

to as the "chief rival to God in our culture."[80] Omnivorous consumerism permeates not merely the selling and purchase of consumable goods, but also inter-personal relationships, which leads to the progressive dehumanization of social relations.[81] People begin to treat friends, work colleagues, family members, and even partners like consumable gadgets—i.e., as "things" to be disposed of as soon as the more efficient, more attractive replacement appears.[82] Within consumer culture the "herd instinct"[83] lures people into finding happiness in the commodities produced by mass culture.

Therefore, instead of thinking and engaging critically with the world, people just show up, behave themselves, obey fashion and follow the fickle tendencies of "public opinion." Almost unwittingly, people capitulate to what German sociologists refer to as the "pressure to conform to the prevailing mass society"[84] and slip into ready-made roles and routines. Like the prisoners in Plato's cave[85] people confine themselves within the conditions of our incarceration and even begin to admire the beauty of their prison walls. The security of routine and dead repetition is preferred to the vulnerability of freedom and responsibility. Thus, as James K. A. Smith rightly maintains, "An important part of revisioning Christian education is to see it as a mode of counter-formation."[86] Noxious forces such as celebrity culture and consumerism must be resisted because, as Berdyaev truthfully maintains, "the religion of Christ is incompatible with the recognition of bourgeois values, with reverence towards wealth, power, fame and the enjoyment of the world."[87]

It has been observed that we are living in very harsh and vulgar times.[88] The recent history of mass culture sometimes reads like an unhappy chronicle of the decay of spiritual values. Grotesque indecency is paraded and packaged by the culture industry and sold to millions of consumers

80. Storkey, "Post-Modernism Is Consumption," 100–107.

81. Marx describes these processes in meticulous detail in the famous first chapter of his major work, *Das Kapital*. In the final part of the first chapter he uses the term "commodity fetishism" (*Warenfetisch*) to describe the dehumanization of human relations within capitalist societies in which social relations among people degenerate into purely economic relations based on market principles. See chapter 1 of Marx, *Capital*.

82. Morgan, *Protestants and Pictures*, 17.

83. Nietzsche, *On the Genealogy of Morals*, 13.

84. Blankertz, *Die Katastrophe der Befreiung*, 237.

85. See Book VII of Plato's *Republic* in Plato, *Six Great Dialogues*, 360–63.

86. Smith, *Desiring the Kingdom*, 33.

87. Berdyaev, *Smysl Tvorchestva*, 260.

88. Leading sociologists, Bauman and Donskis refer to the present "age of modern barbarism." See Bauman and Donskis, *Moral Blindness*, 139.

as entertainment. Insensitivity, meaninglessness and a prevailing sense of nihilism have rendered people indifferent to human suffering. In the words of two leading sociologists, we are witnessing "unparalleled displays of human insensitivity."[89] Society is stuffed with useless, valueless information about the most banal superficialities, which denote the tedious triviality and emptiness of mass culture and fabricated moral sentiment. Under the constant assault of mind-numbing propaganda, people lose their capacity to wonder. Spontaneity and creativity are submerged under the dead forces of repetition and routine. As Dostoevsky put it, "The world is spiritual, but the higher part of human existence is rejected completely and scorned with a sense of triumph, even with hatred."[90]

In a culture that exhibits a "supreme disdain for the things of the soul,"[91] the world is emptied of beauty and depth and becomes flat, dull, tedious, predictable and repetitive. The dominance of secular materialism has ensured that people's souls have been "soaked with secularity."[92] Under the dead weight of commercial and bureaucratic interests, society starts to take on the features of efficiency, calculability, predictability and control that characterize fast food restaurants.[93] The culture industry, the advertising agencies, and the mass media serve as continual distractions that divert people's thoughts away from the deep issues of life and towards the insipid prattle, for example, of soap operas and celebrity gossip.

Even more insidious distractions can be found in the film, tabloid and magazine industries in which degraded conceptions of sex and violence and the lust for power are all found to prevail. Moreover, the language found on the internet is often sadistic. The powers and principalities are at work in the shadowlands of the cybersphere. The anarchy and lawlessness that characterize the unregulated internet environment might even be said to correspond with the primeval chaos of the nothingness (the "formless void") in the biblical creation narratives, which some theologians following Karl Barth, have characterized as the essence of the demonic. Online abuse has spiraled out of control as "verbal orgies of faceless hatred"[94] are unleashed by anonymous trolls against total strangers.

The addictive aspects of internet consumption, together with the constant repetition of degrading and inhumane themes on social media,

89. Bauman and Donskis, *Moral Blindness*, 11.

90. Dostoevsky, *Bratya Karamazovy*, 290.

91. Berdyaev, *End of Our Time*, 78.

92. Willard, *Divine Conspiracy*, 103.

93. Ritzer, *McDonaldization of Society*.

94. Bauman and Donskis, *Moral Blindness*, 11.

television, the advertising industry, and in video games, is harmful in so far as people's inner minds begin to be subtly conformed to the superficial and vulgar material that becomes embedded in our subconscious. Given the alarming proliferation of online pornographic material, it is possible that overall in many parts of today's post-Christendom society, pornography is having a greater shaping power on people's spiritual formation than the gospel. The constant stream of violence, abuse, and sexual perversion trains the mind in destructive thought patterns, thereby impoverishing life and diminishing relationships.

These regrettable tendencies are all symptomatic of an underlying spiritual crisis resulting from humankind's estrangement from God. They testify to the decadence of the world and the process of dehumanization that is occurring in a fallen world buffeted by cruelty and conflict. These trends indicate the desolation of a sinsick humanity that has forsaken God and, in its turn, seems to have been forsaken by God. The world in a post-Christian era continues "as though there had been no redemption and that no anticipatory sign of resurrection had been given."[95]

Such is the seeming absence of resurrection power from the world that the content of modern life in its alienation from God can even be understood as a "negative revelation"[96] of the Christian truth. As Jon Sobrino maintains, the world is "sin, radical negativity, a radical negation of the will of God, and the highest manifestation of the rejection of God."[97] All the baneful developments in the world today—from internet pornography to injustice, fascism, racism, exploitation, poverty, and the degradation of the environment—are derived from a common spiritual source: namely, from sin.

Two Prophetic Witnesses for a Post-Christian World: Nikolai Berdyaev and Dietrich Bonhoeffer

As theology in a post-Christian world seeks to discover its prophetic voice, there are, in my view, two outstanding representatives of the prophetic Christian tradition from whom Christians can learn vital lessons concerning the nature and task of theology today. These are the gifted Russian Christian mystic and free-thinker, Nikolai Berdyaev (1874–1948), and the courageous German pastor and martyr, Dietrich Bonhoeffer (1906–1945).

95. Boff, *Christianity in a Nutshell*, 87.

96. The term, "negative revelation" of God's truth is taken from the writings of the Russian mystic philosopher, Solovyev. See Gajdenko, *Vladimir Solovyev*, 60.

97. Sobrino, quoted in Crowley, "Theology in the Light of Human Suffering," 19.

What marks these two figures out is the way that they saw beyond the superficial events of their times and perceived the raging abyss that was surging beneath the surface of world history. They were endowed with rare and acute powers of spiritual perception that were the fruit of much prayer and suffering. They were so far ahead of their times that, although they were born in 1874 and 1906 respectively, the visions of Christianity set forth by Berdyaev and Bonhoeffer are, arguably, only now coming of age. The philosopher, Isaiah Berlin (1909–1997), once remarked that, "It is one of the marks of writers of genius that what they say may, at times, touch a central nerve in the minds or feelings of men who belong to other times, cultures or outlooks, and set up trains of thought and entail consequences which did not, or could not, occur to such writers, still less occupy their minds."[98] Although Berlin had in mind the Neapolitan philosopher, Giambattista Vico (1668–1744), the same could also apply to both Berdyaev and Bonhoeffer.

For many years now I have had a small framed portrait of Nikolai Berdyaev on my study desk. I regard him as one of the greatest prophets of the twentieth century. His Russian prose is lucid and the profundity of his spiritual insight, which was nurtured by his deep immersion in the biblical vision of salvation, is immense. He has influenced my spiritual outlook more than any other philosopher or theologian I have encountered. Already in his early teens, Berdyaev was fluent in several European languages and deeply acquainted with the works of leading figures in Russian and European philosophy. He was steeped in patristic writings of the Alexandrian and Cappadocian Fathers and well-versed in the classical and mystical traditions of Christian theology.[99]

Despite his formidable learning and the exceptional subtlety of his mind, Berdyaev was no ivory-tower academic. He asserted that, "in my case the desire to know the world has always been accompanied by a desire to alter it . . . I was never a philosopher of the academic type, and it has never been my wish that philosophy should be abstract and remote from life."[100] Berdyaev's greatness consists in his prophetic foresight and spiritual depth that enabled him to expose the falsehood of the pseudo-religions of fascism and communism that were in the ascendency at the time he wrote his prophetic works.

Berdyaev knew what it meant to "suffer for righteousness' sake" (1 Pet 3:14). At the age of twenty-five he was exiled to northern Russia and in 1913 he was charged with blasphemy for an article in which he had criticized the

98. Berlin, *Against the Current*, 151.
99. Seaver, *Nicolas Berdyaev*, 12.
100. Berdyaev, quoted in Seaver, *Nicolas Berdyaev*, 11–12.

clerical abuses of the Russian Orthodox Church. As a Christian freethinker and a dedicated defender of liberty,[101] Berdyaev was imprisoned twice by the Bolshevik regime and was forced into exile by the Bolsheviks in 1922. At the height of Lenin's Red Terror (1918–1922), Berdyaev was interrogated by the Head of Lenin's secret police, Felix Dzerzhinsky (1877–1926). Alexander Solzhenitsyn (1918–2008), in his celebrated book, *The Gulag Archipelago*, describes Berdyaev's encounter with Lenin's interrogators in terms that illustrate Berdyaev's prophetic credentials as one who was unafraid to speak truth to power:

> They wanted to drag him [Berdyaev] into an open trial; they arrested him twice; and (in 1922) he was subjected to a night interrogation by Dzerzhinsky himself . . . But Berdyaev did not humiliate himself. He did not beg or plead. He set forth firmly those religious and moral principles which had led him to refuse to accept the political authority established in Russia. And not only did they come to the conclusion that he would be useless for a trial, but they liberated him.[102]

After his exile from the Soviet Union and his resettlement in Paris, Berdyaev was uniquely placed to understand the pathological tendencies of the emerging totalitarian ideology that had descended upon Europe in the early part of the twentieth century. In a new age of tribalism and the spread of racist ideologies, Berdyaev had the foresight to understand that, "Racism is anti-human and anti-Christian. It is founded solely upon the principle of biological heredity which is highly dubious from a biological point of view. It is an extreme form of anti-personalism and regards the human being as a breed of animals."[103] From this anti-racist perspective, Berdyaev understood that, "Two ideas contend with each other in the world: The first idea is the selection of the strong, of the best, of the genetically-pure, of the aristocrats of blood and race; the domination of certain human beings over others. The second idea is the brotherhood of all human beings, the dignity and worth of every human personality, the acknowledgement of the spiritual foundation of personhood. According to the first idea, a human being is merely part of nature; whereas according to the second idea, the human is a

---

101. Berdyaev remarked that, "Freedom, unconditional and uncompromising freedom, has been the fundamental fountain-head and prime mover of all my thinking"—Berdyaev, *Dream and Reality*, 158.

102. Solzhenitsyn, *Gulag Archipelago*, 130. Berdyaev himself recounts his encounter with Dzerzhinsky in his autobiographical treatise, *Samopoznanie*, 278–82.

103. Berdyaev, *Ekzistentsialnaya Dialektika*, 453.

spiritual being. The truly human is associated with the second idea; the first idea is inhuman."[104]

Berdyaev lamented other dehumanizing forces, such as the increasing collectivization and mechanization of society. He perceived how dangerous these tendencies could become if they were to be harnessed to serve the destructive ends of degenerate ideologies, such as fascism and communism. Under these conditions, the human spirit is crushed and people "are cast into outer darkness in which they are reduced to the semblance of broken puppets."[105] Berdyaev became the most eloquent and perceptive critic of totalitarianism in both its fascist and communist manifestations. He denounced Lenin's communism as "a vast experiment based on the denial of all absolute spiritual elements in personal and social life."[106]

Berdyaev controversially and prophetically ascribed some of the blame for the catastrophe of Soviet Communism to the Christian Church's betrayal of gospel principles concerning the rejection of property and wealth and the fundamental equality of all human beings before God. He famously claimed that:

> Christians who accuse the communists of atheism and anti-religious persecution should not lay the blame exclusively on the godless communists, but they should assume part of the responsibility themselves—a significant part. They should be not only accusers and judges, but also confessors. Have Christians done anything to realize Christian justice in the life of society? Have they helped to realize fraternal relations among the people without hatred and violence with which they accuse the communists? The sins of the Christians, the sins of the historical churches have been very great and these sins bring with them a just retribution.[107]

Berdyaev thus criticized the Christian churches of his day for failing to express their gospel calling to be salt and light by addressing urgent issues of social justice in the public sphere. He thus interpreted the coming of communism as God's just judgement on a sinful Russian Christendom that had prioritized its standing with the state and neglected its duty to serve the poor. If Christians had embodied the truth of communism's commitment

---

104. Ibid.
105. Berdyaev, *Dream and Reality*, 170.
106. Berdyaev, quoted in Lowrie, *Rebellious Prophet*, 146.
107. Berdyaev, *Istoki i Smysl*, 200–201.

to social justice, he insisted, communism's falsehoods would never have prevailed.[108]

Berdyaev lamented the failure of churches to infuse the social space with humane gospel values that would have immunized Russian and German society against the pathogens of communism and fascism respectively. Instead of prophetic resistance to the dehumanizing tendencies of his age, Berdyaev found the Christian churches, on the whole, working in collusion with authoritarian regimes to suppress anarchy and revolution. Despite the strong undercurrent of pessimism that one detects throughout his writings, Berdyaev's message was ultimately one of hope and renewal. He declared that, "When everything seems obsolete and exhausted, when the earth crumbles beneath our feet as it does so in our time, when there is neither hope nor illusion, when we perceive all things uncovered and exposed—it is then that the soil is prepared for a new spiritual awakening in the world."[109]

Berdyaev corresponds with the description of the prophet offered at the beginning of this chapter. He was deeply antagonistic to the prevailing cultural trends that led Europe into two devastating wars that drew the whole world into their destructive capacious orbit. He even claimed that, "Christianity is the revelation of another world, and to make it conform to this world is to betray it."[110] He was distressed by how Christianity had been disfigured and compromised by powerful political ideologies and lamented that, "Men have accommodated Christianity to this world and have greedily seized a thus accommodated Christianity in order to bolster up their role and position in the world."[111] Berdyaev combined political insight with prophetic foresight. He was able to see beyond the facade of surface events and to see his times in light of eternity and to perceive God's redemptive purposes in the world. Most crucially, he understood that Christianity is not a religion of private salvation, but a summons to transform the world in the power of the resurrection. Berdyaev continues to speak prophetically into today's emerging post-Christian world.

Like Berdyaev, Dietrich Bonhoeffer was a prophet for his time. Moreover, like Berdyaev, Bonhoeffer was a formidable theologian, who anticipated the emergence of a new expression of Christianity and attempted to sketch an outline of a theology that would be appropriate for an emerging post-Christian world. With the passion, intensity, and devotion of a prophet, Bonhoeffer initiated a revolution in theology by reminding theologians that

108. Berdyaev, *Dream and Reality*, 229.

109. Berdyaev, *Smysl Tvorchestva*, 626.

110. Berdyaev, *Dream and Reality*, 291.

111. Ibid., 63.

the Christian life is not a matter of adhering to concepts or following rules, but was about lived obedience to the call of God, which expressed itself in concrete actions. The Christian life, in other words, was active, rather than reactive.[112] Bonhoeffer expressed this point eloquently in a letter he sent to his friends around Christmas in 1942:

> If we want to be Christians, we must have some share in Christ's large-heartedness by acting with responsibility and in freedom when the hour of danger comes, and by showing a real sympathy that springs, not from fear, but from the liberating and redeeming love of Christ for all who suffer. Mere waiting and looking on is not Christian behavior. The Christian is called to sympathy and action, not in the first place by his own sufferings, but by the sufferings of his brethren, for whose sake Christ suffered.[113]

What makes Bonhoeffer particularly relevant to the current study is his prophetic vision of a kind of theology that would be required in a post-religious world. Bonhoeffer saw that Christianity was no longer the dominant force in contemporary society and asked searching questions about what this new reality meant not only for academic theology, but for Christian existence in a post-Christian world. In a letter to his close friend, Eberhard Bethge (1909–2000), Bonhoeffer wrote from his prison cell on 30th April 1944 that,

> What is bothering me incessantly is the question what Christianity really is, or indeed who Christ really is, for us today. The time when people could be told everything by means of words, whether theological or pious, is over, and so is the time of inwardness and conscience — and that means the time of religion in general. We are moving towards a completely religionless time; people as they are now simply cannot be religious any more. Even those who honestly describe themselves as "religious" do not in the least act up to it, and so they presumably mean something quite different by "religious" . . . and if therefore man becomes radically religionless — and I think that that is already more or less the case . . . what does that mean for Christianity?[114]

Bonhoeffer realized ahead of his time the demise of "Sunday Christianity." He wanted to expound a vision of theology that recognized that Christ was Lord not just of religion or of church symbols and rituals, but of the whole

---

112. Metaxas, *Bonhoeffer*, 446.

113. Bonhoeffer, quoted in Rasmussen, *Dietrich Bonhoeffer*, 66–67.

114. Bonhoeffer, quoted in Pugh, *Religionless Christianity*, 85.

of life. As Bonhoeffer put it, "Christ is no longer an object of religion, but something quite different, really the Lord of the world." Out of this conviction, Bonhoeffer rejected the fallacy of dividing the world into its sacred and secular dimensions. Bonhoeffer maintained that, "there are not two realities, but only one reality, and that is God's reality revealed in Christ in the reality of the world. Partaking in Christ, we stand at the same time in the reality of God and in the reality of the world . . . Because this is so, the theme of two realms, which has dominated the history of the church again and again is foreign to the New Testament."[115]

One of the key themes that connects the scattered fragments of Bonhoeffer's theological writings is Christ's solidarity with the world in its immeasurable suffering. His aim was to formulate a theology that could come to terms with what Albert Schweitzer (1875–1965) called "the incomprehensible horror of existence."[116] Such a theology, he urged, would need to dismantle the false distinctions of classical theology that had drawn strict lines of demarcation between church and world. "The world," Bonhoeffer affirmed, "is not divided into parts between Christ and the devil, it is the holistic world of Christ, whether or not the world itself knows this."[117] Therefore, "In Christ we are offered the possibility of partaking in the reality of God and in the reality of the world, but not in the one without the other. The reality of God discloses itself only by setting me entirely in the reality of the world and when I encounter the reality of the world it is always already sustained, accepted and reconciled in the reality of God."[118] Accordingly, faith, urged Bonhoeffer, should be joined to every sphere of life, including politics, business and the media, as well as religion and education. Faith must not be confined to private morality or to church life, but the rule of Christ should be extended to all of life in recognition that "the world is the Lord's and all that is therein" (Ps 24:1).[119]

As well as his world-affirming vision of Christianity, Bonhoeffer's prophetic significance also consists in his radical reorientation of theology towards the suffering of God. This tendency had a long pedigree in German theology that stretched back to Martin Luther (1483–1546), who formulated a robust and influential "theology of the cross" (*theologia crucis*), but Bonhoeffer revived this emphasis and gave it a powerful expression for the time of crisis in which he lived. Writing from his prison cell, where he was

115. Stackhouse, *Making the Best of It*, 129.

116. Schweitzer, "The Philosophy of Civilization," 82.

117. Bonhoeffer, quoted in Godsey, *Theology of Dietrich Bonhoeffer*, 215.

118. Bonhoeffer, *Ethics*, 193.

119. Searle and Cherenkov, *Future and a Hope*, 98–9.

being held by the Gestapo, Bonhoeffer famously claimed that "only a suffering God can help us now."[120] To truly follow Christ meant incurring not reward, honor and success, but anxiety, solitude and obloquy.

Bonhoeffer rejected the superficial triumphalism of official Christianity in Germany in the 1930s, which he associated with the vulgar worship of success that he regarded as one of the characteristics of the evil Nazi regime. Instead, he reinstated suffering, rather than triumphalism as the essence of the Christian life. "The cross is not random suffering, but necessary suffering," stated Bonhoeffer. "The cross is not suffering that stems from natural existence; it is suffering that comes from being Christian . . . A Christianity that no longer took discipleship seriously remade the gospel into a solace of cheap grace."[121]

One of the most important legacies of Bonhoeffer's theological fragments is his categorical rejection of "cheap grace." Bonhoeffer defined cheap grace thus: "the preaching of forgiveness without requiring repentance, baptism without church discipline, Communion without confession, absolution without personal confession. Cheap grace is grace without discipleship, grace without the cross, grace without Jesus Christ, living and incarnate."[122]

Cheap grace, in the memorable words of Dorothee Sölle (1929–2003) meant "creeping round the cross."[123] Bonhoeffer taught that for the Christian the cross is not an object to creep around, but a burden to be taken up. Under the illusion of cheap grace, too many Christendom-minded Christians have become accustomed to regarding the cross "not as a burden on the back, but as a decoration on the chest"—as Hans Küng puts it.[124] The cross of compromised Christendom clericalism has become a decorative symbol that confers status, power, and identity, whereas the cross of Christ was an instrument of torture that meant nothing but humiliation, vulnerability and estrangement. For Bonhoeffer, discipleship to the Crucified Christ was always a discipleship of suffering. The integrity and poignancy of Bonhoeffer's theology of suffering were tragically confirmed in his gruesome torture and execution by the Nazis on 9th April 1945, less than a month before the end of World War Two. Despite his tragically premature and violent death, Bonhoeffer, as a Christian prophet, testified that there was a light shining

---

120. Bonhoeffer, *Letters and Papers from Prison*, 361.

121. Bonhoeffer, quoted in Frick, "Imitatio Christi of Thomas à Kempis," 43.

122. Bonhoeffer, *Cost of Discipleship*, 36.

123. Sölle, *Thinking about God*, 134.

124. Küng, *On Being a Christian*, 572. Here Küng had in mind the "pectoral cross" worn on the chest of bishops since the twelfth century and officially prescribed for Mass from 1572.

in the era of great darkness and that not even this darkness could overcome the light of the gospel.

In Bonhoeffer's view, as well as impoverishing the spiritual lives of individual Christians, cheap grace had consequences that extend even beyond the key issue of personal discipleship; this kind of cheap grace also contributed to the rise of Hitler and the Nazis in Germany. Cheap grace had tilled the spiritual soil of the German nation, thus creating a fertile breeding ground for the ideological perversions and theological blasphemies of Nazism. By reducing Christianity to a private, pietistic religion of salvation from sin that had no necessary material connection with the believer's life, character or conduct, the vast majority of German Christians were both morally and spiritually unequipped to resist Hitler. Moreover, since most German Christians had no tradition of thinking theologically or biblically about political events, many were persuaded not merely to accept Hitler's rise to power as "the will of God," but some were prepared even to support the Nazi dictator. Although genocide was an integral part of Nazi ideology, these Christians supported Hitler because he had promised to restore law and order and traditional family values after the chaos and perceived decadence of Weimar Germany.

Unfortunately, many churches in Germany and throughout Christendom have continued to live according to the principles of "cheap grace." For example, in 1988 the Synod of the Evangelical Church in Germany issued the following statement: The church is not "an ideal society, nor are Christians described as better people. Rather, the nature of the church consists in men and women hearing the word of Jesus Christ and as sinners appropriating salvation in proclamation and in the sacraments and handing it on."[125] This is as pure an expression as one will find of what Bonhoeffer had in mind when he spoke about cheap grace. The problem with this understanding of faith, as Bonhoeffer well understood, was that it separates salvation from life and reduces the gospel communication of the newness and transfiguration of life into an insipid message concerning the forgiveness of sins.

The rupture between life and salvation, between faith and obedience, created by "cheap grace," leads to the enfeeblement of the church's prophetic witness to the world. Like the church in Bonhoeffer's time, the response of the Christendom Church to salient issues that emerge from the public sphere has often been devoid of a theological basis[126] and has sometimes directly contradicted fundamental biblical-theological principles.[127] Proph-

---

125. Quoted in Sölle, *Thinking about God*, 147.

126. Searle and Cherenkov, *Future and a Hope*, 2.

127. This is seen, for instance, in the pseudo-theology and anti-Christian hysteria

ets are thus needed in the church today in order to expose the hypocrisy of traditional family values, which upon closer reflection, turn out to be disturbingly anti-Christian.[128] Authoritarian regimes from Hitler's Germany to Putin's Russia offer examples of how Satan can cloak himself in the garb of traditional family values.[129] Tragically, we can also see many examples of how some Christians can be seduced by a "strong delusion" (2 Thess 2:11) into supporting fascist political parties because they pursue their dehumanizing agendas under the banner of the promotion of traditional values.

Therefore, both Bonhoeffer and Berdyaev, each in his own way, cause Christians today to ask themselves some difficult questions, such as: is it even possible to live the Christian life if the entire structure of society requires us to compromise our Christian principles of honesty, openness, integrity, and compassion? If the society is corrupt and if our public institutions are contributing to the dehumanization of society, what can Christians do to address these anti-gospel tendencies? If we lack the moral courage to take upon ourselves the legal responsibility for the government and the situation in our country, then why do we wonder at the immorality of society and the nihilism of ordinary people? If the Christian Church is not in solidarity with the people, then why should the people be in solidarity with the Church? Who needs us if we have nothing to offer? Who will look out for us if we are not willing to be our brother's keeper?

Creating a Curriculum for Prophets

Berdyaev and Bonhoeffer, in common with several other prophets of recent times, have done the great service of making visible to us the urgent spiritual issues with which Christians today must engage. A curriculum in theology today should therefore leave plenty of space to introduce students to the lives and writings of the prophets, because none of the spiritual challenges

---

exhibited by some Christians in the UK who supported Britain's withdrawal from the European Union, as well as in the overwhelming support of many American evangelicals Christians for Donald Trump's campaign to become President of the United States of America. See Joshua Searle, "Fascism and False Messiahs": https://www.christiantoday.com/article/fascism.and.false.messiahs.why.the.world.needs.christ.more.than.ever/103073.htm.

128. Bonhoeffer's critique of conventional, nominal Christianity has invited illuminating comparisons with Kierkegaard. See, for example, Kirkpatrick, *Attacks on Christendom.*

129. Bonhoeffer denounced the Nazi emphasis on such "traditional values," expressed in the slogan, *Kinder-Küche-Kirche* (Children-Kitchen-Church). See Rasmussen, "Ethics of Responsible Action," 211.

posed by a post-Christian society can be addressed in any depth by theological graduates who have only been taught how to conjugate Greek verbs, or who have spent their productive study hours in acquainting themselves with the theory of Real Presence in the so-called Eucharist.

In a Bible college or university, theology students may discover, for instance, that the first five books of the Bible were probably not written by a single author or that Arius disputed with Athanasius concerning the consubstantiation of God the Father and God the Son, but these discoveries will hardly equip students to be change agents of the Kingdom of God once they have finished their studies. If graduates of theological seminaries can discourse at length upon nuances of Trinitarian theology, but have nothing to say about relationships, popular culture, the human costs of a post-Christian society and the spiritual implications of living through a "crisis of compassion," then how do they expect to engage with the world in a meaningful way?

Courses in biblical studies and systematic theology are often laden with Christendom assumptions and are geared towards the training of pastor-teachers; it is doubtful that they contribute to the formation of missional disciples. Such courses are not conducive to the creation of genuinely prophetic figures among the Christian community. In fact, some church and seminar institutions have become so moribund that if a prophetic figure were to emerge, they would probably do so either outside of the church or at least from its margins, often in opposition to the established church as was the case with other prophetic figures in Christian history from Francis of Assisi to Martin Luther King Jr.

Christendom could produce effective church planters and even charismatic evangelists, but it was incapable of forming prophets. Christendom represented the exhaustion of western culture's creative powers, the enfeeblement of the human spirit and the captivity of a dynamic and world-transforming faith within institutional structures. Such a context was not conducive to the formation of those imbued with a prophetic vocation. In post-Christendom, students must be trained to resist the insipid conformity to cultural norms, which is demanded by Christendom churches and the wider society. Theology has been trapped in an iron cage of bureaucracy and smothered under the dreary ferment of performance targets, assessment criteria and regimes of quality control. Funding targets are met, boxes are ticked and arbitrary enhancement criteria are fulfilled, but creative scholars are side-lined and treated as little more than walking CVs, whose publications that can be cannibalized to bolster the department's next submission to the Research Excellence Framework.

Academic freedom and scholarly creativity are undermined by the incessant need to fulfil the metrics of impact and productivity in order to generate funding. "What has happened," explains Leonidas Donskis, "is a revolution of bureaucrats speaking in the name of freedom and competition but each day tearing these values down."[130] Whereas universities were once widely recognized as citadels of culture, many have been pressured by market forces into offering what some commentators have referred to as the pedagogical equivalent of fast food.[131] The market pressures on the university sector have increased to such an extent that there is now serious doubt concerning whether or not universities will even survive the current century as recognizable scholarly communities that promote the virtues of truth, critical inquiry and creativity.[132] What is needed is a new vision of transformative knowledge that is "attuned to basic principles of social justice, the respect for human decency and diversity, the rejection of false universalisms; the affirmation of the positivity of difference; the principles of academic freedom, antiracism, openness to others and conviviality."[133]

In post-Christendom the demand is surfacing for new reformers, for committed innovators and principled leaders who can combine Christlike humility with a bold prophetic mandate. The time has come for courageous, yet responsible, prophetic leaders who are willing to take risks for the sake of the gospel. Like orchids that can grow in a desert, in a greenhouse or in a nature reserve, leaders do not all emerge from the same source. This is why one must know not only the church, but also the related spheres that can produce Christian leaders.

Post-Christendom transfers the center of gravity of Christian faith from the center of society to its periphery and thus enables a proper connection between prophetic vocation and theological formation. Insipid curricula overloaded with modules on doctrine and liturgy do not contribute to the formation of missional disciples in a post-Christendom culture; rather they stifle creativity by producing religious functionaries who can perpetuate the system and the *status quo*. Instead of acquainting students with historical and doctrinal minutiae, theological education should be thought of as a creative task that leads students to perceive the depth, meaning and character of life in all its mystery and abundance. If theology can be envisioned in these terms, one of the benefits that may accrue would be

130. Donskis and Bauman, *Moral Blindness*, 136.

131. This process has been referred to as "McDonaldization of Higher Education." See the book of this title, edited by Hayes and Wynyard, published in 2002.

132. Donskis and Bauman, *Moral Blindness*, 135.

133. Braidotti, *Posthuman*, 11.

the respect and recognition of the wider academic community that theology has something meaningful to contribute to discussions concerning the future of the earth and the welfare and flourishing of its inhabitants.

3

The Marginalization of Academic Theology
in Post-Christendom

The tendencies of our time are converging toward an immediate future that will demand a radically new vision of Christianity and the church. The post-Christendom shift provides a clear choice for theologians: they can either remain preoccupied in the internal affairs of the church and navel gaze on parochial issues such as the meaning of the sacraments and so-called apostolic succession, or they can take a leap of faith into the real world of science, the academy and the public sphere, responding to these areas of life and transforming them with the presence of the transfiguring Word. Public theology (i.e., the study of the transfiguring *Logos* within the world) should set the agenda for theology in post-Christendom. Theology in a post-Christendom key, in other words, needs to be uncoupled from moribund church structures and must jettison its myopic preoccupation with internal ecclesiastical affairs. In post-Christendom academic theology, as a result of its connection with church institutions, has shared the church's fate: it has become marginalized, scorned or simply ignored.

From "Queen of the Sciences" to a Marginal Esoteric Pursuit: A Brief History of Theology

There was once a time when theology was the Queen of the Sciences. Even before theology assumed the characteristics of a science, instruction in the faith was prevalent in the earliest origins of the Christian movement. Teaching was central to Jesus's ministry. The Gospels describe how He taught about the Kingdom of God wherever He went—not just in the synagogues and temples, but in the market places, by the lake, in people's homes, and, most notably, on the hillside (Matt 5–7). Moreover, Jesus taught not through memorization of ancient texts or the authority of past scholars, but "as one who had authority" (Mark 1:22). Not only did Jesus teach with authority, but He also demonstrated what He taught through His life. His ministry of compassion can even be understood as an enacted commentary on the principles that He taught His followers, particularly in the Sermon on the Mount.

Teaching remained central to the faith vision of the early Christian movement. The book of Acts demonstrates the central place of teaching in the apostles' ministry. The ability to teach was key to the selection of Christian leaders and the Epistles refer to teaching as an enterprise that is empowered by the Holy Spirit to build up the Body of Christ (1 Cor 12:20; Eph 4:11–12). The early Christian movement was diverse in faith and practice and many kinds of theology thrived as theology was understood as a means to live in the power of the Holy Spirit and to continue the work that Jesus had begun, when He had announced that the Kingdom of God had arrived. The early Christians were united not by creeds and confessions or ecclesial structures, but by spiritual bonds of solidarity, which were consolidated by the ubiquitous persecution suffered by these communities.

Unfortunately, as the early Christian communities transitioned from what Harvey Cox calls an "age of faith" to an "age of belief," church institutions began to take over and to introduce creeds to which Christian communities were expected to adhere on pain of excommunication. The Kingdom of God started to be conflated with the church. Berdyaev explains that, "in place of the Kingdom of God, the Church took shape, and Christianity, having become historical, began to adapt itself to this world, to the kingdom of Caesar . . . The prophetical side of Christianity was weakened and disappeared almost entirely. Historical Christianity took on an organized dogmatic and authoritarian character. The historical Church was regarded as the coming of the Kingdom of God."[1]

Under these new conditions, diversity of faith and forms of belief was regarded as deviation from institutionally-endorsed dogmas. Church officials assumed doctrinal authority, which entitled them to identify and counter alleged departures from accepted beliefs. Instead of being a general concern of the whole faith community, theological education was delegated to ecclesial specialists, who began to produce catechisms that codified the consensus of the clerical elite into systems of doctrine. Theology was now monopolized by an ecclesiastical structure, calling itself the church, which

1. Berdyaev, *Divine and the Human*, 19.

arrogated to itself the right to determine which doctrines were to be deemed acceptable and to punish those who departed from its teaching.

It has been claimed that "in the ancient Church there were almost no theological academies dedicated to the systematic study of the subject."[2] Although this claim is well founded, several leading figures, such as Justin Martyr, Gregory of Nyssa, and Cyril of Jerusalem emerged during the early patristic period. These influential churchmen addressed the issue of theological education and responded to the dominant ideas of Hellenistic philosophy in an *ad hoc* manner. The question concerning the extent to which Christian teaching was compatible with the pagan literary and philosophical works of classical antiquity was one of the questions that vexed these early theologians. Many of the patristic writers, such as Justin Martyr, discovered what they called "seeds of the word" (*logos spermatikoi*) in the writings of non-Christian philosophers and poets.[3] Some early Christian writers even claimed that Plato had derived the central tenets of his philosophy directly from the Old Testament. Commenting on the extent of the assimilation of Hellenistic philosophy by the early Christians, Christopher Stead mentions that key tenets of Greek Patristic theology, such as the "reality of God, his creation and providence, the heavenly powers, the human soul, its training, survival and judgement could all be upheld by the appropriate choice of Platonic texts."[4] In order to enable Christians to converse with the pagan people, the early Christian "cathedral schools" of this period began to offer instruction not only in preaching, prayer and doctrine, but also in pagan philosophy and literature. The theological curriculum included a study in philosophy, logic and rhetoric. The encounter of Christian faith with Hellenistic philosophy, in particular the writings of Plato and Aristotle, was to leave a lasting mark on theology.

In AD 313, one of the most fateful dates in the history of the Christian movement, the Emperor Constantine (c.272–337) issued the Edict of Milan, granting toleration to Christians throughout the Roman Empire. Christians no longer suffered persecution and could worship freely. This new freedom ushered in a period of relative peace that led many contemporary Christians to believe that Constantine's conversion was "a fortuitous, indeed perhaps divinely ordained, eventuality."[5] Among Constantine's early admirers, the most eloquent was Eusebius of Caesarea (c.260–c.340), who

2. Nichols, *The Shape of Catholic Theology*, 282.

3. McGuckin, "The Trinity in the Greek Fathers," 56–58.

4. Stead, *Philosophy in Christian Antiquity*, 14; cf. Freeman, *Closing of the Western Mind*, 145.

5. Hall, *The End of Christendom*, 11.

lavished praise on the "emperor loved by God," whose reign the obsequious Eusebius associated with the inauguration of the Kingdom of God on earth: "From that time on, a day bright and radiant, with no cloud overshadowing it, shone down with shafts of heavenly light on the churches of Christ throughout the world, nor was there any reluctance to grant even those outside our community the enjoyment, if not of equal blessings, at least of an effluent from an a share in the things that God has bestowed on us."[6]

Notwithstanding this extravagant praise bestowed by his contemporaries, more recent historians and theologians have accused the "Christian" emperor of propagating "a willful falsehood by a solemn and deliberate perjury" in so far as he used "the altars of the church as a convenient footstool to the throne of the empire."[7] The new religion had its advantages as a means of reinforcing imperial power, as Edward Gibbon (1737–1794) explained: "The passive and unresisting obedience [of Christians], which bows under the yoke of authority, or even of oppression, must have appeared, in the eyes of an absolute monarch, the most conspicuous and useful of the evangelic virtues."[8] Harvey Cox explains that, "the most critical and regrettable turning point for Christianity came … with the alleged "conversion" of Constantine, and his insistence that in the interests of imperial unity, the squabbling bishops had to compose a creed to which everyone would have to adhere, or else. At that point, "official" Christianity ceased being a way of life and began to clot into a clerically led and doctrinally defined religion fiercely enforced by imperial power."[9] The "Constantinian turn"[10] revealed that Christianity was not only a revolutionary, prophetic and messianic faith; Christianity could also have a social use for those who wanted to establish the Kingdom of Caesar on a religious footing.[11]

This strict enforcement continued under Constantine's successors. In 356, Constantine's son, Constantius II (317–361), passed an imperial decree

---

6. Eusebius, *History of the Church*, 383–84.

7. Gibbon, *Decline and Fall*, 379.

8. Ibid., 372.

9. Cox, *Secular City*, xix. Constantine's most formidable critic in twentieth-century theology was John Howard Yoder—see Yoder, "Constantinian Sources," 135–45 and Wright, *Disavowing Constantine*. The censure of Constantine as a hypocrite, heretic, anti-Semite and ruthless tyrant has found also expression in popular history and fiction—see, respectively, Carroll, *Constantine's Sword* and Brown, *Da Vinci Code*. Others have attempted to defend the sincerity of Constantine's conversion—see Leithart, *Defending Constantine*. In 2013, a volume was published that contained several essays written in response to Leithart's thesis—see Roth (ed.), *Constantine Revisited*.

10. This notion of the "*konstantinische Wende*" has been a prominent feature of recent German scholarship. See, for instance, Girardet, *Der Kaiser und sein Gott*.

11. Berdyaev, *Istoki i Smysl*, 202.

banning the worship of non-Christian images. In 380, Emperor Theodosius I (347–395) issued the Edict of Thessalonica, which declared the Nicene Trinitarian Christianity to be the only legitimate religion permitted in the Empire. When Christianity became the official religion of the Roman Empire, Christians enjoyed greater freedom of worship and access to high positions in the civil and academic administration. The church grew in power and status and became the bearer of civilization and enlightenment throughout the Roman world. Summing up these momentous changes, the eminent philosopher, Alfred North Whitehead (1861–1947), emphasized the contrast between the caesaropapism of Christendom with the gospel simplicity of the "Galilean vision" of Jesus and His first followers:

> When the Western world accepted Christianity, Caesar conquered; and the received text of Western theology was edited by his lawyers . . . The brief Galilean vision of humility flickered throughout the ages, uncertainly . . . But the deeper idolatry, of the fashioning of God in the image of the Egyptian, Persian, and Roman imperial rulers, was retained. The Church gave unto God the attributes which belonged exclusively to Caesar. There is . . . in the Galilean origin of Christianity, yet another suggestion which does not fit in very well . . . It does not emphasize the ruling Caesar, or the ruthless moralist, or the unmoved mover. It dwells upon the tender elements in the world, which slowly and in quietness operate by love, and it finds purpose in the present immediacy of a kingdom not of this world. Love neither rules, nor is it unmoved; also, it is a little oblivious as to morals. it does not look to the future; for it finds its own reward in the immediate present.[12]

Christianity began as a minority persecuted sect. "Its followers," Hubert G. Locke reminds us, "were a persecuted and despised band who knew what oppression meant and what life on the periphery of society was like."[13] As a result of the Constantinian turn, Christianity, according to Charles Freeman, was "transformed from a religion of outsiders to one of insiders, a transformation of incalculable importance for western history."[14]

The dramatic shift in the status of Christianity from a forbidden religion (*religio illicita*) to an imperial religion (*religio imperium*) produced a new Christology. Roman theologians clothed Christ in the elegant, yet ill-fitting purple robes of imperial power. They emphasized the power of

12. Whitehead, *Process and Reality*, 342–43.
13. Locke, *Learning from History*, 30.
14. Freeman, *Closing of the Western Mind*, 155.

Christ as the cosmic Lord who legitimated earthly power, rather than the Suffering Servant who had declared that control of political power is in the hand of Satan (Matt 4:9).[15] From its origins as a movement of peaceful subversion of worldly power, Christianity transitioned into "a religion of conquest and domination."[16] The Catholic theologian, Leonardo Boff, thus concludes that, "The Church, which until AD 312 was more of a movement than an institution, became an heir of the empire's institutions: law, organization by diocese and parish, bureaucratic centralization, positions, and titles. The Church-institution accepted political realities and assumed inexorable uniformity."[17]

The transition of Christianity into an imperial religion had a profound and lasting impact on the way that theology was taught. Whereas early church fathers, such as Tertullian (c.155–c.240) had sought to warn Christians against the infiltration of pagan philosophy and culture into Christian thought and practice,[18] later generations after Constantine developed a more nuanced approach to the relationship between philosophy and theology. For instance, Augustine of Hippo (354–430), while rejecting pagan myth and religion, admired the philosophy of classical antiquity. Augustine even asserted that, "If those who are called philosophers, and especially the Platonists, have aught that is true and in harmony with our faith, we are not only not to shrink from it, but to claim it for our own use."[19] However, Augustine maintained that although it was possible for Christians to obtain knowledge from the "pagan" philosophies of Plato and Aristotle, true theological reflection was concerned with *sapientia* (divine wisdom), rather than with *scientia* (knowledge originating from human sources).[20]

The subordination of philosophy to theology was a feature of the intellectual life of Europe during the Middle Ages and was expressed in Anselm of Canterbury's definition of theology as "faith seeking understanding." Faith was not so much a result or objective of knowledge, but its precondition and point of departure. Faith, rather than reason, set the agenda for all other branches of knowledge from arithmetic to jurisprudence. Theology

15. These changes are described with insight and erudition in Weaver, *The Nonviolent God*.

16. Boff, *Global Civilization*, 37.

17. Boff, *Church*, 50–51.

18. Henri de Lubac (1896–1991) claimed that Tertullian's opposition to the scholarship of classical antiquity—as expressed in his rhetorical question, "what has Athens to do with Jerusalem?"—has been exaggerated and that his position on this issue was far more nuanced. See de Lubac, *The Church: Paradox and Mystery*, 71.

19. Augustine, quoted in Freeman, *Closing of the Western Mind*, 144.

20. Howard, *Protestant Theology*, 17.

was referred to as the "Queen of the Sciences." The undisputed reign of theology over the intellectual life of Europe continued into the later Middle Ages.

Theology was the basic starting point of knowledge and was understood in propositional form. Under the influence of medieval scholasticism, theology was studied in terms of a systematic inquiry into the nature of divinity, according to certain principles that fused biblical teaching with the logical methods and metaphysical theories of classical antiquity, particularly the philosophy of Aristotle. This approach was followed by leading medieval thinkers, such as Anselm of Canterbury (c.1033–1109), Peter Abelard (1079–1142) and Thomas Aquinas (1225–1274). There were other theologians and educators who maintained that the plenitude of the divine being overflows and overwhelms human understanding. The mystical tradition of Meister Eckhart (1260–1328), Richard Rolle (c.1290–1349), Julian of Norwich (c.1342–c.1416), Teresa of Avila (1515–1582), John of the Cross (1542–1591), Jacob Boehme (1575–1624) and William Blake (1757–1827), and others emphasized the "direct and transformative presence of God."[21] According to the mystics God could be apprehended only through love and faith, rather than through rational analysis and logical deduction. God was to be approached "not in categories of reason, but in the revelations of spiritual life."[22] Although mysticism was marginalized by the mainstream churches, its insights can be applied as a salutary corrective to contemporary academic theology, which has tended to prioritize cognitive reflection over against creativity, imagination and spiritual experience.

The Protestant Reformation, with its renewed emphasis on the "priesthood of all believers," generated the conviction that education was not an exclusive entitlement of the wealthy and those training for church service. The argument that all children should receive an education and that this was the responsibility of the state, rather than the church, can be traced back to Martin Luther (1483–1546) himself.[23] Luther rejected medieval theology, which he denounced as "scholastic barbarism," for its alleged preoccupation with hair-splitting metaphysical minutiae to the neglect of the simple gospel truths concerning faith and salvation.[24] Theology, Luther argued, must have a direct pastoral application and be directed towards practical formation.[25]

---

21. McGinn, cited in Deane, *History of Medieval Heresy*, 155.

22. Berdyaev, quoted in Lowrie, *Christian Existentialism*, 52.

23. Karpova, "Martin Luther and Philipp Melanchthon," 190.

24. Luther, "Disputation," 13–20.

25. Leinsle, *Einführung in die scholastische Theologie*.

Despite Luther's revolutionary break with the Catholic Church, his theology has been described as "non-revolutionary, theoretically as well as practically,"[26] because he taught that the secular authorities should be accepted, even if they are unjust, and that the state, rather than the church, should be responsible for people's education. Although Luther and other magisterial reformers, most notably John Calvin (1509–1564), demonstrated their willingness to cooperate with the political authorities, other radical reformers, such as the early Anabaptists faced severe persecution, not only from the state powers, but also from the new Protestant churches and the established Catholic Church. In contrast to other Christian communities, these radical believers were not permitted to establish seminaries or official centers of learning and theological formation. Their educational activities were thus restricted to private study (mainly of the Bible in the vernacular languages) and unofficial gatherings in homes.[27]

In the first half of the seventeenth century religious intolerance converged with nationalistic enmity and the result was the Thirty Years War (1618–1648), which traumatized the European continent and led to new reforming impulses. In the aftermath of a war fueled by competing dogmatic claims of Catholics and Protestants, philosophers began to search for new methods of establishing truth that were, in the words of Stephen Toulmin, "independent of, and neutral between, particular religious loyalties."[28] The alleged permanence of reason stood in contrast to the incessant flux of religious beliefs. As Miroslav Volf explains, "The rational method as an antidote to violence was part and parcel of the Enlightenment's optimistic vision of the civilizing process as a story of humanity emerging from presocial barbarity into peaceful social civility."[29] In this period reason began to supplant revelation as the source of true knowledge. The late seventeenth century Europe was a period of extraordinary ferment in philosophy and theology that provoked what the leading historian of ideas, Paul Hazard (1878–1944), famously called the "crisis of the European conscience."[30]

Out of this intellectual upheaval a new philosophy emerged that attempted to establish "a new rationality, a new, universal way of thinking that by its assurance and clarity could banish the dark clouds of human enmity and error."[31] This new rationality manifested itself in a new scepticism

26. Tillich, History of Christian Thought, 255.

27. Sunshine, "Protestant Missions," 19.

28. Toulmin, Cosmopolis, 70.

29. Volf, Exclusion & Embrace.

30. Hazard, La Crise de la Conscience Européenne.

31. McClendon, Witness, 207.

towards "revealed religion" and hostility towards the clerical hierarchies of church institutions. This attitude was expressed in the memorably un-nuanced words of the outspoken secular humanist, Ludovico Settembrini, in Thomas Mann's great novel, *The Magic Mountain* (1924): "Our Western heritage is reason—reason, analysis, action, progress: these, and not the slothful bed of monkish tradition!"[32]

Modern theology has been shaped to a profound degree by the forms of thought that originated in the European Enlightenment (c.1650–1800). It has been argued that the paramount preoccupation of the Enlightenment was the formulation of a new "Science of Man."[33] The impulse towards a new scientific conception of human nature instigated a revolution in philosophi-cal anthropology which had deep and lasting implications for theological formation. James K. A. Smith explains that, "Many Christian schools, col-leges and universities—particularly those in the Protestant tradition—have taken on board a picture of the human person that owes more to modernity and the Enlightenment than it does to the holistic, biblical vision of human persons."[34] He remarks that since the Enlightenment, "Christian education has absorbed a philosophical anthropology that sees human persons as pri-marily thinking things."[35]

Moreover, the rationalistic tendencies of the Enlightenment contrib-uted to the marginalization of theology as a pursuit unworthy of scientific status. Denis Diderot (1713–1784), one of the leaders of the French Enlight-enment, thought that the graduates of theological faculties were "the most useless, intractable and dangerous subjects of the state." Diderot's friend and philosophical collaborator, Baron d'Holbach (1723–1789), similarly regard-ed theology as an "insult to human reason."[36] Theology was downgraded because it was perceived not to be founded upon universal reason, but on myths and traditions. The philosopher, Immanuel Kant (1724–1804), in his 1784 essay, "An Answer to the Question: What is Enlightenment?," summed up the essence of Enlightenment in a memorable exhortation: "Have the courage to use your own understanding!" This was a striking reformulation of the classical dictum of *sapere aude* ("dare to know")[37] and presents an

---

32. Mann, *Magic Mountain*, 379.

33. See, for instance, Pagden, *The Enlightenment*.

34. Smith, *Desiring the Kingdom*, 31.

35. Ibid.

36. Diderot and d'Holbach, quoted in Howard, *Protestant Theology*, 2.

37. This phrase is attributed to the classical Roman poet, Horace (65 BC–8 BC). See Horace, *Epistles*. I, 2, 40.

illuminating contrast with Proverbs 3:5.[38] The Kantian formulation under-
lined a general tendency towards the secularization of learning and a new
emphasis on reason which supplanted divine revelation as the foundation
of all knowledge. Kant understood the essence of religion to consist not in
the revelation of *a priori* truth, but in its practical capacity to enable people
to interpret moral duties as divine commands.[39]

These secularizing impulses forced theology to adapt by adopting a
new critical stance towards the Bible, which was regarded not as a spirit-
inspired or sacred text, but as a historical account of the human religious
experience. These trends contributed to the emergence of Liberal Christianity, which tended to regard Christianity—together with all other religions—
as a cultural phenomenon and as a by-product of the evolution of human
consciousness through the course of history. Christianity and religion *per
se* were regarded as necessary stages in the "development of the human
spirit,"[40] rather than as a divine revelation of transcendent and universal
truth.

Theology inevitably participated in the downgrading of Christian
faith within the academy. The perception of theology as an esoteric, obscure
pursuit was reinforced by leading thinkers of German Idealism, which lay
many of the foundations upon which modern theology was constructed.
For instance, the fourfold division of theological studies into exegesis, dogmatics, history and practical theology can be traced back to the scientific
theology (*wissenschaftliche Theologie*) that originated in the German university system of the early nineteenth century.[41] Under these influences,
theology was side-lined as "a minor and often disparaged area of academic
commitment."[42]

Theology was accepted as a legitimate discipline only to the extent
that it confined itself to textual criticism, historical analysis and practical
ministerial training. For instance, the distinction that emerged between
theology and biblical studies and which is still reflected in theology faculties and seminaries today, is a product of post-Enlightenment attempts to
divide theology into the two principal components of philology and history.
"Philology" referred to the scientific study of ancient biblical texts in the

38. "Trust in the Lord with all your heart; do not depend on your own
understanding."

39. Stern, *Kantian Ethics*, 11.

40. This notion of human "spiritual development" (*geistige Entwicklung*) is associated particularly with Hegel and had a major influence on German idealism from Hegel
to Nietzsche, as Karl Löwith explains. See Löwith, *Von Hegel zu Nietzsche*, 138.

41. Farley, *Theologia*, 84.

42. Howard, *Protestant Theology*, 7.

original languages, whereas "history" involved understanding how people in the past had contributed to the formation and evolution of religious consciousness.[43] Doctrines were understood not as timeless repositories of truth based on revelation contained in biblical texts, but, in the words of Friedrich Schleiermacher (1768–1834), as "accounts of religious affections set forth in speech"[44] Doctrine was seen as a historically-conditioned sentiment that demonstrated changes over time in human perceptions of the divine. Attempts to establish theology on a metaphysical foundation were regarded as futile expressions of ecclesiastical obscurantism.

This tendency towards historical theology acquired a powerful impetus in the writings of Friedrich Schleiermacher.[45] Following the lead of Kant, who confined theology to the realm of "practical reason" (i.e., to moral truths posited from the practical outworking of *a priori* postulates of pure reason) several leading thinkers began to argue for the exclusion of theology from the modern research university.[46] The formidable genius of Schleiermacher ensured that theology retained its place within the emerging university system in Germany in the early nineteenth century, but theology's inclusion came at a price. Theology was required to relinquish its status as a science (*Wissenschaft*) and was admitted on pragmatic grounds as a necessary discipline for the theological training of church ministers.[47] Kierkegaard's damning verdict on the degradation of theology by these developments was characteristically vivid and insightful: "Only our age has had the privilege of getting a philosophy that boasts that Christianity has completely merged with science—that is, Christianity no longer exists. But inverted as thieves' slang always is, we do not say what is the truth—that Christianity no longer exists. No, we say: What terrific progress! Now Christianity has completely become a science."[48] Kierkegaard, who had studied at Berlin University during the high point of German Idealism, was particularly well placed to offer an informed judgement.

Two hundred years after Schleiermacher, post-Enlightenment scepticism, suspicion and even contempt continue to characterize popular attitudes towards theology today. In the opinion of its "cultural despisers,"[49]

43. J. G. Fichte (1762–1814), quoted in Howard, *Protestant Theology*, 164.

44. Schleiermacher, *Christian Faith*, sec. 15.

45. Howard, *Protestant Theology*, 206.

46. Stewart Sutherland traces Kant's 'enormous influence' on theology in Britain in the nineteenth and twentieth centuries in his essay, "Philosophy of Religion," 253–70.

47. D'Costa, *Theology in the Public Square*, 16–17.

48. Kierkegaard, *Søren Kierkegaard's Journals and Papers*, 463.

49. This term is taken from Schleiermacher's famous series of addresses, entitled *Über die Religion*, first published in 1799.

theology is a kind of intellectual fraud. Theology, it is claimed, is based on whim and illusion, deluding people into believing that they are learning something, when in fact they are merely being provided with a megaphone for their deluded prejudices and superstitious fantasies.

In response to the apprehension surrounding theology it is necessary to set forth a meaningful and relevant account of how the post-Christendom shift has affected the status of theology and its relation to other disciplines, most notably to the sciences. Such a response must avoid the pitfall of accommodation, which assumes that theology needs only to mimic cultural trends or follow scientific methodologies in order to become relevant and plausible in the modern world. It is true that the Enlightenment clipped the wings of theology, but some theologians' attempts to make theology amenable to post-Enlightenment epistemologies is like pretending that they would be able to fly "if only they could flap their arms hard enough."[50] What theology in post-Christendom needs is not harder flapping but a new set of wings.

Theology and the Sciences

One of the main tasks of theologians today in the transition to post-Christendom is to accomplish the de-marginalization of their discipline by restoring its full presence in the academy. This can only be accomplished through respectful dialogue with practitioners from other disciplines that, in common with theology, are concerned with the flourishing of the world and the life of its human—and non-human—inhabitants. While professing the Lordship of Christ and the presence of the incarnate Word in all spheres of life (spiritual, material, social, cultural and intellectual), theologians in post-Christendom can affirm science as an instrument for learning about God's world and for growing in wisdom and knowledge.

Theology should certainly recognize and respect the tremendous contributions of science to modern life, but theologians should likewise insist that many of the issues that most concern human life cannot become subjects of scientific methodologies. The key difference in terms of method is that science considers the world under the aspect of necessity within dynamic natural forces, whereas theology considers the world from the perspective of freedom, in accordance with the plenitude of possibility that inheres within the incarnate *Logos*.[51] Science is a rational pursuit of mate-

50. This metaphor is attributed by Richard B. Hays to Oliver O'Donovan. See Hays, *Moral Vision of the New Testament*, 3.

51. Berdyaev, *Smysl Tvorchestva*, 31–34.

rial reality, whereas theology, although not irrational, is a spiritual pursuit of existential potentiality. Theology can never attain to the clarity, precision and objectivity of science, and neither should it aspire to do so. As Berdyaev rightly insisted, "nothing in the world should be scientific apart from science itself."[52]

Neither can theology accept the naive assumptions of materialistic rationalism. Materialism, notes Boff, "reduces the scope of reality" by not including within reality "the phenomena of subjectivity, conscience, life and spirituality" and by failing to recognize that reality is not independent, since "there is no object without subject and no subject without object."[53] Moreover, materialistic rationalism, as Berdyaev correctly observes, is based on irrational "dogmatic presuppositions concerning the rational nature of Being in general, and of material Being in particular."[54] Berdyaev insists that, "those who hope to attain knowledge would be better employed in trying to communicate with the mystery of being than in analyzing and defending the truth of logical propositions."[55] Similarly, James Joyce (1882–1941) is reputed to have remarked, "What is clear and concise can't deal with reality, for to be real is to be surrounded by mystery."[56]

It is remarkable that whereas science today is becoming increasingly aware of the all-pervading mystery at the heart of the universe,[57] theology in Christendom has tended to remain shackled to a mechanical view of reality that no longer corresponds with a postmodern scientific understanding of the cosmos. It is widely recognized that the twentieth century was a time of crisis in all domains of human knowledge.[58] For instance, in physics, Isaac Newton's notion of a static, mechanical, ordered universe of inert matter was being shattered by the Theory of Relativity (A. Einstein), the Incompleteness Theorem (K. Gödel), the Uncertainty Principle (W. Heisenberg), and Chaos Theory (E. Lorenz).

Theologians are cartographers of eternity, rather than mere commentators on the given state of the present world. Theology is the passionate pursuit of truth that involves the application of critical and imaginative faculties towards the creative transformation and enhancement of life. Theology is

---

52. Berdyaev, *Smysl Tvorchestva*, 27.

53. Boff, *Essential Care*, 8.

54. Berdyaev, *Dream and Reality*, 98.

55. Ibid., 88.

56. Joyce, quoted in John Cage, *X: Writings*, 54.

57. On this point, see Barrow, *Impossibility*; for a more popular treatment, see Gleick, *Chaos*.

58. See, for instance, Kuhn, *Structure of Scientific Revolutions*.

an expression of the immeasurable plenitude of the divine-human imagination. Smith offers a useful definition of imagination as a "faculty by which we navigate and make sense of our world . . . in ways and on a register that flies below the radar of conscious reflection, and specifically in ways that are fundamentally aesthetic in nature."[59] Theology in post-Christendom must engage the imagination. Theology must emancipate itself from its "fixation with epistemic matters"[60] if it is to aspire to credibility and relevance in the emerging era of post-Christendom. Accordingly, theology must engage with the kind of vital questions to which Nietzsche alluded concerning the place of vision and the inexpressible ecstasy of forging meaning through creative acts of overcoming.[61]

Theology is thus to be studied not with the intellect alone. There should be a sense of joy and enthusiasm, as well as vision and wonder, that accompanies all theological reflection. Theology thus signifies a mode of knowing which emancipates artistic creativity from the ill-fitting straightjackets of functionalism and utilitarianism. As such, theology is not susceptible to human reasoning and empirical criteria of verification. This does not mean that theology is unconcerned with intellectual credibility or critical rigor. Smith's observation on this point is commendable: "the goal is not to denigrate the intellect; rather, it is to situate theoretical reflection within the wider purview of our fundamental pretheoretical orientation to the world."[62]

Theology is therefore by no means irrational, incoherent or merely sentimental. Rather, theological method relies on a judicious combination of creativity and logic. As Whitehead once quipped: "Fools act on imagination without knowledge, pedants act on knowledge without imagination."[63] Although repudiating any claim to be an empirical science, theology can participate in the discourse of the scientific community, where there are rules, categories and criteria that determine what constitutes plausible knowledge.

In post-Christendom theologians will need to defend their faith convictions in the language of debate, and not from a position of power and authority, formerly conferred by ecclesial institutions and hierarchies.

---

59. Smith, *Imagining the Kingdom*, 19.

60. Ibid., 12.

61. This notion of "self-overcoming" (*Selbst-Überwindung*) recurs throughout Nietzsche's works and has been appropriated by theologians who have discovered thought-provoking parallels between this idea and the gospel notion of "self-denial." See Kleffmann, *Nietzsches Begriff des Lebens*, 276.

62. Smith, *Imagining the Kingdom*, 12–13.

63. Whitehead, quoted in McLean, *Pedagogy and the University*, 69.

Theology has lost its academic privileges in the same way that churches have been stripped of their institutional status. Within the academy even the most cherished beliefs associated with Christian tradition and Scripture cannot be taken as accepted or even respected. The diverse challenges of post-Christendom should be taken as a call for creativity. It is no longer sufficient to appeal to the historical merits or traditional status of theology as the Queen of the Sciences. Attempts to assert the authority of theology by appealing to the Christian provenance of the modern university will not be sufficient—notwithstanding the fact that the greatest historical universities throughout Europe and North America were, in fact, founded and developed by Christians.[64] In post-Christendom it is also futile to expect or demand preferential treatment for theology based on the dominant position that the church used to occupy during the Christendom era.

What is essential is the readiness and ability to compete in a professional environment, to present sound arguments in defence of one's convictions, and finally, to demonstrate those same Christian qualities of character (humility, integrity, respect, tolerance, compassion, etc.) that have always signified more than logical proofs. To be a person of integrity, to be a diligent student or a wise teacher, to be self-critical and broadminded, to respect other approaches and at the same time to have the courage to follow one's principles—these are what theology needs, especially in the current context of post-Christendom in which theology is deprived of its former normative status and institutional authority. In today's universities and seminaries, this personal "courage to be" is more important and persuasive than clerical battles over spheres of influence or myopic debates concerning aspects of church belief and practice.

Post-Christendom necessitates a reorientation of theological discourse in accordance with the "regimes of truth"[65] that govern the discursive practices and diverse semantic fields of contemporary humanities and sciences. Theology enters into respectful dialogue where it can address issues of purpose, motivation and meaning, that lie outside of the sphere of scientific competence. While theology can certainly still make a significant contribution towards understanding pressing issues of public debate, theologians can no longer speak from a position of assumed respect and authority, but must assert their claims to truth in an appropriate language that demonstrates their explanatory power.

---

64. D'Costa, *Theology in the Public Square*, 2.

65. This term is associated with the French philosopher and social theorist, Michel Foucault (1926–1984). For a helpful summary of the term in Foucault's work, see O'Farrell, *Michel Foucault*, 153.

This means that theologians cannot fall back on any church institution which, during the Christendom era, might have provided a platform to contribute to public debates. Instead, they will need to cultivate a respectful dialogue with progressive movements in the "secular" world and explore what Rowan Williams calls "the possibilities of theological discourse outside the confessional structure."[66] It is unfortunate that during the Christendom era from Constantine to recent times, theology and Christian faith in general were monopolized by church institutions and clerical hierarchies, which have become progressively more and more detached from real life. The process which Hans Urs von Balthasar refers to as the "clericalization of theology" has not served theology well in the long run.[67] Les Ball explains that, "Historically the main objective of theological education has been the training of clergy for ministry within a largely Christianized social context. Consequently, the formative component has generally been geared to the formation of a priestly persona, not to transform the individual or society, but rather to conform both to a [traditional] model of Christian belief and conduct."[68] In order to reverse this regrettable tendency, it is necessary to revert to the original vision that inspired the early Christian movement. Although deriving inspiration from the past, such a vision must be oriented towards the future. With the future comes the Kingdom of God, which must become the central object and reference point of theology. One way to achieve this is to reorient theology away from *belief* and towards *faith*.

Faith (Not Belief) as the Basic Object of Theology

Theology in post-Christendom should take as its basic object *not* belief, dogma, history or experience; rather theology should be focused on *faith*. Care should be taken to ensure that faith is not conflated with belief. Harvey Cox neatly explains the difference between faith and belief:

> Belief is not the same as faith. belief hovers near the upper, cognitive stratum of the self. It can come and go. It can be strong one day, weak the next. But faith locates itself in a deeper dimension. It is a matter of fundamental life orientation. The early Christians spoke of their faith as the "way." But in its journey through the Graeco-Roman cultural landscape, Christianity became increasingly identified with a set of beliefs that were then organized into creeds. Still, it did not have to happen that way.

66. Williams, "Theology in the Twentieth Century," 250.

67. Balthasar, *Gottbereites Leben*; cf. Siller, *Kirche für die Welt*, 109.

68. Ball, *Transforming Theology*, 134.

> I have come to the conviction that Christianity has emphasized
> "belief" entirely too much, and is now transmuting itself into a
> stage that is "beyond belief."[69]

This distinction between "belief" and "faith" corresponds to the reorientation of theology instigated by existentialism. Paul Tillich decries the way that "faith has lost its genuine meaning and has received the connotation of "belief in something unbelievable."[70] True faith, insists Tillich, "is not a theoretical affirmation of something uncertain, it is the existential acceptance of something transcending ordinary experience. Faith is not an opinion but a state. It is the state of being grasped by the power of being which transcends everything that is and in which everything that is participates."[71] Faith is, in the insightful words of John Calvin, "a firm and certain knowledge of God's benevolence toward us, founded upon the truth of the freely given promise in Christ, both revealed to our minds and sealed on our hearts through the Holy Spirit."[72] To have faith means to be delivered from the power of darkness and transferred to the Kingdom of God's beloved son (Col 1:13).

Faith in Christ is a matter of having confidence in Jesus and trusting that His words were true and that His way leads into the kind of life that is life indeed. Unfortunately, under the influence of the clericalizing forces in the aftermath of Constantine's conversion, the concept of faith "shifted from being a state of openness to revelation (or directly to the teachings and personal charisma of Jesus as recorded in the Gospels), to one of being ready to accept what is authoritatively decreed by the church hierarchy."[73] As a result, faith was understood not as "the story of our lives but a set of propositions to which [one] must subscribe."[74]

Faith, unlike belief, is revealed in the spiritual realities of transformed lives, rather than in a system of belief or a list of propositions. This kind of belief was criticized by Tozer as "a substitute for obedience, an escape from reality, a refuge from the necessity of hard thinking, a hiding place for weak character." He further noted that, "There is a danger that we take Christ for granted. We suppose that because we hold New Testament beliefs we are therefore New Testament Christians; but it does not follow."[75] True faith is thus more than fidelity to a system of belief. Christian faith has

---

69. Cox and Ikeda, *Persistence of Religion*.

70. Tillich, *Courage to Be*, 158.

71. Ibid., 159.

72. Calvin, *Institutes*, Book III.ii.7.

73. Freeman, *Closing of the Western Mind*, 145.

74. Palmer, "Toward a Spirituality of Higher Education," 77.

75. Tozer, *Man the Dwelling Place of God*.

nothing to do with professing "sound doctrine," but is demonstrated in the spiritual reality of transformed lives. Peter Rollins admirably expresses this point, noting that, "the person of faith is not known by which philosophical outlook she affirms, but rather by her commitment to life."[76] Given the widespread prevalence of "belief" over faith within Christendom, Jesus's troubling question in Luke 18:8 ("when the Son of man cometh, shall he find faith on the earth?") appears, as Kierkegaard noted, perfectly justified.[77] Kierkegaard even speculated that "Christ conceives of the possibility at His coming again the situation might be such that Christianity does not exist at all."[78]

In Christendom, it was sufficient for people to adhere to belief—belief in God, belief in Christ, belief in salvation for sins and eternal life, belief in the church, belief in the creeds and catechisms, etc. In post-Christendom, by contrast, belief is devoid of the customary hold over the public consciousness that it enjoyed in times past. What counts today is living faith. Theology must be directed towards illuminating this kind of faith and empowering people to live authentically amid the prevailing banality and superficiality of contemporary postmodern culture. This present-oriented faith does not, of course, abandon the future hope of eternal life with Christ. As Boff rightly points out, "one can hope in eternity without losing one's foothold in the struggle for a better tomorrow, even here and now in our own day and age."[79]

Faith and Truth in Post-Modernism and Post-Christendom

Postmodernism (or postmodernity) describes a cultural condition in which reality is said to consist not in grand theories, but in local stories that people tell about themselves and each other.[80] Within the conceptual contours of postmodernity, explain Martin Robinson and Colin Greene, "reality ceases to be what we have always believed everywhere and at all times and becomes, instead, a culturally constructed pastiche or simulation of what we imagine the world could really be like and our precarious place in it."[81] Postmodern thinkers have argued that modernity's drive towards a rational society resulted not in a scientific utopia, but in Auschwitz and the killing

---

76. Rollins, *The Divine Magician*, 119.

77. Kierkegaard, *Concluding Unscientific Postscript*, 28–29.

78. Kierkegaard, *Attack upon Christendom*, 46.

79. Boff, *Church*, 124.

80. Žižek, *Living in the End Times*, 164.

81. Greene and Robinson, *Metavista*, 27.

fields of Cambodia and Rwanda, and all kinds of sinister and trivial forms of evil.[82] Some have claimed that postmodernity's deconstruction of the Enlightenment tendency to reduce the world to dead and meaningless matter has resulted in what has been called the "re-enchantment of the world."[83]

This re-enchantment has engendered a new spiritual search arising out of a postmodern disillusionment with secular humanism, leading to a new religious age and a society to which the adjective "post-secular" seems more fitting that "post-Christian."[84] This spiritual search is not confined to notions of individual fulfilment, but has profoundly transformational implications for the public sphere and the role of religion in the public domain. The onset of post-Christendom thus coincides with the emergence of post-secularism. The public space today is no longer considered necessarily secular.[85]

Although this re-enchantment creates obvious opportunities for theology and for the church's reengagement with the public sphere, some Christians continue to view postmodernity and post-Christendom as threatening developments. For some, postmodernity posits a gloomy, somber world in which Nietzsche's prophecy concerning the "death of God" has been fulfilled and the world has been emptied of meaning and purpose. The way to counter this threat of meaninglessness is not through a naive insistence on the plausibility of traditional Christian *belief*, but through a rigorous affirmation of living *faith*. Regrettably, some Christians fall prey to the temptation to offer facile criticisms of the "evils" of postmodernity, which they almost invariably misunderstand and caricature. Some have spent decades tilting against the windmills of postmodernity and, like Don Quixote de la Mancha, they have emerged from the fray looking ridiculous. Postmodernity is threatening only to the propositional edifice of Christian belief; it is *not* a threat to Christian faith itself. In fact, in many ways the postmodern condition offers a particularly auspicious opportunity for Christian faith to assert itself with renewed vigor and confidence, as leading Christian thinkers have compellingly demonstrated.[86]

Post-Christendom theology can empower Christians to respond to the challenges of postmodernity not by prompting panicky appeals to "absolute truth," but with a vigorous affirmation of life and hope, which alone can

---

82. Bauman, *Modernity and the Holocaust.*

83. Berman, *Reenchantment of the World.*

84. Habermas, "Secularism's Crisis of Faith," 17–25.

85. Nynas et al. (eds.), *Post-Secular Society.*

86. Smith, *Who's Afraid of Postmodernism?*; Caputo, *What Would Jesus Deconstruct?*; Rollins, *Fidelity of Betrayal.*

overcome death and despair.[87] This existential affirmation is tested and purified in the fire of suffering, which transfigures the character into the likeness of Christ. Faith affirms, as illustrated most strikingly by Jesus himself, that the way to truth and vigorous affirmation of life leads down the road of radical doubt, despair and even death. The faith that finally emerges out of the fire of despair and devastation will be all the stronger for having dared to stare into the abyss.[88]

Faith is not a comfortable vague assurance that everything will turn out for the best; true faith, rather, is a touching of the void, a radical affirmation of life in the midst of overwhelming adversity, the "courage to be in spite of the experience of a chaotic world and a finite existence";[89] faith is at once paralyzing and invigorating. Theological formation can help people to articulate this faith in our culture by finding a common language between Christian convictions and socio-cultural realities. Christian faith has a role to play in leading people out of the existential wasteland of postmodern culture by witnessing to the good news that there is a more excellent way that leads to enduring joy, lasting fulfilment (John 4:14; 6:35) and the kind of life that is life indeed (John 10:10).

In a postmodern world in which the "truth is stranger than it used to be,"[90] post-Christendom theology is required to repair the broken connections between faith, truth, and subjectivity. Whenever God is thought of as object of contemplation, theology invariably degenerates into idolatry. God is Spirit, not matter. He is subject, not object. He resists the attempts of systematic theology to objectivize Him in human terms of being and essence. Parker Palmer explains that,

> When Jesus is asked, "What is truth?" the readers of John's Gospel know the answer, even though he remains silent in the face of Pilate's question. Jesus taught his disciples, "I am the way and the truth and the life" (John 14:6). He refuses to deal with the objectification of "what." He does not give us propositions—they come later with the theologians. Christ gives us personhood; he gives us himself.[91]

Jesus does not merely teach the truth, but is Himself the Way, the Truth, and the Life (John 14:6), and the one in whom are hidden all the treasures

---

87. Limited time and scope preclude the possibility of developing this point in detail here. For a classic statement of this thesis, see Tillich, *Courage to Be*.

88. Searle and Cherenkov, *Future and a Hope*, 43.

89. Tillich, *Courage to Be*, 189.

90. Middleton and Walsh, *Truth Is Stranger*.

91. Palmer, "Towards a Spirituality of Higher Education," 82.

of wisdom and knowledge (Col 2:3). Leonard Sweet explains that, "For Jesus truth was not propositions or the property of sentences. Rather truth was what was revealed through the participation and interaction with him, others, and the world."[92] To live in the truth means to live according to the costly way of Jesus, which results in the transformation of life in the power of the Holy Spirit. The emphasis is upon life transformation, rather than assenting to a set of doctrines.

Commenting on Kierkegaard's theory of learning, Murray Rae states that, "The question is not whether the learner "knows" the truth but whether the learner is *in* the truth, whether the learner is so related to the truth that it becomes a life in him [*sic*], whether it has transformed him."[93] Truth is not to be attained through objective analysis of the world, but through a living encounter with Christ in the power of the Holy Spirit. Such an encounter is relational and is mediated through personhood and implies the encounter of two subjects, rather than an active subject and a passive observer. Truth is revealed through an existential or "I-Thou" encounter that leads to lasting transformation.[94] This understanding of truth lies behind Berdyaev's insistence that "the mystery of the real reveals itself not in objective contemplation on passive objects, but in reflection on the activity of the subject."[95]

From a Christian perspective, truth cannot be understood in isolation to love. Truth is not just a rational category, but a spiritual reality, which "reveals itself only through the creative activity of the spirit."[96] Truth is to be perceived in the spirit, not in objects. "Truth is the supreme criterion," insists Berdyaev, but he maintains that, "truth is not an objective state, nor can it be apprehended like an object. Truth implies above all man's [*sic*] spiritual activity. Its apprehension depends on the degree of community between men on their communion in the spirit."[97] It is now widely recognized that the reduction of truth to the objective perception of empirical phenomena has shackled the spiritual vitality of life, leading to a massive disenchantment with the world. Reality is not exhausted by data and information received by the five senses. The most important realities are spiritual realities and are thus invisible and, as Vladimir Solovyev forcefully claimed,

92. Sweet, *Post-Modern Pilgrims*, 157.
93. Rae, "Learning the Truth," 102.
94. Buber, *I and Thou*.
95. Berdyaev, *Dukh i Realnost*, 8.
96. Berdyaev, *Smysl Tvorchestva*, 48.
97. Berdyaev, *Solitude and Society*, 152.

"All that we see is simply a reflection, only the shadow of that which is invisible to our eyes."[98]

In reference to Jesus's words in John 20:29,[99] Dallas Willard explains that those who believe without seeing are blessed not because of any special faith exertion on their part, but simply because "the most important things in our human lives are nearly always things that are invisible. That is even true without special reference to God. People who cannot believe without seeing are desperately limited in their relationships."[100] Part of the problem with which the church has had to contend from its inception is the tendency to reduce Christianity to a visible institution that is bound by worldly social conventions. This is an unfortunate accommodation to a conventional mindset that does not routinely believe in the invisible world of the spirit, but believes solely in the world of perceptible things.[101] "The world very easily denies and despises the higher spiritual life, the noble aims of the spirit and spiritual knowledge," notes Berdyaev, who claims that, "the world loves to assert that such things obstruct the path towards the world's orderly construction. This view is enunciated by millions everywhere in the world."[102]

Part of the task of post-Christendom theology is to overcome the enslavement of the human spirit to the mechanization processes that govern the material world and blind people to the spiritual reality of the human condition. Theology thus aims to raise awareness of the depth, mystery and beauty of life and to remind the world that life cannot be reduced to organic processes; life is also a spiritual reality.

Life: A New Starting for Theology in Post-Christendom

Theology in post-Christendom should aim to comprehend the meaning and significance of life within a frame of reference that encompasses the totality of the cosmos, including its ideals and spiritual destiny. This kind of theology must begin in wonder, specifically the wonder at the incommensurable experience of life in all its complexity and vicissitudes. Aristotle averred that, "It was their wonder, astonishment, that first led men

98. Solovyev, quoted in Berdyaev, *Ekzistentsialnaya Dialektika*, 61.

99. "Jesus saith unto him, 'Thomas, because thou hast seen me, thou hast believed: blessed are they that have not seen, and yet have believed.'"

100. Willard, *Divine Conspiracy*, 83.

101. Berdyaev, *Dukh i Realnost*, 121.

102. Berdyaev, *Filosophia Svobodnogo Dukha*, 14.

to philosophize."[103] Karl Barth alluded to the need for astonishment in any theological study:

> A quite specific astonishment stands at the beginning of every theological perception, inquiry, and thought, in fact at the root of every theological word. This astonishment is indispensable if theology is to exist and be perceptually renewed as a modest, free, and happy science. If such astonishment is lacking, the whole enterprise of even the best theologian would canker at the roots. On the other hand, as long as even a poor theologian is capable of astonishment, he [sic] is not lost to the fulfillment of his task. He remains serviceable as long as the possibility is left open that astonishment may seize him like an armed man.[104]

Similarly, Immanuel Kant, once remarked that, "Two things fill the mind with ever new and increasing admiration and awe, the oftener and more steadily we reflect upon them: the starry heavens above me and the moral law within me."[105] Other philosophers, such as G. W. Leibniz (1646–1716), were astonished at the simple fact that the world *is*. Theology, too, begins in the same kind of astonishment, but is specifically astonished at the wonder of life. In the same way that Leibniz himself acknowledged that there was no logical answer to the question of "why is there something, rather than nothing?,"[106] theologians are likewise baffled by the question, "why is there life, rather than death?" A theologian is someone who has never quite been able to get over their astonishment at life.

The deepening and enhancement of life in the Spirit is the goal of theology. The Christian gospel is ultimately not a message of salvation from sin, but of *life* in the Kingdom of God. James C. Wilhoit correctly insists that, "The gospel is the power of God for the beginning, middle, and end of salvation. It is not merely what we need to proclaim to unbelievers; the gospel also needs to permeate our entire Christian experience."[107] The gospel concerns the whole of experience, the fullness of life, and its message of good news implies more than the forgiveness of sins. A preoccupation with sin leads not to repentance and renewal, but to defeatism and indolence. As H. D. Thoreau (1817–1862) quipped, people "will lie on their backs, talking about the fall of man, and never make an effort to get up."[108] A theological

---

103. Aristotle, *Metaphysics* (982b,12).

104. Barth, *Evangelical Theology*, 64.

105. Kant, *Critique of Practical Reason*, 66.

106. G. W. Leibniz, quoted in Schacht, *Classical Modern Philosophers*, 52.

107. Wilhoit, *Spiritual Formation*, 27.

108. Thoreau, *Essays*, 78.

preoccupation with sin can also lead to passivity and inertia as "false infer-
ences have been drawn from the notion of original sin and have been used
to justify every kind of existing evil and injustice."[109] Salvation from sin is
important and is undoubtedly part of the good news, but the gospel evokes a
vision of salvation *for* life, rather than salvation *from* life. Therefore, life and
hope—and *not* sin or fear—must be the starting point of theology, whether
"academic theology" or the "practical theology" of witnessing to the reality
of God's Kingdom in the world.

God made an atoning sacrifice for sin through Jesus Christ not merely
to settle the accounts of heaven, but to make available the fullness of life to
those who put their faith in Jesus. By defeating sin, God did not merely make
a juridical decree about the believer's eternal destiny, but He also removed
every existential impediment to human flourishing that had previously
prevented people from experiencing "life in the Spirit," which, according
to Romans 8:6, is life (*zóé*) and peace (*eiréné*). This life in the Holy Spirit is
eternal. As the Apostle Paul explains, "if the Spirit of him who raised Jesus
from the dead is living in you, he who raised Christ from the dead will
also give life to your mortal bodies because of his Spirit who lives in you"
(Rom 8:11). This life begins not on the day when someone physically dies,
but in the moment when they are reborn into God's new world—the new
creation, the Kingdom of life that God that God brings into being when
anyone is reborn in Christ (John 3:7; 2 Cor 5:17). This message of new life
and the availability of eternal life *now* must be reinstated into the missional
proclamation.

Theology therefore begins with life and culminates in a vision of the
interfusion of divine and human life in a renewed earth and heaven.[110] The
good news of the gospel is that this life is freely available to all. All human
beings—regardless of whether they self-identify as Christian, Muslim, athe-
ist, agnostic, or even if they are completely unaware of any religious affiliation—are divine image bearers. Berdyaev explains that, "Just as the tiniest
drop of seawater, however fouled, contains within itself all the properties
of the ocean . . . so the spirit of man contains within it all the properties,
potentialities and attributes of the divine."[111]

The Christian vision of discipleship involves the disciplined process
through which this principle of divine life gradually subdues the elemental
impulses of fallen human nature. The life of the flesh is supplanted by life in

109. Berdyaev, *Istoki i Smysl*, 202.

110. This vision has inspired a movement within theology, known as "Process Theology." For an understanding of the "interfusion" of the divine and the human from the
perspective of Process Theology, see Faber, *Divine Manifold*, 483.

111. Berdyaev, quoted in Seaver, *Nicolas Berdyaev*.

the Spirit. This is the essence of Christian spiritual formation. As the great Russian mystic, Vladimir Solovyev (1853–1900), expressed it, the goal of spiritual formation was to change "the centre of man's life from his nature as given to the absolute transcendent world" of the spirit.[112] Living according to the spirit involves human participation in the divine nature (2 Pet 1:4), so that life is transfigured into conformity with the beauty and holiness of Christ. Spiritual formation into the likeness of Christ means becoming more fully human, thereby attaining more and more to the perfection and purity of Christ's humanity.

This principle is expressed superlatively by the Romanian Orthodox theologian, Dumitru Staniloae (1903–1993): "The glory to which man is called is that he should grow more godlike by growing ever more human."[113] This aphorism echoes the assertion of Irenaeus of Lyons (c.130–c.202) that "the glory of God is man fully alive" and that "the life of man is the vision of God."[114] This vision lies at the core of the philosophy of Solovyev, who considered the fusion of divine and human life as the basic idea of Christianity.[115] "Humankind," insisted Solovyev, "should not only accept grace and truth given by Christ, but should also seek to realize this grace and truth within the specific conditions of its own historical life."[116]

This is an important point because it correlates with Jesus's teaching concerning life, as recounted in the Gospels. When Jesus referred to life and death, His focus was always on transcendent and spiritual life, which was to be lived in the here and now. Eternal life was not limited to an individual's post-mortem destiny; it did not begin at the point of physical death. Rather, Jesus's message emphasized the availability of eternal life in the Kingdom of God which was a living reality to be experienced in the present. The New Testament recognizes two kinds of life, expressed in the words *bios* and *zóé*. *Bios* refers to physical, organic life that is subject to time and space, whereas *zóé* denotes life that is eternal and transcendent and thus insusceptible to biological processes of decay and death.[117]

Jesus's teaching on life and death is expressed in His injunction to "let the dead bury their own dead" (Luke 9:60). In this instance, Jesus clearly was not addressing people who were literally dead, but was speaking to those who are physically alive, but spiritually dead. Connecting salvation

112. Solovyev, quoted in Copleston, *Philosophy in Russia*, 215.
113. Staniloae, quoted in Kallistos Ware, *Orthodox Way*, 67.
114. Irenaeus, quoted in Oster, "The Other," 305.
115. Solovyev, *Chteniya o Bogochelovechestve.*
116. Solovyev, quoted in Berdyaev, *Ekzistentsialnaya Dialektika*, 545.
117. Foster, "Salvation is for Life," 297–308.

to life, Marcus Borg remarks that, according to Jesus, "Salvation is about leaving the land of the dead, being born again, becoming a new creation."[118] The gospel thus comes as a word of life to people who experience their lives as a form of living death and as a word of hope, spoken to a culture of death. Jesus preaches a message of life that is eternal, rather than merely infinite. In other words, the *zóé* life that Jesus offers as a gift of grace is not merely the extension of life into an unceasing infinity, but is a revelation of the depth of authentic spiritual life that transcends the bad infinity of limited time. Nietzsche expresses this point well in his excerpt entitled, "The Heaviest Burden," in his book, *The Gay Science*:

> What if a demon crept after you one day or night in your loneliest solitude and said to you: "This life, as you live it now and have lived it, you will have to live again and again, times without number; and there will be nothing new in it, but every pain and every joy and every thought and sigh and all the unspeakably small and great in your life must return to you, and everything in the same series and sequence . . . The eternal hour-glass of existence will be turned again and again—and you with it, you dust of dust!"—Would you not throw yourself down and gnash your teeth and curse the demon who thus spoke?[119]

In contrast to the "bad infinity"[120] or the "eternal recurrence of the same,"[121] the new life that Jesus offers is eternal not merely in duration, but also in quality. The message of Jesus is therefore not fundamentally about life after death, but is rather about life before death. Life is possible not only after we die, but before we die. This vision of eternal life in the here and now lies behind Berdyaev's lucid maxim, which he formulates thus: "act so as to conquer death and affirm everywhere, in everything and in relation to all, eternal and immortal life."[122] The gospel of life must be re-established as the basic point of departure for theology in a post-Christian world in which death seems so dominant.

---

118. Borg, *Convictions*, 71.

119. Nietzsche, quoted in Hovey, *Nietzsche and Theology*, 69.

120. This term, "*schlechte Unendlichkeit*" was coined by the German philosopher, G. W. F. Hegel (1770–1831), who contrasted it with "true infinity" (*wahrhafte Unendlichkeit*). For a comprehensive perspective on the importance of Hegel for contemporary theology, see Nicholas Adams' lucid study, *Eclipse of Grace*.

121. This concept is explained at length is the classic study by Löwith, *Nietzsches Philosophie*.

122. Berdyaev, *Destiny of Man*, 322.

4

Mission as Solidarity with the World

In post-Christendom I want to suggest a reformulation of mission away from evangelization and towards solidarity. In other words, *Christian mission should be reenvisioned in terms of solidarity with the world.* The aim of this chapter is to elucidate this understanding of mission and to explore how this paradigm of mission-as-solidarity can be expressed in terms of theological formation.

What Is Mission?

Mission, or more precisely *missio Dei*, should set the agenda for theology in a post-Christendom era. Despite notable advances in our understanding of mission in recent years, the subject of mission is still beset with misunderstandings. It is necessary to dispel these misunderstandings before full consideration can be given as to how theological formation can be directed towards the cultivation of a truly missiological imagination.

Mission has sometimes been defined in terms of "organized effort for the propagation of the Christian faith"[1] or as "verbal proclamation of salvation in Christ to unbelievers" and even as "conversion of the heathen." During the Christendom era, as Christopher Wright remarks, mission tended to evoke "images of white, Western expatriates among 'natives' in far off countries."[2] Moving beyond these popular caricatures, Wright offers a more satisfactory definition of mission: "Fundamentally, our mission (if it is biblically informed and validated) means our committed participation as God's people, at God's invitation and command, in God's own mission within the

1. http://www.britannica.com/topic/missions-Christianity.
2. Wright, *Mission of God*, 24.

history of God's world for the redemption of God's creation."[3] Thanks to the pioneering work of Karl Barth and David Bosch and others, the origins of mission in trinitarian theology have been widely acknowledged. Mission originates in the unique relationship of mutual love that inhere within the Trinity itself.

In recent years this notion has worked itself out into a fully-fledged theological formulation of what is known as *missio Dei*. The English word, "mission," is derived from the Latin, *missio*, meaning literally, "to send." The Latin word, *Dei*, is the genitive form of the word for God, *Deus*. *Missio Dei* thus refers literally to "the sending of God." What is implied here is the sense of the Father's sending of the Son and the sending of the Holy Spirit into the world (Acts 2:17; cf. John 14:16, 26; 20:21). Mission, according to this *missio Dei* perspective, arises not out of an ecclesial community but from within the Sacred Trinity: God the Father, sent His Son into the world. As a result of the Son's faithfulness unto death (Phil 2:8), the Father raised Jesus from the dead "and seated Him at His right hand in the heavenly places" (Eph 1:20), giving Him "all authority on heaven and earth" (Matt 28:18). The Risen Son now sends His people into the world in the power of the Holy Spirit "to make disciples of all the nations" (Matt 28:19–20).[4]

In light of this Trinitarian understanding, mission is now widely interpreted in terms of human participation in the divine sending. Drawing on his survey of how mission is depicted in the Scriptures, Christopher Wright argues that, "All human mission . . . is seen as a participation in and extension of this divine sending."[5] Since mission reflects the heart of God, mission should, accordingly, be personal, relational, and compassionate, rather than prescriptive, programmatic and target-driven. In other words, mission is expressed in holistic living, rather than merely in church activities and programs.

Missio Dei and Missio Ecclesiae

The emphasis on activities and programs points to another error of Christendom approaches to mission: namely, their tendency to focus narrowly on the church as the object and point of departure for the theory and practice of mission. Among evangelicals, such ecclesiocentric thinking continues to prevail both in academic theology and in the popular folk theology of

3. Wright, *Mission of God,* 22–23.

4. These themes are explored in detail in notable works, such as Tennent, *Invitation to World Missions*; Flett, *Witness of God.*

5. Wright, *Mission of God,* 63.

many churchgoers. In Christendom mission was usually understood as being synonymous with evangelism. The common understanding among Christians within the Christendom mentality was that mission amounted to external activity, whether by individuals or churches, in order to obtain converts to Christianity. Mission thus meant inviting people to attend events and programs organized by a church and to hear the gospel message within the clearly defined confines of religious gatherings under the direction of church authorities.[6]

The implicit theological assumption of this approach was that God could only truly be present in church activities and that successful mission would result in the convert being accepted into the membership of a church. In Christendom, the missionary impulse was essentially centripetal or inward looking; the aim of evangelism was usually regarded in terms of attracting individuals to church so that they could hear the gospel, repent, and be saved from their sins in order to ensure their eternal destiny in heaven when they died.

The shortcomings of this approach are evident in the light of a biblical understanding of the nature, aims and scope of Kingdom-centered mission. The emphasis on personal salvation and gaining individual converts has been misguided: these emphases have been carried away with narrowly-defined personal issues at the expense of social responsibility. Moreover, any kind of mission that is aimed solely at eliciting individual repentance through dire warnings about hell and eternal damnation raises serious concerns about the motivations of the convert. Pete Rollins explains:

> if someone is convinced that there is a place where they will be tormented after death, and that the only way to avoid this terror is by affirming that Jesus Christ is Lord, then they will no doubt make that affirmation, regardless of whether they are genuinely moved by Christ or not. This type of discourse endeavors to compel individuals to bow their knee regardless of their motives or the nature of their desire. Like a lover of nuts who is offered thousands of shells with no center, so we offer God thousands of "converts" with no hearts.[7]

These words call to mind the disturbing words of Jesus, who said: "Woe to you, teachers of the law and Pharisees, you hypocrites! You travel over land and sea to win a single convert, and when you have succeeded, you make them twice as much a child of hell as you are" (Matt 23:15). The danger of preaching exclusively for converts if further highlighted by Blumhardt,

6. Frost, *Exiles*, 278.

7. Rollins, *How (Not) to Speak*, 36.

who claimed that, "The conversion of individuals is only a temporary measure. Individual conversion by itself risks the sin of pharisaism. A single converted person can so easily flatter himself, thinking that he is now a special person able to give others a spiritual kick now and then."[8] James McClendon has even argued that the focus on making converts constitutes a demonic perversion of the true task of mission. "The perversion associated with evangelism," notes McClendon, "is potentially the more demonic . . . just to the degree that in a crass way it succeeds. Members are added; the institution grows; but in this phony evangelism, the gospel is choked out by that growth." This is what happens when the highest goal of mission becomes the making of converts, which results in "an infinite regress of mere recruitment" that takes the place of any "real (or realistic) understanding of the point of evangelism."[9]

Mission, from this exclusively conversionist perspective, was reduced to evangelism, which was understood as programs and activities organized by Christians with the aim of attracting more people to attend church and affirm a set of core beliefs. Within post-Christendom, the differences between evangelism and mission are becoming increasingly apparent. Bosch has made a compelling argument concerning the connection between mission and theology:

> Just as the church ceases to be the church if it is not missionary, theology ceases to be theology if it loses its missionary character. The crucial question, then, is not simply or only or largely what church is or what mission is; it is also what theology is and is about. We are in need of a missiological agenda for theology rather than just a theological agenda for mission, for theology rightly understood, has no reason to exist other than crucially to accompany the *missio Dei*.[10]

Such an understanding of missional theology has rightly provided a more biblical understanding of the role of the church in witnessing to the Kingdom of God in the world. *Missio Dei* teaches that God is already in the process of saving the world beyond the missional activity of the Church. The Holy Spirit was at work in the world before the church came into being and long the concept of "Christian mission" had even been conceived.

Granted the church, at its best, can become a vehicle through which the *missio Dei* is accomplished, it should also be recognized that in many cases the church can also be an irrelevance, and, in the worst case, a hindrance to

8. Blumhardt, *Everyone Belongs to God*, 35.

9. McClendon, *Doctrine*, 439.

10. Bosch, *Transforming Mission*, 494.

the coming of the Kingdom of God "on earth as in heaven." David P. Gushee laments that, "Christian churches are far too often seduced by the powers and ideologies of this world, to the point that the churches sometimes actually end up opposing rather than participating in the actual work of the kingdom of God."[11] This, tragically, has been the case throughout church history from the Crusades through to the Jim Crow laws in the American South and the system of Apartheid in South Africa, when the institutional churches promoted violence, racism, and segregation. Such a church has no use in God's purposes, except to be thrown out and trodden underfoot. In the same way that God will cause the rocks to cry out if people do not worship him (Luke 19:40), so too will God cause unbelievers to fulfil His purposes if the church is found to be either unwilling or unable to participate in the *missio Dei*.

In post-Christendom, *missio Dei* rather than *missio ecclesiae* is the defining essence of Christian mission. Mission is not restricted to verbal proclamation of propositional statements concerning God, sin, salvation and eternal life, but is rather an incarnational act that makes the gospel visible to a world which God loves and for whose salvation He gave His only Son (John 3:16). God loves the world and cherishes every human being upon it. To say that "God is love" means that He "cannot accept the thought of even one single person not belonging to him."[12] The goal of mission is not that churches should grow numerically, but that the glory of God should fill the universe (1 Cor 15:28) and that "the Kingdoms of this world are become the Kingdoms of our Lord and of his Christ" (Rev 11:15).[13] Attempts to grow churches through aggressive evangelizing techniques, Blumhardt reminds us, "do not spring from the love of God, but from the spirit of business."[14] Today, thanks to the *missio Dei* impulses described above, there is a growing recognition that mission implies not only the salvation of individuals from personal sin, but the coming of God into the world, which results in salvation on a truly cosmic scale.[15]

Therefore, theology in post-Christendom must challenge the monopolization of mission by the church. Although some continue to assert that the church is the "sole agent of mission," this is no longer the normative assumption.[16] Thankfully, there is now a growing recognition that, "A narrow-

11. Gushee and Stassen, *Kingdom Ethics*, xiv.

12. Blumhardt, *Gospel of God's Reign*, 5.

13. Stamoolis, *Eastern Orthodox Mission*, 51.

14. Blumhardt, *Everyone Belongs to God*, 45.

15. Searle and Cherenkov, *Future and a Hope*, 7.

16. For a critical discussion of such ecclesiocentric perspectives, see Bevans and

ly church-centered perception of the *Missio Dei* means that Christians fail to catch glimpses of God at work in the world," and that such approaches also lead "to a condescending attitude towards those among whom the Church ministers."[17] Other theologians, writing from a post-colonial perspective, have similarly argued convincingly that, "The church cannot domesticate mission and manage it. It simply "gets-in-behind" the Spirit of God who is witnessing from within the world and within human hearts to the movement of the new creation that God incessantly brings about"[18] By unduly exaggerating the importance of the church in mission, many evangelical churches, in particular, have relinquished the gospel imperative to make the Kingdom of God a visible reality in the world and have usually been content with making occasional forays into society for testimony and to catch a few converts and bring them into the church.

Mission in post-Christendom, however, looks very different. Mission becomes more holistic and is more concerned with *going* out (Matt 28:16–20), rather than *reaching* out. Moreover, mission in post-Christendom signifies movement in two directions. The church not only teaches the world that which God reveals inside the church, but also learns from what God reveals to the church through the activity of the incarnate *Logos* in the world. This conception of mission is particularly significant in post-Christendom in which the barriers between the sacred and the secular and the religious and the spiritual are becoming increasingly blurred. The transfiguring Word incarnates itself both inside and outside those spaces which Christendom had arbitrarily designated as either sacred or secular.

According to this two-way understanding of mission, the church ceases to be a holy place that is rigidly separated from the secular world. Mission is not about reaching out from religious sanctuaries in order to grab a few converts into the church; it is, rather, a dangerous and costly call to vulnerable, sacrificial living in order to transform the kingdoms of this world into the Kingdom of God after the pattern of Revelation 11:15—"The kingdoms of this world are become the kingdoms of our Lord, and of his Christ; and he shall reign for ever and ever." Mission is defined by a "holistic involvement with the local context, personally and as a community of the followers of the Way of Jesus Christ, as an authentic witness for the Kingdom of God, bringing hope in cultures of fragmentation and despair."[19]

Schroeder, *Constants in Context*, 40–1. See also Kim and Anderson (eds.), *Edinburgh 2010*, 77.

17. The Archbishops' Council and the Trustees for Methodist Church Purposes, *Fresh Expressions*, 123. On this point, see also Walton, *Reflective Disciple*, 69.

18. Duraisingh, "Toward a Postcolonial Re-visioning," 355.

19. Parushev, quoted in Searle and Searle, "Monastic Practices and the Missio Dei,"

It is customary, even among theologians who led the reorientation of missiology towards *missio Dei*, to assume that mission is about the church going out into the world and teaching the world that which God reveals to the church. However, mission signifies not merely a movement from the church into the world, but also a constant Christian presence in the world, not only through evangelistic activity, but also through the sacrament of living. Mission is not only a course of action; it is also a way of thinking and being and implies a critical disposition towards the world and a creative awareness of the presence of God's Kingdom in the world. God's mission in the world is expressed in imperatives to the Christian community to proclaim and encourage, send and convert, to go and teach, but also in non-binding forms, such as being, living, sympathizing, loving, salting, and shining the light of Christ in places of darkness.

The Great Commission of Christ calls not only for preaching about the need for personal repentance from sin, but also for the committed participation in God's work of cosmic salvation. Mission is about aligning the world towards God's good purposes. "Those who respond to the invitation to participate in God's mission," contends Stuart Murray, "are involved in all kinds of activities that anticipate the fulfilment of God's purposes: evangelism, working for justice, care for creation, church planting, political activism, education, reconciling enemies, cultural renewal, healing minds and bodies, offering hope and imagination."[20] This kind of participation in the *missio Dei* is what it means to become part of the answer to the prayer that the Kingdom of God would come to earth, so that God's will be done "on earth as it is in heaven" (Matt 6:10).

The Missionary Nature of Christian Existence

Post-Christendom entails the transition from an understanding of mission as the spiritual work of a few professional missionaries to the idea of holistic mission, covering all spheres of life and mobilizing all Christ's followers to participate in God's mission of building the Kingdom. In other words, post-Christendom theology facilitates the expansion of the social base of mission in terms of a transition from a ministry of *professional missionaries* to a movement of *missional professionals*. It follows that in the new missional context of post-Christendom, theological training courses that are aimed at training an ordained caste of professional clergy to run churches

Journal of Missional Practice.

20. Murray, *Vast Minority*, 86.

will become increasingly irrelevant to the new context in which there will be fewer churches that are able to pay the salary of fulltime minister.

Instead, Christian leaders will need to think creatively about how to unleash the gifts of all believers and to share resources creatively, rather than outsourcing mission to a select group of evangelists. It must be understood that the mission to proclaim, envision and embody the good news of God's coming Kingdom is given to all the people of God, rather than entrusted to a few people with a particular calling. On the 500th anniversary of the Reformation, it is time for Luther's vision of the "priesthood of all believers" to find its proper expression. A reaffirmation of the idea of the "priesthood of all believers" for our times provides impetus to a theological understanding of mission as a responsibility delegated to all the people of God.

Post-Christendom theology envisions Christian life from the perspective of mission. Mission is not a specialist activity to be delegated to a specific group of experts, but is the basic condition of what it means to be a follower of Christ. Charles Haddon Spurgeon (1834–1892) once quipped that, "Every Christian is either a missionary or an imposter."[21] McClendon rightly maintained that, "authentic Christian existence is always missionary, possessed only to be imparted to others."[22] Within post-Christendom, to be a Christian has nothing to do with a tribal identity that confers nominal belonging to a religious tradition; rather Christian existence is bound up with mission and discipleship. From the perspective of post-Christendom theology, Christian faith is inconceivable without mission and discipleship. Christian faith without a missional impulse degenerates into a sectarian mentality and self-satisfied smugness and private piety that reduces the gospel to a self-help aid for personal comfort and happiness. Instead of complacency and self-satisfaction, post-Christendom propels the missional self-understanding of the Christian community towards a posture of indefatigable solidarity with the world in its pain and suffering.

Mission as Solidarity with the World

In light of the foregoing discussion, it makes sense to talk about solidarity with the world as a missional imperative. Solidarity is a humanizing force in social life that resists the dominant currents of apathy and ignorance that denigrate and devalue human life in the world today. Martin Luther King Jr. once remarked that, "Nothing in the world is more dangerous than

21. Spurgeon, quoted in Searle and Cherenkov, *Future and a Hope*, 11.
22. McClendon, *Witness*, 20.

sincere ignorance and conscientious stupidity."[23] There is an old joke that goes, "what's the difference between ignorance, apathy and ambivalence?" to which the answer is given, "I don't know, I don't care, and it doesn't really matter either way!"

Unfortunately, the solidarity deficit in the world today is no laughing matter, but betokens a "crisis of compassion"[24] or a "loss of sensitivity"[25] that has taken hold of the public consciousness. Dostoevsky perceived in his time that "the notion of serving humanity, of fraternity and solidarity among peoples is become increasingly scarce and indeed is viewed with distain."[26] Apathy and ignorance are prevalent even among Christians, "the salt of the earth." Often the church looks on while the world commits spiritual suicide. I have often wondered why Christians are not raging against the fact that right now up to 500 million men, women and children throughout the world are literally starving and double this number are undernourished? The world is weeping from the constant assault of inhumanity and cruelty. Christ remains on the cross; God continues to be crucified every day because of the greed, cruelty and selfishness of human beings. It is vain to claim to be a Christian, to follow the Suffering Servant, to be a disciple of the Crucified Messiah while exhibiting a thoughtless indifference towards suffering people. Indifferent Christians—apathetic believers whose hearts do not blaze with indignation at the folly and injustice of a sin-intoxicated world that has gone mad with injustice—are of no use to God. They are "no longer good for anything, except to be thrown out and trampled underfoot" (Matt 5:13).

Reflection on the manmade degradation of the natural world—revealed in phenomena such as carbon-dioxide emissions, acid rain, nuclear waste, deforestation, the industrial plunder of remote wildernesses and the poisoning of topsoil—has led some radical theologians to refer poignantly to the "crucified creation."[27] Wars are waging, prisoners are being tortured, diseased children are perishing, people are starving, homeless people are shivering and dying on our streets—and all the while people, including many Christians, seem inert, unmoved by obscene levels of structural injustice and poverty that coexist alongside such abundance and prosperity in every part of the world. The prophetic spirit of visionary Christian leaders,

23. King, *Strength to Love*, 37.

24. O'Donohue, *Eternal Echoes*, 374.

25. Bauman and Donskis, *Moral Blindness*.

26. Dostoevsky, *Bratya Karamazovy*, 290.

27. Sobrino considers the "crucified creation" in conjunction with his notion of the "crucified people." See his book, *The Principle of Mercy*.

such as Dietrich Bonhoeffer and Martin Luther King Jr. seems to have been shackled by a consumer-oriented Christianity that is concerned more with self-fulfillment than self-denial and is incapable of expressing solidarity with the world and the immeasurable suffering of its inhabitants.

It is now time to rediscover the prophetic spirit of Martin Luther King Jr., who once insisted that:

> As long as there is poverty in the world I can never be rich, even if I have a billion dollars. As long as diseases are rampant and millions of people in this world cannot expect to live more than twenty-eight or thirty years, I can never be totally healthy even if I just got a good check-up at [my] clinic. I can never be what I ought to be until you are what you ought to be. This is the way our world is made. No individual or nation can stand out boasting of being independent. We are interdependent.[28]

"Everyone shares or ought to share in the suffering of others and that of the whole world," remarked Berdyaev, who claimed that, "Human beings are divided into two categories. There are those who are painfully conscious of the sufferings of the world and of people, and there are those who are relatively indifferent to them."[29] This dividing line does not run neatly between the superficial categorization of "Christians" and "non-Christians." It is possible within Christendom to uphold church doctrines and to self-identify as a Christian and, at the same time, to disregard Christ in the world. Yet no-one can read the accounts of Jesus's life and ministry and come to the conclusion that to have compassion, pity, and mercy on those who suffer is not an absolute, non-negotiable gospel imperative.

I Suffer, Therefore I Am

Mission as solidarity with the world—this is the keynote of theology in post-Christendom. The fissure that breaks the organic link between faith and compassion is the result of a neglect of solidarity that has affected liberal, evangelical and nominal Christians alike. Indifference to suffering is the polar opposite of solidarity with the world. The illusory comforts and distractions of consumer culture can conceal the essential truth concerning the existential necessity of suffering as the basic condition of being in the world. As Berdyaev rightly remarks, "The wastage of life in the world is appalling, the meaningless perishing of innumerable lives which are doomed

---

28. King, quoted in Ojara, *Tragic Humanity and Hope*, 15.
29. Berdyaev, *Ekzistentsialnaya Dialektika*, 412.

to carry on a torturing struggle for existence . . . Suffering is the basic fact of human existence. In this world the fate of all life which has attained to individuality is suffering. Man is born with pain and with pain he dies."[30] From a theological perspective suffering should not be limited to particular instances of pain or hardship, but must be understood in existential terms as a phenomenon that is "massive, cruel, unjust, structural and enduring"—to use the words of Jon Sobrino.[31] To live is to suffer—*patio ergo sum* (I suffer, therefore I am), or, as the Irish playwright, Samuel Beckett (1906–1989) put it, "He weeps, therefore he lives."[32]

The duty of solidarity has not been adequately emphasized in Christian theology. This may explain why solidarity has become something of a forgotten virtue in contemporary public discourse, even among Christians.[33] In fact, "forgetfulness about solidarity"[34] is a phenomenon that cuts across religious, national and ethnic lines. Christoph Blumhardt expressed a profound truth when he asserted that the issue is "no longer religion against religion, Christians against non-Christians, but justice against sin, life against death."[35] The basic conflict in the world is, in the words of the Russian philosopher, Vasily Vasilyevich Rozanov (1856–1919), "the struggle between the denial of life and its affirmation."[36] It will come as a moment of great liberation for many Christians when they realize that the true conflicts in the world have nothing to do with Christians vs. Muslims or any other religion or ideology. God's favor is upon the suffering and the oppressed in the world, regardless of whatever religion, if any, they adhere to or happened to be born into. As Blumhardt remarks, "Whether people are pagan, Muslim or Christian, or find it impossible to believe, Jesus hears

30. Berdyaev, *Divine and the Human*, 65.

31. Sobrino, quoted in Brackley, "Theology and Solidarity," 7.

32. In in his play *Endgame*, Beckett has Hamm say of his father, Nagg: "He weeps therefore he lives." See Kearney, *Navigations*, 183.

33. Over the past few years, I have consciously listened out for the word, "solidarity," in sermons that I have heard preached in church services that I have attended. From 2012 to 2016, I heard the word only on one occasion and this was in a service in German in the Schlosskirche in Lutherstadt-Wittenberg in August 2016, in which the female preacher gave an excellent address in which she encouraged the congregation to resist populist anti-immigrant sentiment and demonstrate solidarity (*Solidarität* in German) with refugees fleeing from Syria and Iraq.

34. In the same way that Heidegger regarded the "forgetfulness of Being" (*Seinsvergessenheit*) as the Original Sin of philosophy since the time of Socrates, would it be possible to censure Western Christendom theology in similar terms for its "forgetfulness of solidarity" (*Solidaritätsvergessenheit*)?

35. Blumhardt, *Everyone Belongs to God*, 83.

36. Rozanov, *Dostoevsky and the Legend of the Grand Inquisitor*, 12.

their cries."[37] The love of God is wide enough to embrace the whole world, especially those whom the world regards as undeserving of such love.[38]

In order to practice mission as solidarity with the world, it is necessary to abandon the conventional Christian view that posits strict dichotomies that divide the world into "us" and "them" or between "Christians" and "non-Christians," "the saved" and "the damned," or "church" and "world." These kinds of polarizing categories, which are hostile to solidarity, are like spiritual cholesterol, clogging the arteries of love, causing sclerosis of the spirit and enervating the spiritual vitality of Christlike compassion. These detrimental dichotomies are caused by over-consumption of spiritual junk food of popular, folk theology—what Dorothee Sölle castigated as "a botched theology which belittles human beings and reduces God to a potentate."[39]

God does not divide the world in two and neither should Christians. God created one world, not two, and this one world—together with *all* the people upon it—is precious to God.[40] Especially precious to God are those who are experiencing the pain and indignity of suffering and injustice. The division of human beings into two categories of the elect and the reprobate is hostile to the spirit of the gospel,[41] even though such a division can be—and often has been—justified by appeals to certain biblical proof-texts quoted out of context. These dichotomizing judgements can engender complacency among those pious Christians who consider themselves to belong to the saved and who thus express little more than pretentious concern for the souls of those who do not share their beliefs whom they consider to be damned. Berdyaev argues persuasively that "Christianity does not allow of dividing mankind [sic] into two camps—"the good" and "the wicked," "the righteous" and "the sinners" . . . The Gospel does not recognize a race of the good who are going to heaven and a race of the wicked who are going to hell."[42]

These dichotomies have become so entrenched in the Christendom-evangelical mentality that it may be necessary for a new generation of post-Christendom theologians to defend unbelievers from pious Christians who would condemn them. Such so-called unbelievers include those who have been left behind by society—the drug addicts, the homeless, the poor, the abused and people in various desperate circumstances, who through no

---

37. Blumhardt, *Everyone Belongs to God*, 84.

38. Pope, "On Not Abandoning the Historical World to Its Wretchedness," 51.

39. Sölle, *Thinking About God*, 1.

40. Blumhardt, *Everyone*, 77.

41. Berdyaev, *Destiny of Man*, 6.

42. Berdyaev, *Destiny of Man*, 145.

fault of their own have never been anywhere near a church or read a word of the Bible. These are the afflicted ones with whom Christ makes common cause. To these suffering people, as Sobrino rightly comments, "God shows his love by . . . being in solidarity with them, completely and forever."[43] God is with these suffering people through their experience of figurative crucifixion (i.e. their humiliation, shame and death) all the way through to their resurrection and their inheritance of eternal life. "The promise of resurrection," explains Elaine Graham, "is that the God who brings redemption, who repairs the separation between God and creation, is the same one who is in solidarity all along with the godless and godforsaken."[44]

The gospel message thus brings with it both hope for the world and judgement upon the world. The judgement of God is real, but the way this judgement operates often defies our all-too-human expectations. Christians who take refuge in systems of sound doctrine and who turn their face away from the pain of the world are playing with hell fire, because the judgement of God comes to Christians as the cries of the "crucified people," the suffering humanity.[45] Solidarity is not just a social question, but a soteriological (salvation) question. To ignore the cries of the poor and suffering is to incur the wrath of God.

The Theology of Solidarity: Who Is Christ for Us Today?

Solidarity in suffering is the key theme that emerges from a plain exegesis of the Parable of the Sheep and Goats (Matt 25:31–46). Jesus clearly indicates in this passage that there will be many who have not made any conscious confession of Christ who will obtain an internal inheritance in God's Kingdom as an unmerited gift of grace, simply because their hearts were opened to those in pain. Commenting on this parable, Harvey Cox remarks that, "What he [Jesus] said then no doubt shocked his listeners. He insisted that those who are welcomed into the Kingdom of God—those who were clothing the naked, feeding the hungry, and visiting the prisoners—were not "believers" and were not even aware that they had been practicing the faith he was teaching and exemplifying."[46]

Another outstanding feature of this text is the unambiguous way in which Christ demonstrates His solidarity with the outcast and the marginalized and oppressed, even to the point of identifying directly with

43. Sobrino, quoted in Pope, "On Not Abandoning the Historical World," 51.

44. Graham, *Rock and Hard Place*, 218.

45. Alison, *Living in the End Times*, 158.

46. Cox, *The Future of Faith*, 19.

them—"inasmuch as ye have done it unto one of the least of these my breth-ren, ye have done it unto *me*" (Matt 25:40).[47] Hans Küng insists that, "No amount of discussion can conceal the fact that Jesus was a partisan for the poor, the mourning, the hungry, the failures, the powerless, the insignificant . . . Success, social advancement mean nothing to him: anyone who exalts himself will be humbled—and vice versa."[48] The most definitive expression of divine-human solidarity was the event of the incarnation, in which for the sake of love God became flesh with all its limitations and weakness in order to "empathize with our weaknesses" as one who was "tempted in every way, just as we are—yet he did not sin" (Heb 4:15). The incarnation was a demonstration of the power of God's love. Through His incarnation, Jesus "offered the chance of being human to those who were set aside by society's standards at the time: the weak, sick, inferior, despised."[49]

In answer to Bonhoeffer's question, "Who is Christ for us today?"[50] another even more provocative question can be posed: "Where is Christ be-ing crucified in the world today?" Several answers could be proffered which would lead us into richer insights concerning mission as solidarity with the world. The "crucified people,"[51] who represent the suffering of Christ in the world today, are to be found in various guises: in the imprisoned, the starving, the refugee, the Alzheimer's patient, the cancer sufferer, the child caught up in a genocide, and in the rugged countenance of the homeless on the streets of our cities who die in solitude, unknown and unpitied without anyone even to mourn their loss.[52] These are the abandoned ones who, in their despair and desolation, God takes into His arms like a lost sheep. Upon those people who walk in the darkness, a great light has dawned (Isa 9:2).

These tormented ones now embody "the historical continuation of the suffering servant of Yahweh."[53] Therefore, it follows that the mission of Christ's followers in the world today is manifested in acts of compassion to those in need. Christ identifies with these people because *they* now em-body the sufferings of the world. These people include "the unsuccessful

---

47. Graham, Walton and Ward, *Theological Reflection*, 172–74.

48. Küng, *On Being a Christian*, 268.

49. Ibid., 266.

50. "*Wer ist Christus für uns heute?*"; see Jürgenbehring, *Christus für uns heute*.

51. Ellacuria, "The Crucified People," 580–603.

52. This theme of God's solidarity with all people, particularly the suffering and stigmatized, is expressed poignantly in Field's thought-provoking hymn, *God of the Moon and Stars*. The same theme is likewise conveyed in the heart-rending lyrics of the German vocalist, Reinhard Mey, in his songs, *Selig sind die Verrückten* and *Ich glaube nicht*.

53. Ellacuria, "Discernir los signos," 17, 58.

revolutionaries, prisoners, those condemned to death . . . the incurably sick, the complete failures, those who weary of life and those who despair of themselves and of the world," as well as "those who are worn out by boredom, crushed by fear and poisoned by hatred, forgotten by friends and ignored by the media."[54] These are the ones who are "filling up in their flesh what is still lacking in regard to Christ's affliction" (Col 1:24). They "suffer with Him, so that they may also be glorified with Him" (Rom 8:17).

Solidarity is thus the cornerstone of the emerging post-Christendom theology—solidarity with the kind of people that Kierkegaard called "the most abandoned scum of humanity," who are particularly close to God's heart.[55] Within the new spiritual and socio-economic configurations of post-Christendom, the ability to stand in solidarity with the lowly and downtrodden is particularly imperative, regardless of whether or not these forgotten ones confess Christ as Lord. "There must be," insists Hans Küng, "a commitment to liberation for all who are legally destroyed as human beings and who have no real opportunity to be Christians."[56] Spiritual formation must be envisioned in terms of following Christ in costly obedience to a vulnerable way of life that could incur scorn, ridicule, violent persecution and even death.

In this light, we can understand the prophetic statement of Dorothee Sölle that, "Belief in Christ concerns our whole life and does not draw us out of history into a private salvation history, but connects us more deeply and unavoidably with the others around us."[57] Professing sound doctrine and offering intellectual assent to a creedal proposition is useless—perhaps worse than useless because a pious profession of belief in Christ could easily become a smokescreen that one uses to hide from the scandalous and unsettling reality of Christ in the world.

It is helpful to understand Bonhoeffer's question ("Who is Christ for us today?") in conjunction with 1 John 4:7–21, in which the Beloved Apostle exhorts his readers to remember that they cannot claim to love God who they have not seen, if they neglect to love those people in their very midst. Blumhardt maintains that, "Every person will be judged on the basis of whether his heart has been turned toward his fellow human beings or not."[58] This is a clear gospel principle to which Christian theology must testify: namely, that solidarity with one's neighbor is not simply an issue of

54. Küng, *On Being a Christian*, 576.

55. Kierkegaard, *Attack upon Christendom*, 35.

56. Küng, *On Being Christian*, 563.

57. Sölle, *Thinking about God*, 103.

58. Blumhardt, *Everyone Belongs to God*, 88.

social justice and compassion for the hungry and needy is no mere act of charity that aims to ameliorate human suffering. Rather, these are principles that are infused with soteriological and eschatological significance. "Once we recognize Jesus's identification with the poor," notes David Bosch, "we cannot any longer consider our own relation to the poor as a social ethics question; it is a gospel question."[59] In light of this understanding of solidarity as a spiritual quality and as a gospel imperative, we can understand the meaning of Berdyaev's assertion that, "the question about bread for myself is a material question, but the question about bread for my neighbour and for all people is a spiritual and religious question."[60]

Post-Christendom Theology and the Crisis of Compassion

The crisis of compassion in contemporary society, alluded to previously, is one of the symptoms of dehumanization that is leading the world into a new dark age. The appealing falsehoods of secular humanism and materialistic rationalism have made a wasteland of the human spirit.[61] This crisis has been exacerbated by a world-denying false theology among many Christians, which reduces the gospel of salvation in Christ to a transaction that results in the forgiveness of sins. Instead of being salt and light, the church has tended to avoid concrete issues of solidarity, justice and compassion and has opted instead to concern itself with abstract and distant categories, such as the soul, heaven and eternity.

What results is a kind of "ecclesial docetism"[62] in which the church "excarnates" itself from the concrete realities of a suffering world and focuses instead on offering the transcendent comforts, which it mediates through sacramental and liturgical expressions of religious ritual and dogma. Jon Sobrino claimed that, "The Church is factually in the world, but it has a recurring tendency and temptation to create its own environment of doctrinal, pastoral, liturgical and canonical reality that distances and protects it from the world."[63] Ecclesial docetism results in "dis-incarnation from poverty and incarnation in centers of power, to the search for salvation not in weakness of the flesh, but in power."[64] Commenting on the docetic tendency towards "excarnation," Charles Taylor notes that, "Christianity, as the faith of the

---

59. Bosch, *Transforming Mission*, 437.

60. Berdyaev, *Istoki i Smysl Russkogo Kommunizma*, 218.

61. Berdyaev, *Smysl Tvorchestva*, 534–6.

62. Gaillardetz and Clifford, *Keys to the Council*, 51.

63. Sobrino, *Witnesses to the Kingdom*, 140.

64. Sobrino, *Witnesses to the Kingdom*, 141.

Incarnate God, is denying something essential to itself as long as it remains wedded to forms which excarnate."[65] The best way to overcome this docetic temptation, is to understand Christian mission in terms of solidarity with the world. This involves not just ameliorating suffering or offering charity, but feeling the problems, perceiving the demands, sharing the agonies and cooperating with suffering people.[66] Our vocation to participate in the *missio Dei* requires us to find creative and compassionate ways of "taking the crucified people from the cross,"[67] as Sobrino puts it.

Solidarity is thus a matter of seeing the world from the angle of what Ignacio Ellacuría called the "crucified people."[68] "It is impossible to make any progress," insists Boff, "without a genuine spirit of solidarity, which is not a matter of doing something for the poor, but of engaging with them and seeing things from their point of view."[69] This conviction was powerfully expressed in the writings and living witness of Dietrich Bonhoeffer. Reggie Williams accurately summarizes the key point that, "For Bonhoeffer, Christians must see society from the perspective of marginalized people since faithful Christianity is calibrated from the perspective of suffering rather than from dominance. This is costly yet crucial to true Christian discipleship."[70] Bonhoeffer, Berdyaev, and now an increasing number of theologians from the Global South openly profess that the gospel of Christ is a summons not merely to act on behalf of the poor, marginalized, and persecuted people but to be with them and to see the world from their perspective.

This perspective does not come naturally to the suburban middle class churches of Christendom, which tend to offer charity, rather than liberation, for the poor and marginalized. As Sobrino puts it, the church "acts in support of the weak, but does not enter into confrontation with the oppressors."[71] Commenting on Sobrino's prophetic theology, Dean Brackley notes that, "From the perspective of the poor, the world looks different; and from that perspective, when one reads the Bible or studies doctrinal formulations, one sees things one would not otherwise see."[72]

---

65. Taylor, *Secular Age*, 771.

66. This sentence is closely paraphrased from Hennelly, *Liberation Theology*, 91.

67. Sobrino, *Witnesses to the Kingdom*, 155.

68. Ellacuría, *El Pueblo Crucificado*.

69. Boff, *Die Wahrheit ist größer*, 44.

70. Williams, *Bonhoeffer's Black Jesus*, 140.

71. Sobrino, *Witnesses to the Kingdom*, 143.

72. Brackley, "Theology and Solidarity," 5.

One example of a doctrine which can be elucidated from the perspective of solidarity with the world is the incarnation of Christ. In the classical theological tradition of western Christendom, the incarnation has usually been understood in connection with the atonement and as an arrangement that God makes to deal with human sin. From the perspective of suffering, the incarnation can be understood as the supreme demonstration of divine solidarity with suffering humanity. Anselm Kyongsuk Min explains the meaning of Christ's incarnation in these terms: "The infinite God does not remain merely infinite but became a determinate flesh, demanding that we too incarnate our faith, hope and love for God in determinate acts of justice, peace and love."[73] This divine-human solidarity reaches its culmination on the cross where solidarity, grace, forgiveness and compassion find their ultimate expression. Incarnation from this perspective signifies the unbreakable solidarity between God and the suffering world. Jesus enters into "the human experience of those who suffer in a world pervaded by injustice"[74] and identifies directly with those who have been crushed by unjust economic and political forces. Jürgen Moltmann even claims provocatively that in Christ's crucifixion, "God humbles himself and takes upon himself the eternal death of the godless and the forsaken, so that all the godless and godforsaken can experience communion with him."[75]

Liberation Theology has brought this sense of solidarity into a sharp and poignant relief. Liberation Theology places a strong emphasis on the notion that God identifies directly with oppressed people by sharing in their suffering and striving with them for dignity and freedom. This view has found powerful expression in the Black Theology movement, led by James Cone and others, who rightly condemn the "white caricature of the gospel," which interprets the saving work of Jesus from the perspective of privilege and power, and thus distorts it. According to Cone, "To know God means to be on the side of the oppressed, to be one with them and to have a share in the goal of liberation."[76] Cone argues passionately that, "Because God has made himself known in the history of oppressed Israel and decisively in the Oppressed One, who is Jesus Christ, it is impossible to say anything about him without seeing him as being involved in the contemporary liberation of all oppressed people."[77] Cohn thus concludes that, "We must become black

73. Min, *Solidarity of Others*, 84.

74. Pope, "On Not Abandoning the Historical World," 49.

75. Moltmann, *Crucified God*, 286.

76. Cone, quoted in Sölle, *Thinking about God*, 97. Cohn is speaking of blackness in this sense not as a racial category, but as an ontological condition of suffering and oppression.

77. Cone, *Black Theology of Liberation*, 116.

with God." As Dorothee Sölle put it, "If God is on the side of the oppressed, then God cannot be 'white.'"[78]

These thought-provoking perspectives challenge theologians in the economically affluent but spiritually impoverished West to reconsider the nature and goals of theology and the "perlocutionary" effects[79] of theological discourse. "The language of theology challenges social structures," insists Sölle, "because it is inseparable from the suffering community." Accordingly, "Theology cannot be neutral or avoid taking sides with either the oppressor or the oppressed."[80] These are the kinds of prophetic voices that must be heard within the emerging post-Christendom theology. Sölle rightly concludes that the "clarity of thought of Black Theology in the context of racial conflict produces a quite different existential depth from any that would be conceivable were it merely to take over white theologies. Christology, too, is rethought in this perspective: a white redeemer cannot help us. Christ was black. Unless we think of Christ as Black (Black theologians say), as a brother of the Black, we are not thinking of Christ, but of a symbol of domination."[81] With clarity and insight derived from his Liberation perspective, Boff contends that, "The more official Christianity reinforces its mechanisms for subjugating all to the power of hierarchies; the more it affirms its dogmatism, controls the doctrines, imposes its liturgies and shows itself as having the higher moral ground, the more it shows its Western face, and thus, the more fallible it shows itself, the more incapable of stimulating hope and of communicating to those who are outside its sphere of influence."[82]

Although no perspective can monopolize theology and posit itself as universal or normative, it is essential for Christians in post-Christendom to assimilate the key insights yielded by these Black and Liberation approaches. Liberation Theology and Black Theology have reminded Christians in the post-Christian West that solidarity is not simply a matter of responding compassionately to specific instances of suffering; true solidarity requires costly confrontation with the material root causes of such suffering. Compassion also involves spiritual warfare with the powers and principalities that incarnate themselves in unjust structures and institutions and which contend against the flourishing and fulfilment of the earth and

78. Sölle, *Thinking about God*, 97.

79. This is a term associated with the Oxford philosopher, J. L. Austin (1911–1960). Perlocutionary acts are acts of speech that are intended to produce a certain action or elicit an emotional state in the hearer. See Austin, *How to Do Things with Words*; see also Chapter 5 of Searle, J., *Making the Social World*.

80. Sölle, *Thinking about God*, 97.

81. Ibid., 100.

82. Boff, *Global Civilization*, 39.

all its inhabitants. Although many Christendom churches have a very long record of remarkable work among the poor and marginalized, many others have regarded the alleviation of poverty and suffering as a distraction from the apparent priority of saving souls.

The image of hell as an infernal torture chamber to which God consigned people who did not hold correct beliefs about Jesus has often led to the assumption that the church should devote its energies exclusively to conversion activities. Moreover, since the world, as one of the stanzas in the well-known hymn *Amazing Grace* put it, would "soon dissolve as snow," any attempt to confront poverty and injustice in this life, so it seemed, would be a futile gesture, akin to polishing the brass on a sinking ship.[83] Unfortunately, such a view often induced passivity, inertia and apathy towards the pain of the world. Christians seemed to forget that biblical teaching concerning the end times is "not an invitation to escape into a private heaven: it is a call to transfigure this evil and stricken world."[84] Moltmann states emphatically that, "the original hope of Christians was not turned towards another world in heaven, but looked for the coming of God and his kingdom on this earth."[85] Post-Christian theology must be able to hope in eternity without losing sight of the urgent gospel imperative to realize the Kingdom of God as a visible reality in the world here and now and in the midst of life in our times.[86]

Solidarity and Salvation

Taking flight in pious platitudes and wishful aspirations for heaven, popular evangelical theology has tended to undermine the gospel imperative of solidarity. With some justice, Sölle claims that, "The confession of "Jesus Christ—my personal savior" brings no hope to those whom our system condemns to die of famine. It is a pious statement which is quite indifferent to the poor and completely lacking in hope for us all."[87] Therefore, as Gutierrez put it, "for the Church to proclaim the Gospel in the heart of the world of poverty means witnessing to life amid the reality of death."[88]

---

83. This attitude was summed up by Moody, who remarked that, "I look upon this world as a wrecked vessel. God has given me a lifeboat and said, 'Moody, save all you can'"—Moody, quoted in Marsden, *Understanding Fundamentalism*, 21.

84. Berdyaev, *Dream and Reality*, 291.

85. Moltmann, *Source of Life*, 74.

86. Boff, *Church: Charism and Power*, 124.

87. Sölle, *Thinking about God*, 103.

88. Gutierrez, quoted in Aguilar, *Religion, Torture and the Liberation of God*, 84.

Similarly, the bonds of solidarity that bind all people together in the unity of Christ have been weakened by a self-seeking, complacent theology that reduces the astonishing universal affirmation of the gospel of life to an insipid message about forgiveness of sins and imputed righteousness. Christianity is sometimes misunderstood as a religion of private salvation, based on crude utilitarian calculations about avoiding the pains of hell and securing for oneself eternal bliss. Marcus Borg (1942–2015) thus criticized the tendency among some Christians to reduce their faith to what he calls "a religion of self-preservation."[89] As Berdyaev noted, "Man's quest for salvation may prove to be only the supernatural projection of his terrestrial egoism."[90] Therefore, he continues, the actions of some Christians have been "inspired not by striving for perfection but by the desire to avoid eternal torments"[91] and Christians have wanted "not so much the change and transfiguration of their characters, as absolution from their sins."[92]

Morbid fear of perdition and an obsessive fixation on the issue of whether one is counted among the elect or the damned results in an impoverished spiritual condition of soteriological utilitarianism. Instead of a utilitarian concern for personal salvation, post-Christendom theology needs to instill a spirit of solidarity, which like the Apostle Paul, can consent to be separated from Christ, if this is the price to be paid for the salvation of a whole people (Rom 9:3). Rather than religious consumers who are eager to avoid suffering and condemnation, we need more Christians with the same self-sacrificial love of the French mystic, Marie des Vallées (1590–1656),[93] who offered herself to suffer eternal torments for the sake of those who had been condemned to hell.[94] Post-Christendom needs fewer Christians elbowing their way into heaven—and shoving others to the side on their way there—and more people like Mother Teresa of Calcutta (1910–1997), who once declared movingly that, "If I ever become a saint—I will surely be one of "darkness." I will continually be absent from Heaven—to light the light of those in darkness on earth."[95]

The gospel message of salvation penetrates the whole created world with its redeeming light and reaches into the darkest recesses of the human

---

89. Borg, *Convictions*, 64.

90. Berdyaev, *Solitude and Society*, 149.

91. Berdyaev, *Destiny of Man*, 338.

92. Berdyaev, *Ekzistentsialnaya Dialektika*, 432.

93. Dermenghem, *La Vie admirable et les révélations de Marie des Vallées.*

94. This notion is magnificently illustrated in Dostoevsky's "Parable of the Onion" in his greatest novel, *Brothers Karamazov*.

95. Mother Teresa, quoted in Chawla, *Mother Teresa*, 268.

condition. Everything in the cosmos is illuminated by the transfiguring light of the gospel. "Christianity," asserts Berdyaev, "is comprehensive and universal; it is the salvation of the whole world, of everyone and everything, right down to the last grain of dust; it is a summons to all to attend the messianic feast."[96] McClendon rightly contends that, "Christ's salvation is for the whole human reality, in all its social, economic, political, and religious dimensions, overcoming all divisions and ending all injustice and oppression."[97] Sobrino laments that, "The Church no longer speaks, as it once did, of transforming structures . . . of bringing in the kingdom of God. It tends to focus on and promote individual or at most family salvation—which is also good and necessary—rather than the salvation of a people: internal rather than historical salvation."[98]

Therefore, within the Christian eschatological imagination, personal salvation cannot be understood in isolation from the salvation of humankind or of the cosmos.[99] "My immortality," contended Berdyaev, "cannot be separated from the immortality of other people and of the world. To be absorbed exclusively in one's own personal salvation is transcendent egoism. If the idea of personal immortality is separated from the universal eschatological outlook, from the destiny of the world, it becomes a contradiction of love."[100] Berdyaev insisted that, "Every human being should take upon themselves the pain and anguish of the world and all its inhabitants and share their fate. All are responsible for one another, for I cannot conceive of my personal salvation if the world and its people are condemned to oblivion."[101]

The notion of Christianity as a religion of personal salvation has diminished the gospel, depriving it of its rightful saving power. The gospel has often been reduced to a "false piety that limits God to saving individuals, but not the world itself."[102] Evangelical theology in post-Christendom must

96. Berdyaev, *Smysl Tvorchestva*, 269.

97. McClendon, *Doctrine*, 427.

98. Sobrino, *Witnesses to the Kingdom*, 143.

99. Snyder and Scandrett, *Salvation Means Creation Healed*, 99–101. Post-Christendom theology must cultivate a new attentiveness towards the natural world and deconstruct the destructive ideologies that have contributed towards the degradation and exploitation of the environment. Unfortunately, it lies beyond the scope of this book to develop this argument, but Snyder's and Scandrett's book offers several useful perspectives. For a classic account of environmental theology, focused on the healing of creation, see Moltmann, *God in Creation*.

100. Berdyaev, *Divine and the Human*, 165.

101. Berdyaev, *Dukh i Realnost*, 166.

102. Blumhardt, *Everyone Belongs to God*, 27.

emphasize love and solidarity with the world over narrow conceptions of "personal salvation" and "Jesus, my personal Savior," which have more in common with post-Enlightenment western individualism than they have with the gospel of Christ.[103] What is required is a renewed focus on the saving power of the gospel in terms of the resurrection and the unbreakable bonds of solidarity that join together God, humanity and the whole cosmos. Theology thus needs a new language that bypasses the stifling formalism and rationalism of traditional systematic theology. Such a language would be able to resonate with the depth and substance of the gospel in terms of its original meaning and contemporary significance. The banal and discursive language of popular folk theology is incapable of expressing the fecundity and depth of the gospel in ways that can both challenge and inspire people today.[104] There are signs today, as Christopher Rowland observes, that theology is beginning to "move away from an individualistic piety to the cosmic dimension of divine activity."[105]

To express solidarity in suffering (i.e., to share each other's burdens) is the fulfilment of the law of Christ (Gal 6:2; cf. 1 Cor 12:26). Solidarity requires that "No one should seek their own good, but the good of others" (1 Cor 10:24; Phil 2:2–4). Leading theologians and philosophers have argued persuasively that solidarity and care are constitutive of the human condition.[106] As William Blake remarked, "Man liveth not by Self alone but in his brother's face."[107] The solidarity formula is expressed evocatively by C. F. Blumhardt: "You belong with me, and I belong with you, for both of us belong to God," who remarks that, "It's amazing how this truth changes people."[108] Solidarity from a gospel perspective means to uphold the dignity of the other, particularly when the other is a foreigner, an adherent of a different religion, a child, or a sick person. What is required is a new vision of "an all-consuming solidarity with the pain and sufferings of the world and

---

103. Thiselton, *The Hermeneutics of Doctrine*, 188.

104. O'Donohue makes a similar point in his book, *Anam Cara*, 94, 143–44.

105. Rowland, *Open Heaven*, 447.

106. Heidegger, argued that *Mitsein* (Being-with) is a fundamental mode of being that is the condition of possibility for *Dasein* (Being-there). See Olafson, *Heidegger and the Ground of Ethics*, 45–46. It should be noted that some philosophers, including the eminent Lithuanian-French Jewish thinker, Levinas, criticized Heidegger's notion of solidarity, which he associated with the camaraderie of fascism and communism, which suppressed the immediacy of the face-to-face encounter. See Critchley, *Ethics of Deconstruction*, 277–79.

107. Blake, *The Four Zoas*, IX, 636–42.

108. Blumhardt, *Everyone Belongs to God*, 81.

an undaunted readiness to serve and sacrifice"[109] oneself for the sake of love towards God and neighbor. This kind of solidarity must become the cornerstone of mission in today's post-Christendom era. The question that arises is how this kind of solidarity can be nurtured through theological formation.

Cultivating a Missional Imagination

To participate in the *missio Dei* means to live according to the reality of the presence of the Kingdom of God that is "now at hand" (Mark 1:15), adopting spiritual disciplines and practices that are consistent with Kingdom values for the benefit and transformation of the world. Such participation involves joining in what Dallas Willard aptly calls God's "cosmic conspiracy to overcome evil with good." [110] Participation in the *missio Dei* means costly discipleship. Christians are called to exhibit an attentive availability to God and to their neighbors. The call to discipleship is also a call to vulnerability, as the world that the Christian seeks to love and serve is in the grip of powerful forces that are opposed to God and His Kingdom. It is these spiritual forces, which incarnate themselves in social structures, causing society to grow "more and more fragmented and inhumane."[111] These powers and principalities have been unleased in the world, which has taken leave of God.

In Christendom churches God was preserved in symbolic form and represented in liturgy and ecclesiastical rituals. However, the spiritual presence of God as a tangible, incarnated reality in the midst of real life in the world was disregarded. The vision of God as the one who "became flesh and made his dwelling among us . . . full of grace and truth" (John 1:14) was marginalized. As a result, Willard explains, "The idea of an all-encompassing, all penetrating world of God, interactive at every point with our lives, where we can be totally at home and safe regardless of what happens in the visible dimension of the universe, is routinely treated as ridiculous."[112] To be a Christian in post-Christendom is to be part of a dwindling minority in a world that is passing through a painful era of godforsakenness.

In the transition to a post-Christendom era, Christians are thus becoming increasingly aware of their marginal status as a pilgrim people. Living in a condition of exile can be a disorienting experience that can evoke feelings of lament and nostalgia. However, exile can also be a time of rebirth

109. Berdyaev, *Dream and Reality,* 279.

110. Willard, *Divine Conspiracy,* 103.

111. Willard, *Spirit of the Disciplines,* 233.

112. Willard, *Divine Conspiracy,* 103.

and new beginnings. Commenting on the experience of Ancient Israel in the Old Testament, the Irish theologian, Cathy Higgins, remarks that, "At the heart of that exilic experience there emerged creativity and hope. Out of exile came a new identity, a new sense of purpose, and a new vision of God."[113] Exile, for all its suffering and lamentation, was an opportunity for the people of God to renew their vision and to engage their imaginations in order to recognize the "new song" that God was singing and to perceive the "new thing" (Isa 42:10; 43:19) that He was doing in their midst.[114]

Although the analogy should not be taken too far, the post-Christendom era evinces some of the characteristics of exile. Post-Christendom, for all its challenges, presents new opportunities for the church to present the "gospel as public truth"[115] in the midst of a society, which, in its depths, is not as secular as it may appear on the surface.[116] Within contemporary culture, various "surrogate forms of transcendence," such as nationalism, humanism, consumerism, and culture itself have stepped into the breach and assumed the guise of what Terry Eagleton calls "displaced forms of divinity."[117] McClendon observed that, "The religious dimension of culture [is] no longer to by symbolized by the church . . . Now the religious dimension was to be found in the various autonomous spheres of *secular* society."[118] There is a conspicuous transcendental residue that lingers on in an ostensibly material age and expresses itself in the midst of mundane life.[119]

The ability to perceive the sacred depths of ordinary life requires the engagement of a missiological imagination that can recognize the ways in which God is at work in the world amid the routine events of everyday life. As J. Richard Middleton aptly remarks, "Imaging God thus involves representing and perhaps extending in some way God's rule on earth through ordinary communal practices of human sociocultural life."[120] The obvious problem with attempting to perceive the signs of God's activity in the world is that, as Jesus said, "the Kingdom of God cometh not with observation" (Luke 17:20). Moreover, if anyone claims that the Kingdom has come into the world by identifying anyone or anything with the coming Messiah, Jesus

113. Higgins, *Churches in Exile*, 9.

114. These themes are developed with skill and insight in Brueggemann, *Prophetic Imagination*.

115. This term is taken from Newbigin, *Truth to Tell*.

116. Küng, *On Being a Christian*, 27.

117. Eagleton, *Culture and the Death of God*, ix.

118. McClendon, *Witness*, 37.

119. Eagleton, *Culture*, 177.

120. Middleton, quoted in Smith, *Desiring the Kingdom*, 163.

explicitly warns His followers not to believe it (Matt 24:23). Therefore, since the activity of the incarnate *Logos* in the world is not susceptible to precise definition, it is necessary to exercise the discernment of what some thinkers have called the "sanctified imagination." One theologian offers a helpful perspective on how this imagination operates:

> Through the imagination sanctified by God's Spirit the saint sees everything as related to divine mystery . . . The saint sees the world as stamped as part of divine creation and subject to God's intervening wrath and love. He [sic] sees everything in the world as consisting of images or shadows of divine things. The world is not only symbolical but sacramental in the sense that the regenerate eye beholds it as existing within the unity of divine meaning.[121]

The sanctified imagination can be used in the service of the *missio Dei* if it is combined with the missiological imperative of going into the world and transforming the nations in the power of God's truth. One helpful perspective in this regard is offered by Paul Tillich, who claimed that Christians should not restrict their theological horizons to explicitly Christian or church-related symbols and practices. Instead, he called on Christians to learn to perceive the "religious substance" within apparently secular spheres of culture. Such a quest for the divine presence in culture lay behind the work of Harvey Cox who maintained that "we meet God not just in religion or in church history, but in all of life, including its political and cultural aspects."[122]

This view is based on the understanding that the Great Commission is fulfilled not just by Christians operating out of church contexts, but also involves the whole world. The fulfilment of the Great Commission depends on the witnessing power of the Holy Spirit in the world among those who submit themselves entirely to God's will. God's Spirit is effective in the world beyond the activities of churches. As Blumhardt rightly remarks, "The Holy Spirit is at work everywhere. It is not a spirit of churches and confessions, parties and nations. The Spirit belongs to all humankind. It is the Spirit before whom all the differences between us, though they do not disappear, become meaningless."[123] The Great Commission is thus fulfilled not merely when people participate in church activities or adhere to particular beliefs, but when the Holy Spirit, having been poured out on *all* people (Joel 2:28;

---

121. Simonson, *Radical Discontinuities*, 39.

122. Cox, *Secular City*, xii.

123. Blumhardt, *Gospel of God's Reign*, 19.

cf. Acts 2:17), is at work in the world, often in subtle and even imperceptible ways.

Therefore, in order to recognize the work of the Holy Spirit in the world, normal sight is often inadequate. Today, as in days gone by, sometimes God sings a new song and His people do not perceive it (Isa 43:19). What is needed is an optic of the missiological imagination. When the Spirit is at work in the world, He brings new life, redemption, reconciliation, forgiveness, and compassion in His wake. The transformation that takes place is often subjective and imaginative, rather than objective and empirical. In terms of human life, the most fundamental change that can take place is the spiritual process that leads to the transformation of character into the likeness of Christ.

The missiological imagination is oriented towards character formation. This means that the mission of the Christian university should be envisaged more in terms of transforming character, rather than disseminating information.[124] Smith advocates "a holistic education that not only provides knowledge but also shapes our fundamental orientation to the world."[125] Smith formulates the notion of a "pedagogy of desire" as a theoretical point of departure from which to castigate the captivity of contemporary theological education to a flawed anthropology that falsely privileges the intellect to the detriment of the imagination.[126] He contends that instead of being fixated on questions of knowledge and worldview, theological education should be conceived as a holistic and integrated task that is directed towards the transformation of those "material practices that shape the imaginative core of our being-in-the-world."[127] Putting the Kingdom of God at the center of the Christian witness helps us to understand the task of theological learning and spiritual formation from the perspective of the Great Commission. As Sölle explains, "learning is a process in which people develop a relationship to God and his way of truth, justice and peace, so that they can follow this way obediently in their relationship to one another and extend it to all peoples."[128]

---

124. As Smith notes, "the Christian college is a formative institution that constitutes part of the teaching mission of the church." See, Smith, *Desiring the Kingdom*, 34.

125. Smith, *Imagining the Kingdom*, 4–5.

126. Smith, *Desiring the Kingdom*, 33.

127. Smith, *Imagining the Kingdom*, 15.

128. Sölle, *Thinking about God*, 145.

Participating in the Great Commission

Mission involves committed participation in the Great Commission. The ultimate textual reference point for theological formation is thus the Great Commission of Matthew 28:16-20. The primary goal of the Christian university or seminary is not to offer new theories about the nature or God or to induct students into a Christian worldview. When seen from the perspective of the Great Commission, the ultimate task of theological education is the formation of disciples. The renewal of theological formation as mission will require a reconnection between mission and discipleship. In order to participate in the *missio Dei*, Christ commissions His followers to go into the world and "make disciples of all the nations," which means "teaching them to observe all things that I have commanded you" (Matt 28:19–20).

Christ is speaking here not only about a hasty transfer of the truth or information about salvation, but also about the long and difficult work of teachers with students. Christ is referring not primarily to church planting and the need to preach for converts, but to the Christian enlightenment of nations and the formation of entire peoples. If God's purpose for individuals is Christlikeness (i.e., that they be conformed to the image of His Son—Rom 8:29), then His purpose for nations is Kingdom-likeness (i.e., that they be conformed to the image of His Kingdom—Matt 6:10; Rev 11:15). To be a theologian is to be an active participant in the *missio Dei*. It is imperative, as Joel Carpenter remarks, that Christian scholars "recover the idea that what we are called to do as intellectuals is missionary work."[129]

The Great Commission thus helps us to think of the task of theological formation and mission in cosmic terms. Arguing from a similar perspective, James K. A. Smith maintains that, "the primary goal of Christian education is the formation of a peculiar people—a people who desire the Kingdom of God and thus undertake their vocations as an expression of that desire . . . the Christian college is a formative institution that constitutes part of the teaching mission of the church."[130] According to this understanding, Christian colleges in post-Christendom can be reenvisioned as formation centers that equip and empower students to participate thoughtfully and passionately in the Great Commission. Theological formation, focused on the Great Commission, must equip people to lead lives "in a manner worthy of the calling with which [they] have been called" (Eph 4:1).

---

129. Carpenter, "Mission of Christian Scholarship," 72.

130. Smith, *Desiring the Kingdom*, 34.

Concluding Remarks on Theological Education as Mission

A basic conviction that underlies this chapter is that theology and theological education can serve as a catalyst for change that will enable the church to fulfil its existential imperative to participate in the *missio Dei*. The future of theology in post-Christendom will depend on the recovery of the vital organic link between the life of the Christian community, missional practice and Christian formation. Christendom tended to separate these areas which has led to the fragmentation or compartmentalization of theology and the structures of theological education.

5

The Kingdom of God as the Focal Point of Theological Formation

Introduction to Chapter 5

The key contention of this chapter is that theology in post-Christendom must shift its focus from the church towards the Kingdom of God. The aim is to explore the meaning and significance of the Kingdom of God as the organizing principle of all theological formation and the point of departure for a new theological agenda that is attuned to the activity of the Holy Spirit in the world today.

Theology is directed towards the transformation of the world into the likeness of the Kingdom of God (Rev 11:15). Theology must stimulate the awakening of Christianity from its captivity to church institutions and dogmatic systems. Church-oriented (ecclesiocentric) theology is often devoid of prophetic witness. Theology that takes the Kingdom of God as its starting point will be concerned with the development of a creative vision of Christian faith, which has social transformation as one of its fundamental aims.[1]

However, the Kingdom-oriented theology that we are advocating understands Christianity *not* as a social religion, but as a progressive revelation of transforming truth and empowering justice to all spheres of life at its cosmic, social and individual levels. From this perspective, the essential message of Christianity concerns neither the forgiveness of personal sins (i.e., evangelical fundamentalism) nor the renewal of society (i.e., liberal theology, Social Gospel, etc.), but the regeneration of life, resulting from a new birth in the spirit (John 3:7; 2 Cor 5:17; 1 Pet 1:3; Jas 1:18) that propels

1. Berdyaev, *Istoki i Smysl*, 221.

the cosmos towards the Kingdom of God. Post-Christendom theology cannot be identified as either liberal or fundamentalist. It is not founded on human experience or social reality. Theology cannot be permitted to reduce the gospel to the promotion of social values, such as equality, liberation and tolerance. Neither does this approach make naive and indolent appeals to literalist readings of Scripture, which have served only to exacerbate the rift between theology and the real world. Post-Christendom theology takes as its departure point not a supposedly inerrant biblical text, but the vision of transfigured life in the Kingdom of God to which that text testifies authoritatively.

The good news of the gospel is that the Kingdom of God is "now at hand." The Kingdom of God is a present, living reality in the here-and-now that has the power to bring salvation. This message of the coming Kingdom lies at the heart of Christian proclamation. The gospel is addressed in the first instance not to any particular community (i.e., the church), but to the world. Virtually every time Jesus is heard speaking in the Gospels, He is referring not to any religious organization, but to the Kingdom of God. Nowhere is the gap between the original message of Jesus and the dominant emphasis of today's churches more strikingly revealed than in the contrasting emphasis placed on the proclamation of the Kingdom of God. Whereas the Kingdom was constantly on the lips of Jesus and formed the imaginative fulcrum of His entire teaching, the Kingdom is largely absent from the ecclesiocentric theologies Christendom. This chapter aims to highlight and account for this theological deficit, before setting out a positive vision of integration between the church and the world in terms of the Kingdom of God.

The Gospel as Good News of the Coming Kingdom of God

The gospel is the message of good news that Jesus came to proclaim concerning the universal availability of the Kingdom of God. At the heart of gospel proclamation is a radical, inclusive and all-encompassing vision of the Kingdom of God. The gospel issues in a call to *metanoia*, a summons to reorder one's life in response to the "new thing" (Isa 43:9) that God is doing in the world. The gospel calls not only for personal repentance from sin, but also for cosmic transformation. "The gospel is the joyful tidings concerning the coming of God's Kingdom," contends Berdyaev, "rather than a revelation of an ascetic method for the salvation of the soul."[2] The gospel is not concerned in the first instance with the salvation of individual converts

2. Berdyaev, *Dukh i Realnost*, 83.

through the profession of correct beliefs; rather the gospel is a messianic announcement that a new reality has dawned upon the earth, the consequences of which are cosmic in scope.

There is always something scandalous about the gospel, for it is, at the same time, a message of salvation for the earth and judgement upon the world; it is both "good news (*eu-angelion*) for the poor" (Luke 4:18) and "bad news" (*dys-angelion*) for those who trust in "the deceit of riches" (Mark 4:19). The gospel brings a word of comfort to the sinner, but a stern word of warning to the pious and to those who consider themselves to belong to "the good and the just."[3] Shirley Guthrie (1927–2004) is correct when he explains that Jesus "almost never mentioned hell except when he spoke to the scribes and Pharisees—the moral, religious, church-going people of his day who wanted above all else to preserve the 'moral values' and 'religious traditions' that 'once made our country great.'"[4] Blumhardt adds that, "It is true that certain scripture passages regarding damnation cause difficulty. Yet the sternest warnings of Jesus are addressed to the devout, not to unbelievers and sinners."[5]

It is crucial to note just how antithetical the gospel is to the prevailing attitudes and values that determine contemporary social reality. As Berdyaev explains, "The morality of the Kingdom of God proves to be unlike the morality of the fallen world, which is on this side of good and evil. The Gospel morality lies beyond the familiar distinction between good and evil according to which the first are first and the last are last."[6] Gospel morality is scandalous because unlike any other ethical system ever devised by human ingenuity, the gospel insists that "the tax collectors and sinners" enter the Kingdom of God before those the world considers to be good and just (Matt 21:31). In other words, "The Gospel is opposed not only to evil but to what men consider good."[7] The Gospel thus "transcends and cancels the ethics of the law, replacing it by a different and higher ethics of love and freedom."[8] Berdyaev, again, lucidly illustrates the contrast between the gospel of the Kingdom and the customary assumptions that govern the world:

---

3. This term, "die Guten und Gerechten," is taken from Nietzsche, *Also Sprach Zarathustra*, 168.

4. Guthrie Jr., *Christian Doctrine*, 396.

5. Blumhardt, *Everyone Belongs to God*, 41.

6. Berdyaev, quoted in Witte and Alexander (eds.), *Teachings of Modern Orthodox Christianity*, 163.

7. Berdyaev, *Destiny of Man*, 158.

8. Ibid., 128.

> [According to the Gospel] publicans and harlots go before the others into the Kingdom of God. But the world thinks that the good, the righteous, the pure, those who have fulfilled the law and norm, lead the way. One must come through the narrow gate. The world goes through the wide gate . . . The Gospel tells us to be as carefree as the birds of the air and the lilies of the fields and take no thought for the morrow. But the whole life of the world is based upon care and upon taking endless thought for the morrow. A man ought to leave his father, mother, wife, and even to hate them if they hinder him from seeking the Kingdom of God. But the world requires first of all love for one's nearest—for one's father, mother, wife. It is difficult for the rich to enter the Kingdom of Heaven. But the world esteems the rich above all, honours them and regards them as first.[9]

Using more present-day illustrations, John Caputo makes a similar point about the Kingdom that Jesus preached:

> His kingdom was an ironic kingdom from the point of view of Roman power and Roman kingdoms and Roman thrones, for it meant that God rules precisely among the powerless and the disenfranchised, the little ones and the nobodies, the homeless and starving, the lepers and the lame, that is to say, all the victims of Roman—read worldly—power. God rules not in Rome but in the victims of Rome. God rules not in the churches but in the inner cities . . . God rules not in respectable upper middle class mostly white suburban families but among the unwed mothers and fatherless children of the inner cities whom the churches, perfidiously in league with the right wing, teach us to resent and despise as lazy freeloaders. Wherever the kingdom rules, the tables in the temple, the councils of the powerful wherever they are to be found, are in trouble.[10]

The gospel therefore signifies a "transvaluation of values" in which customary assumptions that govern the world concerning good and evil are refuted and nullified, the mighty are brought low and the humble are exalted.

The good news that Christ proclaimed cannot be reduced to a set of rules and dogmas passed down by traditions. The gospel is the living power of God for the redemption of the world. The power of the gospel should not be underestimated. Paul defined the gospel as "the power of God that brings salvation to everyone who believes" (Rom 1:16). The gospel signifies the

---

9. Ibid., 159–60.

10. Caputo, *Prayers and Tears of Jacques Derrida*, 247.

power of grace and the transfiguring Light that overcomes the darkness of the world. The Kingdom of God upsets the social and political status quo. The simplest gospel statement, "Jesus is Lord," in its positive expression is a theological statement; in its negative expression it is a political statement, because it necessarily implies that "Caesar is *not* Lord."[11]

To the extent that it is bound up with justice and acts as a stumbling block to the rich and powerful and the religiously complacent, the gospel is a message that is invested with political, as well as spiritual, meaning and significance. Leonardo Boff explains that, "The sign that the Kingdom of God approaches and begins to abide in our cities is that the poor have justice done to them . . . and that they are raised in terms of their dignity and defended against the violence they suffer at the hands of the current economic and political system."[12] The coming of the Kingdom is manifested not in people streaming into churches on Sunday mornings, but in the enactment of righteousness and justice as the preeminent values governing the general life of a society. The Kingdom of God is transfigured life that is immersed in the reality of God's presence.

Therefore, any attempt to reduce the good news of Jesus to a simplistic message concerning the atoning efficacy of the cross results in a distortion of the gospel. The *ultimate* good news of the gospel is not the cross, but the resurrection. The resurrection has conquered sin, for "if Christ has not been raised, your faith is futile; you are still in your sins" (1 Cor 15:17). Christ saves not only by His death, but pre-eminently through His life: "For if, while we were God's enemies, we were reconciled to him through the death of his Son, how much more, having been reconciled, shall we be saved through his life!" (Rom 5:10). This verse testifies to the new life in the Kingdom of God and the saving power of Christ's resurrection life. This is why, as Tom Wright persuasively argues, "we must be sure that whatever we say about the death of Jesus, it clearly and visibly belongs with the good news of the kingdom of God."[13]

When we recognize the Kingdom of God from the perspective of life, we understand why the resurrection occupies such a central place in the gospel proclamation. The resurrection is God's great "Yes" to life.[14] The resurrection demonstrates that life, not death has the final say in human existence and cosmic destiny.[15] Death is hostile to life and acts as a nega-

---

11. McKnight and Modica, *Jesus Is Lord, Caesar Is Not.*

12. Boff, *Church*, 25.

13. Wright, *Simply Good News*, 66.

14. Muers, *Keeping God's Silence*, 80.

15. Barth, *Faith of the Church*, 162–63.

tive spiritual force that aims to reduce God's good creation to non-being. The Kingdom of God is the sphere of divine life and the resurrection is the assurance that this life is indestructible.

Unfortunately, under Christendom the message of the universal availability of the divine life was gradually whittled down to a thin message about salvation from sin through Christ's death. Dallas Willard explains that, "Christ's transcendent life in the present Kingdom of heaven is what drew the disciples together around Jesus prior to his death. And then resurrection and post-resurrection events proved that life to be indestructible." The cross, he explains, only emerged centuries later as the symbol of Christian hope. "The cross," Willard remarks, "came to the center because the force of the higher life [of Christ's resurrection] was allowed to dissipate as the generations passed by." As a result, "The church's understanding of salvation then slowly narrowed down to a mere forgiveness of sins, leading to heaven beyond this life" and "the basic structure of the redemptive relationship between us and God came to be pictured in a way radically different from its previous new Testament conception." Willard concludes that as a result of these regrettably trends, Christ's life and teaching came to be regarded as "nonessential to the work of redemption and were regarded as just poignant decorations for his cross, since his only saving function was conceived to be that of a blood sacrifice to purchase our forgiveness."[16]

One unfortunate consequence of this neglect of the saving power of Christ's life is the tendency among many evangelical Christians to abstract the issue of salvation from Jesus's proclamation concerning the Kingdom of God. The whole meaning of the gospel of salvation in Christ is sometimes reduced to an arrangement that results in the forgiveness of sins and the settling of heaven's accounts by the atoning sacrifice of Christ on the cross. Tom Wright explains this point with force and clarity:

> Most people who regard the statement that Jesus died in your place as the center of the gospel place this truth, this beautiful fragment, into a larger story that goes like this. There is a God, and this God is angry with humans because of their sin. This God has the right, the duty, and the desire to punish us all. If we did but know it, we are all heading for eternal torment in hell. But this angry God has decided to vent his fury on someone else instead—someone who happens to be completely innocent. Indeed, it is his very own son! His wrath is therefore quenched,

---

16. Willard, *Spirit of the Disciplines*, 34–38.

and we no longer face that terrible destiny. All we have to do is to believe this story and we will be safe.[17]

Wright adds that this presentation of the gospel, although "not completely wrong," is nevertheless "deeply misleading." A proper understanding of the saving power of Christ's life, supremely demonstrated in His resurrection, and an awareness of the application of this life towards the transfiguration of the cosmos into the likeness of the Kingdom of God will help post-Christendom theology to avoid these kinds of distortions of the gospel message. Post-Christendom theology must rediscover the saving power of Christ's resurrection life within the all-encompassing vision of the Kingdom of God as the centerpiece of all gospel proclamation.

The Kingdom of God: Towards a Brief Definition

What, therefore, is the Kingdom of God? Put simply the Kingdom of God is rejuvenated reality; it is the meeting point between Christian vision and social reality. However, the Kingdom of God is a transcendent reality and cannot be confined to the phenomenal world of things and objects. The Kingdom of God eludes our efforts to grasp it. It exceeds the capacities of human language to describe it. As a spiritual reality, it is to be perceived spiritually (1 Cor 2:14–15). By insisting that the Kingdom of God is spiritual, it must be clear this does not mean it is abstract or disconnected from the concrete realities of life. The Kingdom of God breaks into history and inaugurates the new world that God is bringing into being in the power of the Holy Spirit and the transfiguring Word. The Kingdom, maintains Boff, "is not a territory; it is rather an expression of being or a situation in which justice reigns, mercy is in place, love governs, life triumphs and the feeling of God flourishes in people and in the whole of creation."[18]

The Kingdom of God establishes itself in human communities that are covenanted together within the love of Christ. In such communities, the Kingdom becomes a visible reality when the gospel values of compassion, healing, hospitality, forgiveness, reconciliation and solidarity are embedded in the material realities of life and relationships. Communities that express the Kingdom of God are established on gospel principles of grace, freedom and reconciliation, rather than authority, submission and punishment. As well as transforming human communities, the Kingdom of God also signifies the liberation of the whole world from the destructive forces of sin,

17. Wright, *Simply Good News*, 69.
18. Boff, *Global Civilization*, 41.

death, injustice and cruelty and the emancipation of creation from degradation and devastation. The Kingdom of God becomes a reality when the groaning creation is healed through the revelation of the sons of God (Rom 8:19–22). From this perspective, the Kingdom is "the liberation from everything that breaks the covenant of co-living and solidarity between beings and also liberation from the gap that distances God."[19]

The Kingdom of God is both a vision and a reality; it is a threshold, a point of conceptual connection between what is and what could be. To this extent, the Kingdom of God is a utopian ideal. Philosophers from Plato to Marx have understood that while human beings seem able to live without God, they cannot live without striving for utopia. Just as space is inconceivable without motion, so religion is inconceivable without utopia. This is because the human being, as a religious being (*homo religiosus*), is continually projecting transcendent aspirations onto the world.[20] This does not mean, of course, that the Kingdom is an imaginative fiction or that it does not exist. The Kingdom of God is an eschatological and spiritual reality. The Kingdom of God posits an eschatological reality that is at once beyond human comprehension and yet an integral part of our humanity. The Kingdom of God is a meeting point of time and eternity, of grace and law, of spirit and matter, of freedom and authority, of power and weakness, of transcendence and immanence. The Kingdom of God signifies the potential of divine-human creativity to transfigure the world in the power of the resurrection. The Kingdom denotes the healing of creation and the vision of a salvation that encompasses the whole cosmos.

The Imagination of God

The Kingdom of God is not only the place where the *will of God* is done; it is also the place where the *imagination of God* is expressed in its immense fecundity. The imagination of God is expressed superlatively in the creation of the world in its immeasurable diversity and in the effulgence of the cosmos.[21] A proper emphasis on the imagination of God enables theologians to understand the universe as constituting an "immense, living and open-ended network of spontaneous interactions."[22] God acts in freedom,

19. Ibid.

20. The notion of the human being as *homo religiosus* can be traced back at least as far as Thomas Aquinas.

21. Ford, *Spiritual Masters for All Seasons*, 145–46.

22. Keller, *On the Mystery*, 23.

creativity and love in order to achieve His purposes for the flourishing of His good creation.

The imagination of God encompasses infinite possibilities, which means that "the future is fully and radically open."[23] God interacts with His world on the basis not of top-down authoritarian sovereignty, but through His creative, compassionate synergy with creation. Bulgakov remarks that from the perspective of the "kenotic Christ" (i.e., the God who empties Himself of power for the sake of love—cf. Phil 2:6–8), it can be argued that God's "relation to the world is now based not on omnipotence but on providential interaction."[24] God incarnates Himself not as a sovereign monarch, but as suffering love. God, maintains Berdyaev, "was never incarnate as worldly power, but only as crucified truth . . . God's power is spiritual and in no way resembles the manifestation of power in this world."[25]

God interacts with His world on the basis of creative freedom rather than unilateral sovereignty.[26] Human beings are therefore co-workers with God, working together creatively towards the fulfilment of God's purposes, which will culminate in the comprehensive realization of God's Kingdom on earth. The culmination of this creative process will be "communion with God, in which the righteous will be finally transfigured by light in communion with the Holy Trinity. It is this communion with God, in which the righteous will be finally transfigured by light and will themselves become as resplendent as the sun, which constitutes the beatitude of the age to come—the deified state of creatures, where God will be all in all."[27] The only certainty on the way to this eschatological communion is the final victory of the Lamb of God and the ultimate triumph of the powers of light over darkness, love over hate, and the kingdom of God over the rule of Satan. The manner and means of this victory remain a mystery. Paul Fiddes remarks that, "while the end is certain, God can always do new things; God fulfils promises in unexpected ways, and we can hear the divine voice of promise in many ways. While the end is certain, it is also open because of the freedom of God, and because of the freedom God gives to human beings to contribute to the project of creation."[28] The fulfilment of God's good

23. Cobb and Griffin, *Process Theology*, 113.

24. Bulgakov, *Lamb of God*, 184–85.

25. Berdyaev, quoted in Lowrie, *Christian Existentialism*, 276.

26. This thesis is explored in detail in Fiddes, *Creative Suffering of God*.

27. Lossky, *Vision of God*, 133.

28. Fiddes, *Promised End*, 38–39.

intentions remains in the hands of His human protagonists who must work creatively towards the realization of His purposes.[29]

The imagination of God is also manifested in the parables that Jesus told to illustrate the Kingdom. The Kingdom of God, said Jesus, is like unto a mustard seed, leaven in the bread, treasure hidden in a field, and various other images besides. Jesus used these vivid images to illustrate the character of God and the reality of life in God's Kingdom to which His hearers should aspire. Jesus did not convey His message in terms of moral postulates. He did not communicate the truth about God in theological propositions about sin and salvation. He did not give people a catechism or a list of propositions to which they needed to give their assent in order to obtain eternal life. Rather, He told stories or parables that illuminated a specific truth about God's Kingdom. Neither did Jesus give His hearers information about how they could meet the "minimum entrance requirements" for going to heaven when they died.[30] Instead, He used a series of creative images from His Kingdom-oriented, Spirit-inspired imagination in order to shatter conventional wisdom. These images or parables surprised, unsettled and sometimes even outraged His hearers.

The Kingdom of God is the Kingdom of Truth that is set apart from the alluring falsehoods of the contemporary world. The Kingdom of God welcomes and embraces all people, regardless of social or economic circumstances or ethnicity; the Kingdom of this world excludes and divides people and threatens them with fines and deportation, if they do not produce the right documents. The Kingdom of God blesses the meek and the poor in spirit, the widows and the orphans and the "least of these," whereas the Kingdom of the world rewards the rich and powerful, the arms manufacturer, the banker, and the stock market speculator. The gospel message is therefore an invitation to participate in the dawning reality of God's Kingdom—a new community of love in which the humble are exalted, the poor are dignified and the values of solidarity, hospitality and justice pervade all relationships. "When we open the writings of the New Testament," write Willard and Simpson, "we discover that we are called to live in the awareness of another world, to join in 'the kingdom of the heavens' and to participate in the divine nature."[31]

The natural overflow of personal transformation into Christlikeness is the extension of the Kingdom of God so that social structures are

29. Searle, J., "Ideology, Convictions and Eschatology," *Baptistic Theologies* 3, 99–115.

30. Willard, *Living in Christ's Presence*, 54.

31. Willard and Simpson, *Revolution of Character*, 9.

transformed to the extent that justice will "roll down like waters, and righ-teousness like an ever-flowing stream" (Amos 5:24).[32] Living in the reality of God's Kingdom means to exhibit a profound awareness of the world as a place pulsating with the mysterious presence of God. The Scriptures set out a vision of the world as a grand theatre in which God is living and active in redeeming the world through subtle—but transformative—initiatives of divine compassion. This is the "divine conspiracy" to which Dallas Wil-lard—both in his life and in his writings—testified so eloquently.

Addressing the Kingdom Deficit in Christendom Theology

Christoph Blumhardt once asked the following pertinent question: "Why is it so hard for people to imagine anyone coming to God without walking through church doors?"[33] I would hazard a guess that one of the reasons for this difficulty is the scant attention that evangelical theology has paid to the Kingdom of God. Nothing less than a paradigm shift in the evangelical consciousness is required to recast theology as the servant not of the church, but of the coming Kingdom of God. Leonardo Boff asserts that, "Jesus did not preach the church but the reign of God. His intention was directed at humankind and was not restricted to a portion of it, to Judaism or to the church. He did not have in mind a new religion but a new man, a new woman, a new heaven, and a new earth."[34] Theology, accordingly, should be concerned primarily with the transformation of life within the Kingdom of God, rather than with the religious instruction of particular people for church ministry.

The Kingdom of God, rather than the church, must become the point of departure for theology in post-Christendom. Unfortunately, the course of theology during the Christendom era has been set by a powerful eccle-siocentric impulse. Consequently, the Kingdom of God has tended to be subsumed into the church.[35] Ever since Augustine of Hippo, (354–430), there has been a tendency to regard the Church and the Kingdom of God as practically synonymous.[36] According to Augustine's anti-prophetic theolo-gy, the thousand years' reign of Christ, as prophesied in the book of Revela-tion (20:1–6), had already been fulfilled in the establishment of the Catholic Church. "In the course of history," explains Berdyaev, "the Church tried to

32. Searle and Searle, "Monastic Practices and *Missio Dei.*"

33. Blumhardt, *Everyone Belongs to God*, 31.

34. Boff, *Christianity in a Nutshell*, 50.

35. Grenz and Franke, *Beyond Foundationalism*, 243.

36. Augustine, *City of God* 20.9, 725–27.

render harmless the moral change wrought by the Gospel."[37] One way the Church attenuated the radical demands of the gospel of the Kingdom was by presenting Christianity as a symbolic or liturgical religion, rather than as a movement for the realization of the Kingdom of God as a visible reality within the world.

Therefore, part of the immediate task of post-Christendom theology is to deconstruct the ecclesiocentric edifice of theology and return the Kingdom of God to its rightful place of prominence. In post-Christendom any theology that does not serve the realization of the Kingdom of God as a visible and concrete reality in the world is no longer good for anything, except to be thrown out and trampled underfoot. To paraphrase the Scottish philosopher David Hume (1711–1776): When we go through our theological libraries, persuaded of the principle that theology must serve the Kingdom of God, what havoc must we make. If we take in our hand any volume, let us ask: Does it contain dogmatic claims that attempt to assign a sacred or sacramental character to church institutions? Yes. Does it focus narrowly on issues of authorship, context and reception of ancient texts? Yes. Does it set forth a vision of life in the Kingdom of God that can be understood and applied by ordinary thoughtful people? No. Does it help readers to expand their horizons of compassion and imagination in the power of the Holy Spirit? No. Does it lead readers into new insights about how to enact and embody the gospel imperative to love God and neighbor? No. Commit it then to the flames: for it can contain nothing but dogmatic platitudes and distortions.[38]

Perhaps it is not necessary to consign such a book to flames, but it should be removed from the theology section and placed in whatever section would be relevant—Philology, Religious Studies, History, Sociology, etc. Theology is concerned with the Kingdom of God, which does not reveal its inner workings or even outward manifestations to scientific or empirical methodologies. Part of the difficulty with taking the Kingdom of God as the starting point of all theological endeavor is the teaching of Scripture concerning the subtlety and imperceptibility of the Kingdom as a visible reality in the midst of life. Jesus explained that the "Kingdom cometh not with

---

37. Berdyaev, Destiny of Man, 144.

38. Hume, Enquiry concerning Human Understanding, 120. The original quotation from Hume reads as follows: "When we run over libraries, persuaded of these principles, what havoc must we make? If we take in our hand any volume of divinity or school metaphysics, for instance, let us ask, Does it contain any abstract reasoning concerning quantity or number? No. Does it contain any experimental reasoning concerning matter of fact and existence? No. Commit it then to the flames, for it can contain nothing but sophistry and illusion."

observation" (Luke 17:20), but is realized only through spiritual conversion or "metanoia" (μετάνοια—Matt 3:2; 4:17), which has been mistranslated as "repent" in most English Bible translations.[39] The Kingdom of God becomes a tangible reality only through spiritual enlightenment and a lived experience of rebirth in the Holy Spirit.

From the perspective of a pragmatic academic culture in the grip of scientific materialism and social utilitarianism, the spiritual reality of the Kingdom of God may thus seem eccentric or even ridiculous; it might appear as the prophecy of the "Superman" to the "Last Men" in Nietzsche's *Thus Spake Zarathustra*; that is, as "a laughing-stock, a thing of shame." Therefore, seeking to avoid ridicule and to make their theological claims seem relevant and meaningful, Christendom theology tended to appeal to the lowest common denominator of rational criteria in such a way that left no room for the Kingdom of God.

Prophetic voices within Christian theology have sought to redress the conspicuous Kingdom deficit that has shackled the potential for theology to make a decisive and transformative contribution towards the renewal of faith in the world today. Dorothee Sölle insisted that, "The concept of the kingdom of God stands at the center of the original proclamation of Jesus. This kingdom . . . is understood as God's nearness to men and women which is experienced in justice, peace, and above all joy."[40] Harvey Cox explains that, "the phrase 'Kingdom of God' is one of the most misused and misunderstood in the entire Bible. It is too often thought of as where you may go after you die, or something that begins after this world's history is over, or something that is entirely inward. However, the Hebrew prophets, Jesus himself, and the last pages of Revelation . . . all teach that the Kingdom of God is something that happens in and to *this* world."[41]

It is widely acknowledged by biblical scholars that the announcement of the Kingdom of God "formed the substance of Jesus's ministry on earth" and that "all of his teaching in parables, his miracles of healing, his ethical instruction to the disciples, revolves around this central idea of the 'kingdom of God,' much as in the physical world the planets in our solar system revolve around the sun."[42] Whereas the Kingdom has tended to be misrepresented and misunderstood, it has more often been neglected, downplayed or even ignored outright. The prominent New Testament scholar, I. Howard Marshall (1934–2015) noted that, "during the past sixteen years I can recol-

---

39. Boda and Smith, *Repentance in Christian Theology*, 80.

40. Sölle, *Thinking about God*, 138.

41. Cox, *Future of Faith*, 44.

42. Kreitzer, *Gospel According to John*, 49.

lect only two occasions on which I have heard sermons specifically devoted to the theme of the Kingdom of God . . . I find this silence rather surprising because it is universally agreed by New Testament scholars that the central theme of the teaching of Jesus was the Kingdom of God."[43] As far back as 1974, the evangelist Michael Green challenged delegates at the Lausanne Conference with a provocative question: "How much have you heard here about the Kingdom of God?" In answer, he said, "Not much. It is not our language. But it was Jesus' prime concern."[44]

In contrast to the relative absence of the Kingdom of God, the church has occupied a very prominent place in the landscape of evangelical Christendom theology. This ecclesiocentric theology lies behind various initiatives to promote "church growth." In the UK, these include "Decade of Evangelism" and "Alpha," as well as models that originated in North America, but have become popular in parts of the UK, such as "Purpose Driven Church" and "Seeker-Sensitive Church"; "House Church"; "Café Church"; "Emerging Church"; and even "Pub Church."

These initiatives had some value in so far as they aimed, in theory, to mobilize the gifts of their members and to create friendly and hospitable environments where newcomers felt welcomed. Their basic shortcoming was their preoccupation with the church. They took the church, rather than the Kingdom of God, as their focus, and relied on "attracting new members to an essentially passive, audience-oriented model of church."[45] The evangelistic impulses behind these initiatives were laden with Christendom assumptions about the purposes of evangelism. The goal of mission was thought to consist in persuading one's family members, friends and strangers on the street to attend a church service or to show up at an evangelistic rally in the hope that they would hear the gospel and go through the standard conversion process—from conviction, to repentance, to confession, to regeneration, to sanctification. Christian faith was presented as "just another consumer choice, a private matter for consenting adults, but not something that [could] possibly represent public truth."[46]

Therefore, although many of these initiatives have been quite energetic and have helped people to connect with church activities, they have served more as church growth or church renewal strategies, rather than dynamic movements that represent the fullness and comprehensive world-orientation of God's Kingdom. Despite all the quixotic attempts to revive

43. Marshall, quoted in Willard, *Divine Conspiracy*, 69.

44. Green, quoted in ibid., 69.

45. Greene and Robinson, *Metavista*, 178.

46. Ibid.

the dying churches of western Christendom and the commendable new initiatives connected with "missional church," it remains the case, regrettably, as Greene and Robinson remark, that, "a concern for the missional church once again shifted the focus away from culture and towards ecclesiology."[47] Post-Christendom theology should therefore serve the *missio Dei* by developing a robust biblical-theological rationale for missional *cultures*, rather than missional *churches*.

In simple terms, whereas Christendom theology said, "Church, Church, Church!"; post-Christendom theology now says, "Kingdom, Kingdom, Kingdom!" The Kingdom-oriented missiology of post-Christendom theology must recognize that the church is the means rather than the end of mission. "One of the most important things Christians need to know about the church is that *the church* is not of ultimate importance," claim the leading missiologists, Stephen Bevans and Roger Schroeder. The point of the church, they insist, is "to point beyond itself, to be a community that preaches, serves and witnesses to the reign of God."[48] In terms of *missio Dei*, it is essential that mission should have a theocentric, rather than an ecclesiocentric, focus and point of departure.[49] Put simply, mission serves *not* the church, but the Kingdom of God.

Responding Creatively to the Challenge of Post-Christendom

The reorientation of theology towards the Kingdom of God coincides propitiously with spiritual shifts that are occurring in contemporary culture. In the same way that theology is no longer the Queen of the Sciences, neither is the Christian religion the dominant or normative force in the world. For the western church, post-Christendom is the great new fact of our times. The worst possible responses to post-Christendom are denial and triumphalism. The triumphalist mentality must be jettisoned if Christians are to navigate the new course in the world with integrity and sensitivity to the leading of the Holy Spirit.

Unfortunately, instead of looking to the future with realistic hope, many churches, still under the spell of Christendom, continue to sing hymns that make baseless declarations about imminent revival. In post-Christendom, the experience of the western church seems to be more like

47. Ibid., 179.

48. Bevans and Schroeder, *Constants in Context*, 7.

49. Bosch, *Transforming Mission*; Kirk, *What is Mission?*; Schenk, *Changing Frontiers*.

exile. The spiritual landscape resembles more a desert than a fertile pasture, although even within the desert there are oases of hope to be found. In his book, *Church After Christendom*, Stuart Murray makes a clear statement concerning the inexorable emergence of post-Christendom:

> The end of Christendom and transition into post-Christendom in Western culture is a paradigm shift. Many Christians are re-sisting this shift in employing familiar tactics of defending the old paradigm, denying its demise, dithering on the cusp of a new era or delaying their commitment to this new reality. But Christendom is fading. We may grieve or celebrate its passing, but we cannot revive, restore or recover it. Post-Christendom is coming.[50]

Making a similar point from an even more radical perspective, John Douglas Hall asks the following question:

> Why are we still so thoroughly wedded to Christendom that we refuse to entertain consciously this great transition through which we are passing, and therefore fail to engage in the kind of radical reassessment and reforming of our calling, our mission, our structures and ministries that would enable us, perhaps, to pass through this paradigm shift with greater understanding and a more faithful and imaginative kind of obedience?[51]

One way to answer to Hall's provocative question would be to attribute the church's inertia to the lack of a coordinated, Kingdom-oriented strategic vision for theological formation. This education deficit may explain why so many church leaders today lack even a basic awareness of the reality of post-Christendom or a workable vision of how to respond to the changing times with prophetic insight and faithfulness to the church's calling. The approach of post-Christendom is marked by a visible diminishing of the old ecclesiastical structures and the invisible formation of a new spiritual impulse in the life of the church. The demise of institutional religion coincides with the resurgence of spirituality within post-secular society.

The future of Christianity in post-Christendom depends on whether it can meet the challenges of the new times. The painful travails of post-Christendom and the arduous disestablishment of Christianity from an institution to a movement are like birth pangs that presage the beginning of a new era of hope and renewal. The genesis of a new Christian movement, unleashed from its institutional Christian trappings, is underway. The

50. Murray, *Church After Christendom*, 7.
51. Hall, *End of Christendom*, 20.

Kingdom of God is poised to break into world history and yield its mighty harvest. The problem is that the harvest is plentiful, but the laborers are few (Luke 10:2). So much has been sowed, yet the yield has been so miniscule.

Education, in terms of the theological formation of the people of God into Christlikeness, will play a key strategic role in helping the worldwide Christian community produce more faithful and effective laborers for God's in-breaking Kingdom. For this hope to become a reality, education in post-Christendom must be reoriented away from church ministry and towards solidarity with the world on behalf of the Kingdom of God. These challenges are a summons to theologians in post-Christendom to pioneer a new trail out of the morass of sacramentalism and religiosity and envision a new theology of solidarity that can serve the renewal of the church and the transformation of culture.

As western society transitions into post-Christendom, the inadequacies of traditional churches are becoming increasingly apparent. The institutional church is fast approaching a dead end from which there will be no turning back. The advent of post-Christendom is a cause for careful reflection, which should include a strong note of repentance and lament. For instance, the church of Christendom must repent of the ways in which it has so often allowed Christianity to be shackled by demonic religious structures of power and domination, which has inhibited the freedom of the Spirit, suppressed the truth of the gospel and impeded the coming of the Kingdom of God in the world. Theology must be reenvisioned in terms that are both more conducive to the changing culture and more consistent with the freedom, compassion and creativity of the gospel.

6

Freedom, Compassion, and Creativity

New Points of Departure for Theology in Post-Christendom

Theology in post-Christendom finds itself at a crossroads. In order to set a course along the path of renewal and new life, theology needs bold and prophetic theologians who can unshackle theological endeavor from the dead weight of dogma and sacramentalism. This chapter is an attempt to offer an outline presentation of a theology that is attuned to the dynamic movement of the Holy Spirit in the present post-Christian world. The fundamental realities of freedom, compassion, and creativity are proposed as central elements of a post-Christendom theology. This triad offers an appropriately Trinitarian focus for theology, since each spiritual reality exemplifies the basic principles of Father (freedom), Son (compassion), and Holy Spirit (creativity), and expresses the unity in diversity of the Sacred Trinity.

In the previous chapter it was argued that theology after Christendom has a unique opportunity to reenvision Christian faith in ways that are faithful to the biblical witness, to the vision of God's coming Kingdom. It was also suggested that there needs to be a general acknowledgement of what perceptive observers already see all too clearly: namely, that the Christendom churches, on the whole, are no longer serviceable to God's great purposes in the world. As part of the repentance process, a new Kingdom-oriented Christianity can take shape. Rather than programs and institutional commitments, the Christianity that will prevail in post-Christendom will be a Christianity that puts freedom, compassion and creativity at the heart of its life and witness, as well as its doctrine.

What will be important for Christianity in post-Christendom will not be participation in religious events and or attendance at church services, but living according to the spiritual realities of "justice, mercy, and faithfulness"

(Matt 23:23) and learning to "act justly, love mercy, and to walk humbly with God" (Mic 6:8). God is to be found not only within the sphere that our society designates as "sacred"; He is also to be pursued and discovered in the world. The whole world is bathed in the reality of God's presence and this presence becomes a visible reality when refugees are offered shelter, when sick people are cared for and healed, or whenever people turn away from the darkness of sin and towards the light of Christ. It follows that God is to be found not necessarily in church sacraments or religious language, but He manifests His presence in the spiritual realities of love, liberty, solidarity and justice. The God who reveals Himself in Christ cannot be understood outside of these spiritual realities. If we do not include these realities in our discourse about God, warns Boff, "then we are speaking of some idol and not of the living God."[1]

The Theology of Freedom

"Now the Lord is the Spirit, and where the Spirit of the Lord is, there is freedom" (2 Cor 3:17). Thus wrote the Apostle Paul to the Corinthian church, expressing a key truth that offers us a useful departure point for envisaging the aim and scope of theology in the midst of the current post-Christendom shift. Long before the institutional sclerosis of Christendom has set in, Christianity made its explosive appearance on the earth as a religion of radical emancipation. Jesus Christ began His public ministry by preaching a revolutionary message of freedom: "The Spirit of the Lord is upon me, because he hath . . . sent me . . . to preach deliverance to the captives" (Luke 4:18). The New Testament is full of exhortations to liberty and affirmations of freedom.[2] In order to recapture the dynamism of pre-Constantinian Christianity, theology should rediscover the meaning of freedom in terms of a gospel imperative.

Freedom, by definition, does not possess any coercive power. This notion of freedom and the nature of God is compatible with a theological understanding of God's activity in the world, for, as Berdyaev argues, "God is spirit, and he acts within the order of freedom and not of objective necessity. His activity cannot be understood in naturalistic terms. He is present not in external things and happenings, to which we attach divine names and in which we perceive a divine purpose, not in the power or powers of this

---

1. Boff, *Church*, 24.

2. For example, see Matt 17:26; John 8:31–36; John 15:15; Jas 1:25; 1 Cor 6:20 and 7:23; 2 Cor 3:17; Gal 4:7 and 5:13.

world, but in truth, beauty, love, freedom, and creativity."[3] Authority and necessity belong to the world in its fallenness and alienation from its spiritual source.[4] Berdyaev is correct to maintain that "Christianity presupposes the spirit of freedom and the freedom of the spirit."[5]

Freedom constitutes the essence of spiritual life. The freedom that inheres in the will of God encompasses the irregularities and vicissitudes of human nature and recognizes that the world contains infinite possibilities, which must be realized through God's providential will. Within the freedom of the spirit, God's summons to human beings is to participate with Him in His grand project of redemption. Human beings are invested by God with the dignity of being able to respond in freedom to this gracious invitation to become co-workers with God in the healing and restoration of the cosmos.

God expects from His creatures not formal adherence to a legal code, but the free and creative response to His self-sacrificing love. The French poet and essayist, Léon Bloy (1846–1917), expressed this idea provocatively: "God suffers and spills His blood when He does not meet the reciprocal love of human beings, when human freedom does not work alongside God in His creative work and when human beings do not place their creative powers at His disposal."[6] Berdyaev thus maintains that, "God expects from every human being a free response to his call, a reciprocal love, and creative collaboration in defeating the darkness of non-being. The human being should demonstrate the great activity of spirit in all the intensity of its freedom, in order to accomplish that which God expects of him [or her]."[7]

This kind of freedom consists in submitting the will to the necessity that inheres in the will of God and realizing this purpose through radical acts of freedom that conform to the character of Christ. Theology thus aspires towards "the glorious liberty of the children of God" (Rom 8:21); it aims to elevate human beings to a new level of consciousness of freedom. This summons to freedom is sometimes better conveyed not in the prose style of the theologian-bureaucrat, but in the vivid language of the poet.

Truth is the basic precondition of freedom and "God has laid upon man the duty of being free, of safeguarding freedom of spirit, no matter how difficult that may be, or how much sacrifice and suffering it may require."[8] The problem that theology in post-Christendom must address is the in-

3. Berdyaev, *Dream and Reality*, 179.

4. Seaver, *Nicolas Berdyaev*, 34.

5. Berdyaev, *Filosofia Svobodnogo Dukha*, 124.

6. Bloy, quoted in Berdyaev, *Filosophia Svobodnogo Dukha*, 210.

7. Berdyaev, *Filosophia Svobodnogo Dukha*, 209.

8. Berdyaev, *Fate of Man in the Modern World*, 44.

ability and unwillingness of people to embrace authenticity and freedom. Freedom certainly comes at a cost. Freedom of choice can lead people into destruction. "Freedom," remarks Boff, "endows the human being with the potential to decide whether to cultivate the good angels or the interior demons."[9]

The Russian novelist and philosopher, Fyodor Mikhailovich Dostoevsky (1821–1881), expressed this paradox with the full force of his lively poetic genius in the "Parable of the Grand Inquisitor," which appeared in his greatest novel, *The Brothers Karamazov* (1880). Dostoevsky's Grand Inquisitor depicts the dilemma of human beings who are paralyzed by the existential tension arising from the tragi-comic situation of being, on the one hand created for freedom, but, on the other, being too feeble and afraid to embrace the risk responsibility and vulnerability that freedom brings. Although human beings may be born for freedom as a bird is born for flight and the fish for swimming,[10] most human beings are crushed by self-imposed burdens that prevent them from expressing their inherent freedom.

Seemingly prefiguring the rise of totalitarian regimes in the twentieth century, Dostoevsky recognized that freedom is identified by most human beings not as a blessing, but as a curse, or—as Berdyaev put it—a "fatal gift" that condemns them to perdition. With great truth Berdyaev remarked that "freedom is a burden rather than a right, a source of tragedy and untold pain."[11] The Grand Inquisitor thus refers to the "great anxiety and terrible agony" that people must endure when they are called upon to make an authentically free decision for themselves.[12] Addressing Christ (who has returned to Seville at the height of the Spanish Inquisition), the Inquisitor remarks, "I tell thee that man is tormented by no greater anxiety than to find someone quickly to whom he can hand over that gift of freedom with which the ill-fated creature is born."[13] The Grand Inquisitor, representing the authoritarian perspective of institutional Christianity, accuses Christ of entrusting weak human beings with the burden of freedom, which is too much for them to bear. He explains to the silent Christ that the Church has taken upon itself the duty to deprive the people of their freedom for the sake

---

9. Boff, *Essential Care*, 109.

10. This notion is well established in philosophy, finding notable expression in the famous opening sentence of chapter one of Rousseau's *Du Contrat Social*: "Man is born free, yet everywhere he is in chains."

11. Berdyaev, *Dream and Reality*, 177.

12. Dostoevsky, quoted in Wake, *Tragedy in Hegel's Early Theological Writings*, 17.

13. Dostoevsky, *Brothers Karamazov*, 230.

of securing their happiness and comfort. The old Inquisitor thus rebukes Christ, asking reproachfully, "why . . . art thou come to hinder us?"[14]

The Grand Inquisitor offers a hyperbolic, but nonetheless illustrative, depiction of how the Church under Christendom operated—often with the best of intentions—to crush human freedom. Recognizing the torment of genuine freedom, the Christendom church entered into an unofficial contract with its members that they would, as Dostoevsky put it, "become free when they renounce freedom." The Inquisitor adds that the Church shall permit the mass of people "an unexciting modest happiness, suitable to the feeble creatures that they are . . . Certainly we shall make them work, but in their spare time we shall organize their life like a children's game, with children's songs and cantatas and innocent dances. We shall allow them even sin, knowing that they are so weak and helpless."[15]

Despite the dangers and uncertainty implied by freedom, Paul Tillich insists that, "There should be no question of what Christian theology has to do in this situation. It should decide for truth against safety, even if the safety is consecrated and supported by the churches."[16] One of the tasks of theology in post-Christendom will be to restate the wildness, danger, freedom and ineffability of God. I remember hearing a talk by the gifted Irish poet and philosopher, John O'Donohue (1956–2008), who said that theologians need to "make God dangerous again." It is a characteristically pagan trait to want to tame one's deities. Christendom tended to make God as palatable as possible by containing Him within predictable systems of dogmatic theology or theories of atonement that set out in a linear way God's redemptive relationship with His creatures.

This tendency to delineate God's plan of salvation in terms of clear, unambiguous arrangements often works in tandem with dubious efforts to present an image of Jesus that is totally opposed to the image of Jesus that emerges from the Gospels. Too often churches have presented a sanitized, domesticated Jesus to would-be consumers of Christianity. This fabricated Jesus never says anything to offend anyone; neither does he ever get angry, tired, upset or irritated. This tame Jesus promises people a safe and comfortable life if they will only affirm the right beliefs about Him. There is nothing wild, unpredictable or dangerous about this "gentle Jesus, meek and mild" of popular theology.

In contrast to this soft, fake Jesus of popular Christianity, the real Savior who confronts us in the Gospels is a Jesus whose anger burns against

14. Ibid., 225–35.

15. Dostoevsky, *Brothers Karamazov*, 235.

16. Tillich, *Courage to Be*, 130–31.

religious systems that enslave and exploit people. As the one who had come to preach deliverance to the captives, Jesus perceived God's call to confront the spiritual powers of darkness. In the eloquent description of Hans Küng, the Jesus of the Gospels was someone who

> took everyone as they were in their weakness and fragility, and treated them with utter seriousness as the people they were, the creatures whom God wanted to be like this . . . He never interrogated anyone in inquisitorial fashion about their beliefs . . . but was able to look into their hearts. He avoided all exaggerated piety, didn't build up any position of sacral power, but went before them in the service of humanity.[17]

Jesus's compassion was not expressed in sentimental platitudes. Jesus understood that to be compassionate in a context of injustice and exploitation involved a costly participation in spiritual warfare against the *archai kai exousiai* (power and principalities) that enslave and denigrate people.[18] Prophets today need to rediscover the essential truth that the real Jesus that we encounter in the Gospels is not a safe, domesticated deity, but a spirit-empowered divine/human being who expressed the wildness and danger of God.

The Theology of Compassion

One way of thinking about theology is to envision it in terms of a phenomenology of compassion. The term, phenomenology, refers to the scientific or philosophical method that examines the way that experiences reveal themselves to human consciousness which then gives shape and form to that consciousness. In this way, we can define a theologian as someone who is learning to interpret and assimilate his experience from the perspective of compassion. Every day a human being accumulates an infinite number of experiences, which can generate responses that cover the whole spectrum of human emotion from pain, joy, bewilderment and certainty. In order to perceive these emotions from the perspective of compassion, the theologian must aspire to a kind of knowledge that is gained only through love.

Compassion from this perspective is not merely a Christian virtue, but a way of being in the world and a pre-critical orientation that structures one's experience.[19] Leonardo Boff explains,

17. Küng, *My Struggle for Freedom*, 32.
18. Searle and Cherenkov, *Future and a Hope*, 14.
19. Smith advances a similar thesis in his *Imagining the Kingdom*.

Com-passion is not a minor feeling of "pity" towards those who suffer. It is not passive but extremely active. Com-passion, as the Latin philology of the word suggests, is the capacity to share passion with the other. It is about coming out of one's own sphere and entering into the universe of the other to suffer with the other, to be happy with the other, to walk with the other and to build life in synergy with the other.[20]

A theology of compassion affirms that "mercy triumphs over judgement" (Jas 2:13) and learns to "judge not, that [it] be not judged" (Luke 6:37). Theologians must reject any collusion with authoritarian political regimes to impose Christian morality by passing legislation, such as laws that discriminate against homosexuals. Such legislation may have a thin veneer of Christianity, but is in fact a denial of Christian compassion, which can never be institutionally imposed or endorsed by ruling ideologies.

The church in post-Christendom must therefore renounce the Christendom tendency to provide a legitimating religious ideology to uphold political systems.[21] The church is responsible not only to the authorities, but also to the people as a whole. A church guided by the gospel of justice and compassion will not aim to build a separate relationship with the State or be lured by promises of patronage, and preferential treatment in return for its loyalty and collaboration. Rather than building a "state church" of officially-endorsed religion, the gospel imperative of compassion requires that theology set forth a vision of open Christianity and church without walls. This kind of Christianity facilitates the development of a generous and hospitable climate within which the gospel virtues of compassion, truth, and justice can flourish. Post-Christendom theology must be free, humble, generous, hospitable, full of grace, and ready not just to judge and criticize, but also to listen, learn, serve, and suffer for the sake of the Kingdom of God.

The trouble is that compassion is hard work. One of the most obvious conclusions to draw from the life of Jesus as described in the Gospels is that a life of compassion requires vulnerability and discipleship. Theology should equip people to love not concepts and ideas *about* God, but to love God and neighbor. "Love," maintains Berdyaev, "can only be directed upon a person, a living being and not upon the abstract good . . . Christian love is concrete and personal, while humanistic love is abstract and impersonal."[22] Post-Christendom theology must resist the tendency to reduce Christianity to humanitarian religiosity and high-minded moralizing. Humanitarian

20. Boff, *Essential Care*, 90.
21. Boff, *Church: Charism and Power*, 113.
22. Berdyaev, *Destiny of Man*, 137.

activism and cosmopolitan philosophizing are useless if they do not issue in concrete expressions of compassion. Jean Jacques Rousseau (1712–1778) justly cautioned his readers to "Distrust those cosmopolitans who, in their books, seek to find far away those duties which they disdain to fulfil around them. A philosopher loves the Tartars in order to be excused from loving his neighbour."[23] Theologians thus need to avoid the danger of lapsing into the same attitude as the doctor referred to by Father Zosima in Dostoevsky's *Brothers Karamazov*, who made this disturbingly honest confession:

> The more I love humanity in general the less I love man in particular. In my dreams, I often make plans for the service of humanity, and perhaps I might actually face crucifixion if it were suddenly necessary. Yet I am incapable of living in the same room with anyone for two days together. I know from experience. As soon as anyone is near me, his personality disturbs me and restricts my freedom. In twenty–four hours I begin to hate the best of men: one because he's too long over his dinner, another because he has a cold and keeps on blowing his nose. I become hostile to people the moment they come close to me. But it has always happened that the more I hate men individually the more I love humanity.[24]

In order to avoid this kind of discrepancy between idealistic aspiration and actual conduct, compassion must be embodied and directed towards real situations of need. The Christian imperative to love human beings in their concrete situations of real life is enjoined by Christ in the Gospels. When Jesus is asked which is the greatest commandment in the Law, His reply is clear and unambiguous: "Love the Lord your God with all your heart and with all your soul and with all your mind." This is the first and greatest commandment. And the second is like it: "Love your neighbor as yourself." All the Law and the Prophets hang on these two commandments" (Matt 22:36–40). This imperative is reinforced by the Beloved Apostle in his epistle: "Whoever claims to love God yet hates a brother or sister is a liar. For whoever does not love their brother and sister, whom they have seen, cannot love God, whom they have not seen (1 John 4:20)."

Love, self–sacrificing love and compassion (ἀγάπη—*agape*) is the ultimate revelation of God. In the incarnation and crucifixion God Himself participates in the existential hell of human suffering in a mind-blowing,

---

23. Rousseau, quoted in O'Hagan, *Rousseau*, 110.

24. Dostoevsky, *Brothers Karamazov*, 48–9. This saying reminds one of the humorous saying of the Peanuts character, Linus van Pelt: "I love mankind; it's people I can't stand."

logic-defying demonstration of His solidarity with humanity in pain. For the "crime" of loving people, the Son of God is betrayed, whipped, spat upon, abused, mocked, tortured, and humiliated. Eventually, He suffers an obscene and excruciating death on a cross. Such a superlative and unrepeatable demonstration of divine solidarity reveals the true character of God. By dying on the cross, Jesus is demonstrating the truth of who God really is: He is the God whose most basic essence is self-giving love and this love is expressed in eternal solidarity with His creatures. God suffers *with* His creatures. As Moltmann maintains, "God and suffering are no longer contradictions, as in theism and atheism, for God's being is in suffering and the suffering is in God's being itself."[25] Berdyaev expressed a great truth when he asserted that, "To deny tragedy in the Divine life is only possible at the cost of denying Christ, His cross and crucifixion . . . God shares His creatures' destiny. He sacrifices Himself for the world and for man whom He loves and yearns for."[26]

A compassion-based spirituality is particularly urgent for today's world. We live in a society that is suffering from a crisis of compassion. The politics of austerity, the promotion of wealth accumulation at the expense of the poor in society, and the rise of xenophobic populist politicians—on both the extreme right and the extreme left—are just some of the surface manifestations of a spiritual malaise at the heart of contemporary society. In situations of injustice, compassion is often obliged to express itself in protest and non-violent forms of resistance and civil disobedience. A theology that is rooted in a gospel vision of compassion, can raise its prophetic voice against social trends that are not consistent with the values of the Kingdom of God. The world still awaits the emergence of Christianity not as a religion of private salvation, but as a gospel movement of universal, creative compassion. My hope for post-Christendom theology is that it can help to envision Christianity in precisely these terms.

The Theology of Creativity

Post-Christendom theology needs a new creative impetus. Theology is a passionate pursuit of truth that engages the intellect in tandem with the imagination. James K. A. Smith rightly laments the tendency during the Christendom era to pursue "flawed models of discipleship and Christian formation that have focused on convincing the intellect rather than recruiting

25. Moltmann, *Crucified God*, 227.
26. Berdyaev, *Destiny of Man*, 38.

the imagination."[27] Theology needs to provide a hospitable environment for the poets and mystics, as well as for the scholars and systematic thinkers. Christendom theology tended to be dominated by what Brian McLaren calls "theologian-accountants, theologian-technicians, theologian-scientists," rather than "theologian-poets."[28]

No words can adequately express "the unspeakable and ineffable apophatic mystery of God's life."[29] Although no human language can encompass the plenitude of the divine reality, scientific and purely rational discourse falls lamentably short. The empirical sciences, despite their great utility in elucidating the relation between causes and effects, do not have a monopoly on knowledge and truth. As Dallas Willard rightly maintains, "most, if not all, of the things that matter most to human beings are not subjects of anything like scientific methodology."[30] Theology should not attempt to establish itself on empirical foundations that adhere to positivistic criteria of verification by corresponding to a proper understanding of observable facts. Attempts to establish theology on such a footing have been tried and have proven to be a road to nowhere.[31]

Theology, in common with human beings themselves, aspires to transcendence and eternity and, as such, cannot be confined to the sphere of observable phenomenon and empirical facts. Theology aspires to elucidate what von Balthasar calls the "infinite, silent firmament of being which arches above all that is existent."[32] Reality is not exhausted by data and information derived from the five human senses. Truth is not to be confused with factuality.[33] There is more to truth than the space-time world of observable phenomena that present themselves to the human mind as facts. Truth encompasses myths, symbols, and the imagination, as well as facts, logic, and reason. Taking creativity as its point of departure, theology posits that a human being is not simply a rational animal motivated by elemental

27. Smith, *Imagining the Kingdom*, 39.

28. McLaren, *Generous Orthodoxy*, 161.

29. Berdyaev, *Dream and Reality*, 99.

30. Willard, "The Bible, the University," 27.

31. For an account of the failure of scientism in this regard, see chapter 1 of Stratton, *Coherence, Consonance, and Conversation*. For an example of an attempt to establish theological method in line with the principles of logical positivism, see Mackintosh, *Theology as an Empirical Science*. In this work, Mackintosh argues that, "if theology is to become really scientific, it must be by becoming fundamentally empirical" (11).

32. Balthasar, *Man in History*, 230.

33. According to Quine, both truth and factuality are dependent upon theory. For a discussion of Quine's understanding of the difference and interrelation between truth and factuality see Orenstein, *W. V. O. Quine*, 119–20.

instincts, but also a visionary being who inhabits a world of metaphor and symbol, which expresses the human yearning for transcendence. Theologians therefore recognize that the study of human nature must go beyond existing empirical facts and take seriously the role of dreams, visions and the imagination as constitutive of the human condition.[34] As John Macquarrie aptly expresses it, "the study of human nature is a study of possibility as much as of actuality."[35]

Since it is concerned with potentiality just as much as actuality, theology is a creative and transformative enterprise. The leading impulse for theological reflection in the power of the Holy Spirit is the creative activity of the divine *Logos*. As the poet, artist, and mystic, William Blake, put it: "I know of no other Christianity and of no other Gospel than the liberty of both body and mind to exercise the Divine Art of Imagination."[36] For Blake and other Christians in the mystic tradition, the imagination is the realm of supreme reality in which God manifests Himself to human consciousness. As a creative pursuit that strives towards transcendence and overflowing the boundaries of the visible world of material reality and social facts, theology thrives on the kind of deep intuitive insight that arises from the creative forces generated by a free imagination. Berdyaev claimed that, "Philosophical knowledge cannot have its source in books or scholastic theory. The source of philosophy is neither Aristotle nor Kant, but the intuition of being. The only philosopher is the one who has an intuition of being and whose philosophy is drawn from a living source."[37]

Taking creativity as its departure point, theology can recognize the importance of narrative to a proper understanding of the Scriptures and the character of God to whom the Bible testifies. The Parables of Jesus testify to the immense plenitude of the divine imagination. Jesus did not present His disciples with a list of propositional statements about the character of God. He did not come with an announcement that God was "omnipotent," "omniscient," "inerrant," "impassible" and "immutable." Instead, He announced the coming of God's Kingdom.

Maintaining that this Kingdom "cometh not by observation" (Luke 17:20), He told creative stories that illustrated the spiritual reality and truth of the Kingdom so that those with eyes to see and ears to hear (Matt 13:15; cf. Isa 6:9–10) would be able to perceive the "signs of the times" (Matt 16:3) and respond in love to this "new thing" (Isa 43:19) that God was doing in

---

34. Searle, J., "The Future of Millennial Studies," 144.

35. Macquarrie, *In Search of Humanity*, 3.

36. Blake, quoted in Manganiello, *Joyce's Politics*, 203.

37. Berdyaev, *Smysl Tvorchestva*, 57.

their midst. Jesus's parables, explains N. T. Wright, "broke into the world of first century Judaism, cracking open ways of understanding God's kingdom and creating hermeneutical space for fresh insight in which people could imagine different ways of thinking, praying and living."[38] Jesus's creative and vivid parabolic imagination summoned His hearers to respond to the gospel message. V. George Shillington offers a helpful explanation concerning the imaginative force of Jesus's parables:

> The parables of Jesus carry provocative power more than they do moral education. The parable invites the audience to step inside an alternate world from where they stand in the received world. The step is taken in the mind, in creative imagination. Participants in the plot fill in the gaps, envision the possibilities, and in this sense become co-creators of the parable. Once inside the parable plot, the participant is caught in the narrative interplay, with no escaping the repercussions of answering the question inherent in the parable.[39]

Jesus, as Lord and Savior is also the Great Teacher, and He understood the power of narrative to transform the heart in a way that propositional statements or moral instruction are unable to do. He understood that if He wanted to depict the character of God, it was better to tell a story than to give His hearers a list of adjectives.

The same principle applies to human character descriptions. For instance, if a man wanted to describe his wife's character to a listening audience, he could enumerate a list of adjectives which seem to correspond to her character. For instance, he could say that she was "kind," "caring," "compassionate," "gracious," "generous," "hospitable," etc., but this may seem rather banal and unconvincing. A more effective way of communicating his wife's character would be to tell a story about her that would allow his hearers to draw their own conclusions based on what the story reveals about her character. The story would need to include a plot, a series of events, and a character illustration or development.[40] For instance, if the man told a story about how his wife rescued a child from a burning house and then organized her church to support the family whose home had burned down, offering them food and shelter during the cold winter, then the man would not even need to use adjectives to describe his wife. The listeners would come to their own conclusion that she was "kind," "caring," "compassionate," "gracious," "generous," "hospitable," etc. Moreover, this creative narrative

---

38. Wright, *Scripture and the Authority of God*, 13.
39. Shillington, "Engaging with the Parables," 18.
40. McClendon, *Doctrine*, 228; cf. McClendon, *Biography as Theology*, 17.

approach avoids the confusing vicissitudes of language, which is constantly changing its meaning. For example, think about how the meaning of the following words has changed even in relatively recent times: "gay," "cool," "sick," "fantastic," "awful," "wicked," etc.[41]

Narrative theology is thus a summons to creativity. Non-propositional presentations of the gospel will become more and more relevant as society transitions further into post-Christendom. Postmodernity, which runs in tandem with post-Christendom but which should not be equated with it, has lost confidence in the explanatory power of propositional language to represent reality. Postmodernity is thus characterized by a rediscovery of the power of narrative to convey or imitate reality. The postmodern shift has generated a new interest in the notion of human beings as *homo fabulans*, or "the being that tells stories."[42] Notable postmodern philosophers have claimed that storytelling is the quintessential human activity. Alasdair MacIntyre maintains that, "Man [*sic*] in his actions and practices, as well as in his fictions, is essentially a storytelling animal."[43] James K. A. Smith concurs that, "We are narrative animals whose very orientation to the world is fundamentally shaped by stories . . . It is a story that provides the moral map of our universe. It is narrative that trains our emotional perceptual apparatus to perceive the world as meaningful."[44] The universal suspicion of the totalizing claims of Grand Narratives (e.g. Marxism, Fascism, Secularism, Liberalism, Modernism, etc.) does not extend to local stories and personal testimonies. Stories have explanatory power because they are "loaded with emotions, symbols and representations to provide explanations of mysteries and important facts" that are indescribable by logic or rationality.[45] Narrative discloses a depth of meaning which propositional statements are unable to elucidate.

Emphasizing creativity as not only a matter of freedom, but also of duty, Berdyaev maintained that "human nature is creative because it is the image and likeness of the Creator-God."[46] Berdyaev moreover emphasized the soteriological significance of creative activity, arguing that "a human being justifies him or herself before the Creator not only by redemption, but also by creativeness."[47] Lamenting the lack of creativity in the life of the

41. The explanatory power of narrative, summarized in this paragraph, is treated at length in Hauerwas and Jones, *Why Narrative?*

42. Pagden, *Enlightenment*, 17–18.

43. MacIntyre, *After Virtue*, 201.

44. Smith, *Imagining the Kingdom*, 108.

45. Boff, *Essential Care*, 33.

46. Berdyaev, *Smysl Tvorchestva*, 117.

47. Ibid.

Christendom church, Berdyaev claims that, "Christianity, in the best case, has justified creativity, but it has never fully realized that it should not only justify creativity, but that through its own creativity, it should justify life."[48] Theology in post-Christendom should be distinguished by a new spiritual orientation towards creativity.

Theological Obstacles to the Kingdom: Fundamentalist and Liberal Theologies

The history of Christendom theology has often been characterized as a clash of two antithetical tendencies: liberalism and fundamentalism. Whereas fundamentalism insists on the objectivity and infallibility of the Bible as unmediated, eternal and unchanging Word of God, liberalism has been characterized by a willingness to accommodate biblical teaching to changing cultural contexts. The challenge of theology in post-Christendom will be to surmount these distinctions by situating theological method and practice outside of the limiting parameters of both tendencies.[49] Post-Christendom theology should be thought of neither as "fundamentalist" nor "accommodating," neither "conservative" nor "liberal." Post-Christian theology should be evangelical, but not in the dogmatic sense of focusing narrowly on a set of traditional beliefs. Rather, all theology—whether Catholic, Orthodox, Protestant or unaligned to any church tradition—should be evangelical to the extent that it gives creative expression to the *euaggelion* (εὐαγγέλιον), the good news of the gospel concerning the coming of God's Kingdom to earth.

The debate about the place of faith in post-Christendom transcends the customary distinctions between liberals and fundamentalists. Christendom has permeated the beliefs and practice of both liberal and fundamentalist theology and each expression is as prone as the other to indulge in fantasies about imminent revival and unrealistic prospects for church growth. Whereas some evangelical churches may entertain exaggerated hopes that all will be well if Christians simply intensify their devotion to the Scriptures or if they pray more fervently for revival, liberal Christians likewise, as Hall notes, "either simply fail to come to grips with the changed circumstances in which they find themselves, or else they opt for methods like "church growth," which permit them to exploit the old, more sedate forms

48. Ibid.

49. Notable efforts have been made to lead theology out of the liberal/fundamentalist impasse. See Franke and Grenz, *Beyond Foundationalism*; Murphy, *Beyond Liberalism and Fundamentalism*.

of Constantinianism a little longer without impinging too conspicuously on the qualms of new liberals respecting Christian exclusivity."[50] The faith that post-Christendom seeks to nurture is neither liberal nor fundamental, but "simply Christian."[51]

The term, fundamentalism, is derived from a set of twelve books published by a group of American Protestants which were collectively entitled, *The Fundamentals: A Testimony of the Truth* (1910–1915). Christian fundamentalists have distinguished themselves historically from other Christians by insisting on the indispensability of five core doctrines: Biblical Inerrancy, the Deity of Christ, the Virgin Birth, Penal-Substitutionary Atonement, and the Physical Resurrection and Bodily Return of Christ to Earth.[52] The fundamentalist emphasis on fidelity to the biblical text is commendable. Theology must recognize the normative status of Scripture as the authoritative witness to the new life in the Kingdom of God that Jesus proclaimed and embodied.

However, the error of fundamentalism consists in the naive, yet aggressive, claim to know the truth of the Scripture to the exclusion of other interpretations. Fundamentalism bypasses theological reflection, the witness of tradition and the need for deep interpretation and settles for the indolent certainty of dogmatic affirmations. The fundamentalist does not seem to realize that the belief in the biblical inerrancy, like all other doctrines, can be affirmed at the expense of other aspects of truth and exaggerated to the point of falsity. Thus, the fundamentalist's appeal to the authority of Scripture easily morphs into the canonization of the fundamentalist's own personal interpretation. Moreover, anyone who disagrees with the fundamentalist's interpretation is condemned as a liberal or a heretic.

Today fundamentalism expresses itself in distrust of academic theology and theological formation and in opposition to supposedly deplorable trends and initiatives, such as ecumenism, secularism and (post-)modernity. Fundamentalist theology elevates the biblical text to the point of idolatry (or bibliolatry) and exhibits a persecuting zeal against those Christians it regards as liberal or charismatic. The tragedy of fundamentalism is that in its desire to be faithful to the Bible, fundamentalism in fact betrays the Bible and turns this life-giving word into a cold and sterile compendium of factual claims. The Bible is full of wisdom and folly, love and conflict and joy and pain. It is a text that is full of humor and humanity. In this sense, the text reflects the complex reality of life, which likewise constitutes a complex

50. Hall, *End of Christendom*, 20.
51. Wright, *Simply Christian*.
52. Searle, J., *Scarlet Woman and the Red Hand*, 11.

synthesis of hope, fear, clarity and confusion. The Bible is the book that breathes life and bristles with pathos, adventure and creativity; it is the "great code of art," in the words of the poets.[53] However, rather than reading the Bible as the book of life that invites readers to discover and experience the depth, beauty, mystery and sacrament of life, the fundamentalist is fixated with approaching the Bible as an academic text that details facts about God.

Furthermore, in its efforts to establish the authority of the Bible, fundamentalism uses words such as "inerrancy," "infallibility," "objective," and "literal," apparently without realizing the irony that these words and concepts originate neither from the Bible nor even from Christian tradition, but from the secular philosophy of the Enlightenment.[54] Alister E. McGrath thus notes that, "The paradox of fundamentalism is that it depends upon secularism for its credibility."[55] By insisting on notions such as "inerrancy" and "objectivity," fundamentalist theology unwittingly capitulates to the agenda of the secular humanist approach known as positivism, which insists that all claims to truth must adhere to a scientific criteria of empirical verification by corresponding to a proper understanding of the facts.

The serious shortcomings of this kind of positivistic foundationalism have been demonstrated by leading philosophers, scientists and theologians since at least the 1950s.[56] The fundamentalist believes that the truth of the Bible must be established by extra-biblical criteria. The truth of the Bible, it is claimed, is bound up with propositional statements that correspond to the facts about God, sin and salvation. Ironically, therefore, in its insistence that the Bible is an infallible repository of inerrant facts about God, Christian fundamentalism has inadvertently become one of the last remaining citadels of positivism in contemporary postmodern culture. Fundamentalism reads the Bible not as the guiding narrative of Christian life that requires creative appropriation, but as a rigid regimentation of thought and behavior that is extrapolated from a distorted interpretation. Instead of reducing the Bible to alien criteria of empirical verification, it is more faithful to the Scriptures to read the Bible, as Peter Rollins aptly suggests, as "a means of approaching its life-transforming truth, a truth that dwells within and beyond words."[57] In contrast to the naive simplicity of fundamentalist interpretation, biblical

---

53. Blake, quoted in De Luca, *Words of Eternity*, 85.

54. McLaren, *Generous Orthodoxy*, 182–83.

55. McGrath, *Future of Christianity*, 75; see also McGrath, *Christianity*, 277.

56. Murphy, *Theology in the Age of Scientific Reasoning*.

57. Rollins, *Fidelity of Betrayal*, 47–62.

interpretation in post-Christendom, as Lloyd Pieterson helpfully proposes, should be "prophetic," "subversive," and "sustaining."[58]

Unfortunately, these nuanced and life-giving approaches to reading the Scriptures are not very popular in contemporary evangelicalism. Much more popular are simplistic and superficial appeals to the inerrancy and the literal meaning of the biblical text that avoid the necessity of having to grapple with the problems of semantics and hermeneutics. For the fundamentalist, "the Bible remains a cold icon, relegated to symbolic significance, or when . . . it is made a graven idol, a "paper pope," receiving the more homage the more it is misread."[59] This misreading can be attributed to the general tendency of fundamentalist theological textbooks towards a superficial "proof-texting" approach to Scripture in which the Bible is plundered for words and phrases that will substantiate the preconceived prejudices of the fundamentalist author.[60] The fundamentalist author can then claim that owing to their alleged grounding in the Scriptures, his (fundamentalism tends to be a male phenomenon) view is thus "biblical." The problem is that, on closer inspection, these "biblical" convictions often turn out to be little more than cultural or ideological prejudices that the fundamentalist has brought to his reading of the Bible.

This accounts for why Christian fundamentalism is so susceptible to conscription by authoritarian political ideologies. The servile notion of divine sovereignty and the depiction of God as a cosmic dictator can easily morph into a pseudo-theological justification of unjust and tyrannical political regimes. This explains why Protestant fundamentalists in Russia can find pseudo-biblical arguments for supporting a corrupt and kleptocratic political regime[61] and why their counterparts in North America can make a similarly dubious biblical case in favor of fascist populism and demagoguery.[62]

58. Pieterson, *Reading the Bible After Christendom*, 211.

59. McClendon, *Doctrine*, 35.

60. See, for instance, the vulgar and flawed—yet representative and influential—work by Grudem, *Systematic Theology*.

61. For example, in May 2014 the Russian Baptist Union sent a letter addressed to Vladimir Putin, which praised the Russian President (who had waged a series of devastating wars in Chechnya, Georgia, and Ukraine that resulted in the slaughter of thousands of people, mainly innocent civilians) for "his contribution to the strengthening of civil peace and harmony in Russian society." See Geddes, "Protestants: Different Views on Ukraine."

62. One particularly notorious example of this is the endorsement of Donald Trump by Grudem, a leading fundamentalist theologian. Grudem penned a 5,000-word article explaining why "I think voting for Trump is a morally good choice." See   http://townhall.com/columnists/waynegrudem/2016/07/28/why-voting-for

According to the severe and rigid doctrines of Christian fundamentalism, animosity to adherents of other religions becomes elevated to the status of a gospel imperative. Historically, the main target of Christian fundamentalism was the Jewish community and, regrettably, anti-Semitism has blighted the Christendom Church from Constantine to Martin Luther[63] and partly explains why the Christian community in Europe did so little to save the European Jews from the Nazi Holocaust.[64] Although anti-Semitism is prominent in some expressions of Christian fundamentalism, nowadays, it is the Muslim community that has become the object of Christian fundamentalist indignation.

Post-Christendom theology must resist this fundamentalist tendency to caricature and scapegoat adherents of other religions. The Christian movement in post-Christendom needs to raise up a new generation of theologians who can refute the islamophobic distortions of contemporary Christian fundamentalism and work towards a more constructive and respectful engagement with their Muslim neighbors. A notable advantage of taking the Kingdom, rather than the church, as the starting point of theology is the fact that the vision of the Kingdom of God surpasses the parochial interests of churches and denominations.

Fundamentalism and the Future of Theology in Post-Christendom

If fundamentalism dominates the theological agenda, the result will be the death of theology in the post-Christian West. Fundamentalism signifies the death of creativity, the enervation of spiritual vitality, the subordination of compassionate grace to legalistic dogma, and the crushing of life in the spirit. "Fundamentalism," claims Leonardo Boff, "blinds important sectors of Christianity to what is obvious and to that central message of Christianity, the message that brings life in abundance. Life is sacrificed in the name of archaic rules and doctrines."[65] Despite the purported emphasis on "irresistible grace," the God posited by Christian fundamentalism is a graceless taskmaster. The stern and disciplinarian God worshipped by fundamentalists is a blasphemous caricature of the gracious God who is revealed per-

---

-donald-trump-is-a-morally-good-choice-n2199564.

63. See the fascinating study by Carroll, *Constantine's Sword*.

64. For a detailed study of Christian apathy and hostility towards the European Jewish community in the first half of the twentieth century, see the volume edited by Spicer, *Antisemitism, Christian Ambivalence, and the Holocaust*.

65. Boff, *Fundamentalism*, 12.

fectly in Jesus Christ and whose heart overflows with compassion. The best way to overcome the stifling tendencies of fundamentalism is to re-establish the broken connection between faith and discipleship and between salvation and life.

The God of fundamentalist Christianity is the product of conceptual hypnosis and sociomorphic debasement of the divine image by sinful human perception. This God of fundamentalism orthodoxy has ossified into brittle systems of sound doctrine that have been abstracted from life. Authoritarian religion takes the place of living faith. For the God of fundamentalism, power is more important than justice and love.[66] Despite its outward concern for the purity of Christian doctrine, the dominant impulse behind fundamentalism is the will to power, rather than the will to truth. To the extent that it expresses the will to power, fundamentalism rejects Christ and His gospel. As Berdyaev noted, "The will to power is always a form of atheism. The will to power is the will to murder. Every man who aspires to achieve a condition of power for himself is a murderer and ought to be judged as such."[67] This murderous impulse arises out of fanaticism, and intolerance, and the sinful instincts and affections of a hate-fueled imagination.

Concerned only with power and sovereignty, rather than truth and compassion, the God of fundamentalism regards human beings as insignificant, worthless and incapable of aspiring to higher values of truth and love. This authoritarian God is all-powerful. He is more at home in a palace than in a stable. This is why fundamentalism often found it so difficult to confess the kenotic Christ (Phil 2:1–11), who empties Himself of power for the sake of love and thus gave a new definition of what it meant to be divine in terms of weakness[68] and self-sacrificial love, rather than sovereignty and top-down authoritarianism.[69] As Berdyaev remarked, "God is in the child which has shed tears, and not in the world order by which those tears are said to be justified."[70]

This fundamentalist Christianity places great emphasis on sin and sees the world from the perspective of sin and judgement, rather than grace and compassion. For all this emphasis on sin, however, there is an apparent unawareness of the most glaring sin that a human being can commit: namely,

66. Sölle, *Thinking about God*, 177.

67. Berdyaev, quoted in Davy, *Nicolas Berdyaev*, 124.

68. See 1 Cor 1:25—"the weakness of God is stronger than human strength."

69. Commenting on Philippians 2:6–8, Bulgakov writes that "this passage talks about not only an earthly event occurring within the limits of human life but also about a heavenly event occurring in the depths of Divinity itself: the kenosis of God the Word"—Bulgakov, *Lamb of God*, 215.

70. Berdyaev, *Slavery and Freedom*, 87–89.

"the sin of the unlived life."[71] There are no sins so fearful and worthy of damnation as sins that blaspheme against the fullness of life in the Spirit. Sin is not merely a matter of individual or collective acts of transgressive behavior. At a deeper level sin, as John Oman (1860–1939) noted, is the result of "a desire to get out of life what God has not put into it."[72] Sin is a spiritual disorder that leads people into misperceiving the character of God and overlooking His presence in the world.

Misperceiving God's character, many fundamentalists believe that their authoritarian God willingly (sometimes even gleefully) consigns to eternal damnation anyone who does not convert to the system of doctrine fabricated by the sinful imagination of the fundamentalist mind. Sometimes this fundamentalism demands not only conceptual affirmation of its creed, but also visible affiliation to a specific church institution, which is regarded as the only path to salvation and the sole interpreter of the divine will on earth. The authoritarian God fabricated by the fallen fundamentalist imagination discriminates against women and apparently demands that his followers do likewise. Fundamentalism suppresses humane gospel values of grace, hospitality, human warmth and generosity. The fundamentalist spirit radiates only fear, negativity, hostility and paranoid rejection of anything that does not fit comfortably within the stifling contours of the prevailing dogma. Not recognizing that "perfect love casteth out fear" (1 John 4:18), fundamentalism invariably falls short of love and truth, because "fear is the father of falsehood."[73]

The rigid regimentation of beliefs and dogmas associated with fundamentalism indicates the absence of the Holy Spirit, for "where the Spirit of the Lord is, there is freedom" (2 Cor 3:17). True faith leads to a deepening of the depth and beauty of life and an expansion of one's horizons of compassion; fundamentalist belief, conversely, leads to a superficial adherence to a life-sapping system of dogma and to a reduction of one's capacity to love. Fundamentalism can even make a person a prisoner within their own life. "Belief should liberate your life," wrote John O'Donohue, who added that, "Anything that turns [life] into a torment hardly merits the title salvation."[74]

Fundamentalism is totally opposed to the true spirit of theology, because whereas theology thrives in freedom, creativity and compassion, fundamentalism requires conformity, inertia and intolerance towards

71. O'Donohue, *Anam Cara*, 159.

72. Oman, *Grace and Personality*, quoted in Bevans, *Models of Contextual Theology*, 21.

73. Berdyaev, *Ekzistentsialnaya Dialektika*, 406.

74. O'Donohue, *Eternal Echoes*, 163.

adherents of other perspectives. Therefore, fundamentalists are often opposed to theological education unless such education is concerned exclusively with instructing students in mindless adherence to stale doctrinal
formulas. For the fundamentalist, the only function that theology can serve
is to perpetuate systems of power, illusion and deception,[75] often under
the guise of upholding "sound doctrine." All Christians, including fundamentalists, have a theology (see chapter 2 above). However, fundamentalist
theology, which looks for meaning only on the surface of "literal readings,"
lacks depth and authenticity and, for all its appeals to the inerrancy of Scripture, lacks a proper biblical basis. The stale platitudes of fundamentalism are
too superficial to be true and too simple to be real.

The fundamentalist sees the world in black and white terms. Boff
remarks that, "fundamentalism is always a closed system based on sharp
distinctions, inimical to the different and blind to the rationale of inclu-
siveness, to the rationale of the rainbow where the plurality of colours lives
with the unity of the rainbow itself."[76] The rigid contours of the myopic
fundamentalist worldview does not allow for grey areas or shades of truth.
Fundamentalism permits neither acceptance nor generosity towards other
viewpoints that diverge from the fundamentalist's personal understanding
of the truth.

The fixation on dogmatic systems of thought and propositional statements betrays a dangerous foundationalism that abstracts God from life and
restricts God to the realm of ideas. Boff explains that within fundamentalism, "Christian experience is replaced by indoctrination in the existing
system—a system that lives in the inferno of terms and doctrines that are
reinterpreted ideologically, again and again, in order to maintain power, an
endless chain of interpretations that loses its reference to the one necessary
element, the Gospel."[77] The fundamentalist invests faith in a system of sound
doctrine, but neglects the vital truth of Christianity that "God is testified to
in the transformed lives of believers rather than in some abstract doctrinal
system."[78] The fundamentalist is usually in error because he knows neither
the Scriptures nor the power of God. With an edifice of sound doctrine,

75. Ibid., 363.

76. Boff, *Fundamentalism*, 29.

77. Boff, *Church*, 86.

78. Rollins, *How (Not) to Speak of God*, 40. This remark is reminiscent of Newbigin's claim that, "the only hermeneutic of the gospel, is a congregation of men and
women who believe it and live by it." In my view, this quotation from Newbigin would
have been even better if he had replaced the word, "congregation," with "community."
See Newbigin, *Gospel in a Pluralist Society*, 228.

the fundamentalist has a semblance of godliness, but denies the power of transformed life in the power of the Holy Spirit.

Fundamentalism has been described as one of the greatest challenges confronting theology in the twenty-first century.[79] Younger theologians are now openly referring to fundamentalism as an "inhibiting factor" not only in theological development, [80] but also in Christian peacebuilding endeavors.[81] By denying academic pursuits, such as theology and science, the right to credibility and relevance, fundamentalists immensely simplify reality and deprive themselves of a true perspective on Christian faith. One leading evangelical scholar thus refers to "the intellectual disaster of fundamentalism."[82]

In the wake of the fundamentalist challenge, theology in post-Christendom now stands at a crossroads. For theology, fundamentalism is a road to nowhere. The only theology that can resonate with gospel values in the emerging post-Christendom condition is a theology that is nourished by a holistic vision of life within the Kingdom of God. In this time of momentous transition, theologians have a choice either to remain in the isolation and inertia of fundamentalism; or they can restore the damaged connections between life and doctrine, "repair the broken altars" (1 Kgs 18:30), and join the fragments of a life-giving and holistic vision of theological formation into Christlikeness.

One of the essential prerequisites towards overcoming theology's captivity to fundamentalism is the formulation of a viable and robust public theology that can express the truth of the gospel in ways that connect transformatively with the concrete realities of life in the world today. The next chapter will offer a vision of public theology for a post-secular world and a post-Christendom church.

---

79. Žižek ironically includes "Christian Fundamentalism" itself as one of the four horsemen of the apocalypse that portent the advent of a secular apocalypse in the world today. The other three are "New Age spirituality," "techno-digital post-humanism," and "secular ecologism"—Žižek, First as Tragedy, Then as Farce, 94.

80. Dubrovskij, "Fundamentalizm kak tormozjashhij faktor," 27–45.

81. Hertog, Complex Reality of Religious Peacebuilding, 191.

82. This is the title of chapter 5 of Noll's book, Scandal of the Evangelical Mind, 109–45.

7

Making the Gospel Visible in the Public Sphere

The Church, Academy, and Society

The time has come for bold and innovative thinking. In post-Christendom it is becoming increasingly apparent that a new vision of authentic Christian existence is required for these changing times. There is still hope for the church in post-Christendom, but the aims and structures of church must be subordinated to the Kingdom of God. Christianity requires revitalization and a new eschatological orientation towards the Kingdom of God. The impulse towards a new vision of Christianity as a movement of universal compassion (rather than a religion of private salvation) comes primarily by the Holy Spirit.

Notwithstanding this divine agency, the realization of this vision requires the active participation of God's people, who must be educated (or formed), firstly, to understand what the incarnate *Logos* is doing in the world, and, secondly, to participate with Him in the power of the Holy Spirit to accomplish the Father's purposes in the world. Theology facilitates the *missio Dei* by empowering the Christian community to work towards the redemption of the world. The gospel penetrates every sphere of life; God is just as concerned with those spheres that we arbitrarily designate as "secular" as He is with the "sacred" dimensions of life. The whole world belongs to God and He cares about the flourishing of all people, not just those who adhere to a Christian system of belief or who are affiliated to a church.

This world-orientation requires a coming of age of theology. Theology awaits its renewal in the new spiritual configurations of post-Christendom and expresses itself not in the preservation of the church, but in the yearning for the Kingdom. The aim of this Kingdom-oriented vision of theological formation is, in the words of Dietrich Bonhoeffer, nothing less than the "realization in our world of the divine and cosmic reality which is given in Christ."[1] In order to realize the gift of Christ's presence in the world, there needs to be a new awareness of the transforming power of the gospel that extends to every sphere of life. Fostering this kind of awareness is how I envisage the task of public theology. The aim of this chapter is to elucidate the meaning, significance and application of public theology towards the renewal of the church, the regeneration of theological education and the transformation of the wider society.[2]

Post-Christendom Theology and the Renewal of the Church

I am aware that my analysis of the church might have appeared to be mainly critical and pessimistic. However, I am keen to stress that this critical posture should not be attributed to any anti-clerical sentiment on my part. This book arises out of a deep commitment to the church and an ardent desire for the church to rediscover its prophetic voice and become a major factor in the positive transformation of the world into the image of God's Kingdom. Although I believe that the attempts to revive Christendom are futile and counterproductive—and notwithstanding my scepticism towards the various attempts to present the church as healthy and poised for imminent revival[3]—my desire is to see the renewal and flourishing of the church in post-Christendom.

On this point, I have often found myself resonating with the sentiment of one of my favorite Russian writers, Vasily Vasilyevich Rozanov, who on his deathbed lamented that he had devoted so many years of his life to the destruction of the church. "God, what madness it was," bewailed Rozanov shortly before he died, "that for eleven years I made every possible effort to destroy the Church. And how fortunate that I failed. What would the *earth* be like without the Church? It would suddenly lose its meaning and get cold."[4] The world without the church would indeed be a bleak and desolate place. Many of the ideals and values, such as freedom, compassion, courtesy and solidarity first penetrated western culture through the influence of Christians and the churches. My personal experience of ministering to

1. Bonhoeffer, quoted in Rasmussen, "Ethics of Responsible Action," 216.

2. This threefold focus on church, academy, and society reflects the approach of the influential public theologian, Tracy, who regarded these three spheres as the distinct constituencies to which theologians should address their discoveries. See Tracy, *Analogical Imagination*.

3. See, for instance, Oliver-Dee, *God's Unwelcome Recovery*. A more academic account is given in Goodhew, *Church Growth in Britain*.

4. Rozanov, quoted in Copleston, *Philosophy in Russia*, 199.

deprived and suffering people in Ukraine has taught me the value of local churches. I am convinced that were it not for the churches in this region, the whole of Eastern Ukraine would descend into complete chaos. The work that churches are doing, such as delivering insulin medicine for diabetics in war-torn regions of Eastern Ukraine, is literally saving lives, even while these Christians sometimes risk their own lives in the process. Moreover, the evidence of history testifies clearly that without the Christian churches, the very ideals which we take as basic to our state, such as universal health-care and education, would not have been possible. In the post-Christendom West, churches have historically been at the forefront of the establishment of schools, universities, hospitals, and hospices. Churches were also instrumental in the foundation of compassionate and humanitarian organizations, such as the Samaritans, Oxfam, and Amnesty International.

Therefore, I am persuaded that the transition to post-Christendom does not and should not necessarily lead to the demise of the church. Nevertheless, the church must be re-imagined in order to ensure its faithfulness to the gospel in these momentous times of cultural change. As the western world transitions into post-Christendom, the time has come for a new vision of Christian existence that expresses itself in solidarity and compassion. The church in post-Christendom can become a powerful movement of the gospel, but only if the church is willing to undergo radical structural transformation, which involves a reorientation towards the pain and *pathos* of the world. Solidarity, rather than separation, is the new missional imperative for the church in post-Christendom.

At their best, churches are inclusive and boundary-pushing communities that offer a foretaste of heaven on earth. They are the emancipatory communities in which people are released from the iron cage of bureaucratization that regulates life in the world.[5] Churches should be communities of warmth, compassion, hospitality and welcome, where strangers and outsiders feel at home and where humane values of dignity and care are recognized and affirmed. Creativity should be valued over productivity; meaning prized over utility. Church, in the ideal scenario, is the site of life in which God manifests Himself among His people. The church is not synonymous with the Kingdom, but if churches express their common life in *koinonia* (compassionate fellowship) towards each other and in *agape* (sacrificial love) towards the world, then such churches can rightly claim to be beachheads of the Kingdom—as places "in which the reign of God

---

5. The term, "iron cage" (*stahlhartes Gehäuse*), was used by the German sociologist, Weber, as a metaphor to describe modern society. See Weber, *Die protestantische Ethik*, 203.

begins to be made manifest here and now."[6] The Kingdom of God, in the words of Jürgen Moltmann, can be regarded as an exemplary prototype of an eschatologically-constituted "new creation of all things"[7] which Christians can experience proleptically by belonging to the church.

Unfortunately, however, in the post-Christendom West, this is not how churches are generally perceived. Public attitudes towards the church tend to fluctuate between benign indifference and hostile antipathy. The term, "church," itself has lost its meaning and is more likely to be associated in the popular opinion with homophobia, bigotry, and hostility towards science, rather than with compassion, solidarity, generosity, or intellectual credibility.

This misperception is partly due to the distortions of the media and an agenda of some secularists to present Christians, particularly evangelicals, as bygone, bigoted obscurantists whose opinions should be ignored or ridiculed. However, Christians themselves have often contributed to the media caricatures by fixating on peripheral issues, such as homosexuality, at the expense of more pressing and central issues of injustice and the crisis of compassion in contemporary society. Within Christendom, many Christians seem to have shown more concern for defending lost privileges, rather than promoting a gospel agenda of social justice in the interest of the common good.[8]

As a result of the church's bad press, Christians are becoming an increasingly ignored—sometimes even despised—minority in a condition of cultural exile. To be a minority without power or social status—this is what it means to follow Christ in a post-Christendom context. The church in post-Christendom will be a church without social status or political patronage.[9] In these changing times it is imperative that churches reform themselves as "communities of discernment and resistance."[10] Adopting a posture of discernment and resistance does not require a Christian community to speak or act from a position of power. Stuart Murray neatly summarizes the role and purpose of such communities:

6. Stassen and Gushee, *Kingdom Ethics*, 230.

7. Moltmann, *Theologie der Hoffnung*, 28.

8. Graham, *Rock and a Hard Place*, 173.

9. For more details concerning the nature and mission of post-Christendom churches, see Murray, *Church After Christendom*.

10. Murray uses this term in his book, *Vast Minority*. The term derives originally from Wink's influential work, *Engaging the Powers*. I would prefer to add another descriptive term to Wink's definition—"communities of discernment, resistance and compassion."

A community of discernment and resistance refuses either to be isolated from or co-opted by the society in which it is set. It reminds its members of its founding story, celebrates this in worship and explores its implications for discipleship. But it also listens carefully to the other stories that are shaping its society, examines their assumptions, exposes their ideologies and un-masks contemporary idols. Discernment means recognizing and affirming what is good and deserving of support as well as identifying malign and dehumanizing influences that call for re-sistance. This is the prophetic role of the Christian community and our pastoral responsibility to each other as we share and test our insights, equipping each other to reflect theologically on family, work, society, study, leisure activities, local community and global issues—asking how we can live as faithful disciples in all spheres of life.[11]

Too often, Christianity has become inert, compromised and conformist. Instead of offering prophetic resistance to the dehumanizing tendencies of this age, many Christians have unwittingly colluded with these anti-gospel forces. Such collusion occurs when Christianity is understood as a religion, rather than a movement, and when church is understood as an institution, rather than as an emancipatory collective of radical disciples.

One of the tasks of post-Christendom theology is to counteract the default tendency of church towards clericalization and institutionalization. Theology can have a purifying effect on Christianity, freeing it of religious elements that are unrelated to its essence. Post-Christendom theology insists that Christianity is *not* a religion and neither is church a religious institution. Blumhardt remarked, "People have made Jesus the founder of religion. No! He is the bringer of life."[12] Within Christendom religion often served as a substitute for faith. There is nothing religious about living a life of faith in loving and disciplined obedience to Jesus Christ.

Christians in post-Christendom must not be content with what Blum-hardt called, "the Christ of religion."[13] The "religious Christ" gives no hope to the world. Only the Crucified and Risen Christ, the real Jesus of the Gos-pels can bring salvation and healing to the world. Christianity is a way of life that is oriented towards the presence of Christ in the world. Theology in post-Christendom must resist the tendency of secular liberalism to classify Christianity as a religion which can be consigned to a safely self-contained sphere or relegated to the status of just another private consumer choice.

11. Murray, *Vast Minority*.
12. Blumhardt, *Gospel of God's Reign*, 33.
13. Blumhardt, *Everyone Belongs to God*, 33.

Post-Christendom theology must thus deconstruct the false dichotomies of church vs. world and sacred vs. secular. Christendom erred in so far
that it posited the institutional church as the locus of the gospel in culture,
whereas the gospel takes root not just in the religious sphere, but in the life
of the world, often in the most surprising and unexpected places. Whereas
Christendom aimed for the Christianization of society, post-Christendom
aims for the socialization of Christianity. This does not involve the accommodation of the gospel to social conventions; rather, it involves the interfusion of the gospel and culture and the transfiguration of society. Christian
mission thus involves "the humanization of society as much as expansion of
the Church."[14]

Crucially, the success of this kind of mission is expressed not in the
triumph of Christianity over society, but in compassion for and involvement in society. Solidarity with the world, not numerical conversions to
church subcultures, is what matters. What is preserved here is the social
responsibility and the desire to influence and change, but without the naive
optimism of Christendom-laden assumptions concerning the top-down
Christianization of society.[15] The "guiding principle" of public theology in
post-Christendom should be, as Elaine Graham maintains, the "salvation
of the world, and not the survival of the Church."[16] This approach, which
prioritizes solidarity with the godforsaken world, requires "a deep sympathy
with the integrity of the godless and a compassionate identification with the
godforsaken."[17]

A proper understanding of solidarity helps us to perceive that the
sectarian division between the church and the world was based not on the
biblical principle of incarnational mission, but on the secular principle of
the division of life into clearly demarcated spheres of influence. The ethic
of separation from the world was motivated by fear, including the fear of
sin and fear of the supposed compromises to the integrity of the gospel
that would ensue unless the church retained its sacramental character and
institutional identity. Any theological perspective that is determined by
fear cannot be truly theological, according to our definition above, for the
animating principle of theology is love and "there is no fear in love, because
perfect love casts out fear" (1 John 4:18).

Within post-Christendom the clearly demarcated lines that used to divide the church from the world have now lost their meaning. As McClendon

---

14. Graham, *Rock and a Hard Place*, 222.

15. Searle, J., *Church without Walls*.

16. Graham, *Rock and a Hard Place*, 223.

17. Ibid., 232.

put it, "the line between church and world pass right through each Christian heart."[18] Church is not an ideal concept that is separated from the world, because it consists of people whose lives are shaped by powerful seemingly worldly or secular forces in contemporary culture, such as the media, arts and politics. Terrence Tilley thus remarks that, "Christian lives are structured not only by the church and its narratives, but also by the world."[19]

The Poverty of Sacramentalism

One of the best illustrations of the prevalence of the Christendom mentality in the church is the inflation of discourse concerning the status of the eucharist in current theology. Christendom theology has sometimes posited that the eucharist constitutes "an entry into the paschal mystery of the Lord"[20] and that it formed the basis of the entire unity of the Christian worldwide community.[21] Over the course of church history the emphasis shifted from the informal celebration of Christ's sacrifice to a sacramental ritual invested with magical qualities. Some have even claimed that "a Christian practice of the political is embodied in the Eucharist."[22]

Post-Christendom theology should expose these dubious assumptions and exaggerated claims concerning the alleged missional significance of church sacraments, such as the eucharist. It is not immediately apparent, for instance, how (in the words of one influential consensus document commissioned by the World Council of Churches in 2013) "the celebration of the eucharist . . . enables the Church to participate in the mission of God for the transformation and salvation of the world."[23] This statement seems to be without foundation in Scripture or experience. As well as the lack of any reference to the eucharist in the Great Commission (Matt 28:16–20), it is difficult to see any connection between *missio Dei* and the eucharist. For instance, how does the consumption of bread and wine by Christians in church buildings empower or enhance the church's witness in the world? Eucharist is a sacramental gesture, rather than a "powerful practice" of world transformation.[24]

18. McClendon, *Ethics*, 17.

19. Tilley, *Postmodern Theologies*, 147.

20. Snoek, *Medieval Piety from Relics to the Eucharist*, 31–64.

21. See, for example, the booklet published by the Anglican House of Bishops, *Eucharist*.

22. Cavanaugh, *Torture and Eucharist*, 2.

23. Faith and Order, *Church*, 2.

24. The term, "powerful practice," is taken from McClendon, *Ethics*, 172–82.

Against the claims that mission should have a eucharistic foundation, post-Christendom theology should insist that mission needs Christocentric foundation that takes its point of departure not from church sacraments, but from the Kingdom of God in the world. How can it be claimed, for instance, that "the eucharist brings into the present age a new reality which transforms Christians into the image of Christ and therefore makes them his effective witnesses"?[25] According to the World Council of Churches, the church "reveals Christ to the world by proclaiming the Gospel" and "by celebrating the sacraments."[26] It is apparent how proclaiming the gospel reveals Christ to the world; less clear is how the celebration of the sacraments fulfils the *missio Dei*. While one may concede the importance of the eucharist[27] as a celebration of the finished work of Christ and as a joyous anticipation of the coming of the Kingdom of God in all its fullness,[28] the attempt to build a whole theology of mission on the eucharist is unwarranted by Scripture, and lacks even a foundation in common sense.

Christendom-minded theologians who persist in asserting the world-transformative power of the eucharist often resemble the flea on the chariot wheel in the parable told by the Italian humanist writer, Laurentius Abstemius (c.1440–1508). Perched on the chariot wheel during a race, the flea looks back and boasts about how much dust he is raising. The flea from this parable is analogous to the Christendom theologians who ascribe sacred attributes to their church rituals and think that by fulfilling their sacramental duties they are contributing to the transformation of the world in the power of the Holy Spirit.

If the Eastern Orthodox and Catholic traditions have tended to inflate the missional significance of the eucharist, then the Baptist churches have tended to exaggerate the importance of water baptism. In contrast to the eucharist, Jesus does refer to baptism in His Great Commission:

> Then Jesus came to them and said, "All authority in heaven and on earth has been given to me. Therefore go and make disciples of all nations, baptizing them in the name of the Father and of the Son and of the Holy Spirit, and teaching them to obey everything I have commanded you. And surely I am with you always, to the very end of the age" (Matt 28:18–20).

---

25. Faith and Order, *Church*, 19–20.

26. Ibid., 27.

27. Most European Baptists would refer to the Eucharist as "the Lord's Supper." See Jones, "Eucharistic Liturgy," in Briggs et al., *Dictionary of European Baptist Life and Thought*, 175.

28. Wright, *Free Church, Free State*, 101–4.

However, when Jesus mentions baptizing people in the name of the Father, Son, and Holy Spirit, He is referring not to a church ritual in which people are plunged into a pool of water upon a verbal confession of faith. Rather, as is clear from the entire testimony of Matthew's Gospel, most importantly the Sermon on the Mount (Matt 5–7), when Jesus speaks of baptizing people in this way, He is referring to the need to immerse people into the reality of a universe that is suffused by the presence of the Trinitarian God. The regrettable sacramentalist tendency is sometimes just as prevalent in non-conformist Baptist traditions[29] as it is in the established churches that claim to stand within the so-called "apostolic succession." Ecclesial bureaucrats who insist on the performance of certain rituals in strictly prescribed ways exhibit a spirit of legalism and control that is at variance to the freedom of the gospel. Christ brought the gospel to the world not so that it could be preserved in a museum or that it could be contained in church rituals, but so that its power could be unleashed upon the world for the realization of life in all its fullness.

To be a follower of Christ involves not a baptism of water, but a baptism of the Holy Spirit and a full immersion in the reality of God's life. What matters is not the performance of a ritual, but the transformation of life and the awakening of the heart and mind to the life of the spirit. This awakening may lead to church membership, water baptism and participation in the life of a local church, but what matters ultimately is the spiritual formation of the believer into the likeness of Christ. Spiritual formation encompasses every aspect of life. Spiritual reality suffuses everyday human experience and cannot be confined to the supernatural. Blumhardt correctly observes that, the "human trait of seeking divine revelation outside the realm of human experience has ruined all religions," including Christianity.[30]

God is to be discovered not in church sacraments, but in the sacrament of everyday life. The truth to which the Scripture testifies is true not merely for the church, but is true for the whole world. The gospel is public truth and requires the "public use of reason," which does not require institutional authorization in order to be influential and transformative.[31] Protestant Chris-

---

29. In the United Kingdom, several leading Baptist theologians have advocated a sacramentalist understanding of ministry. For a summary of these developments, see Fowler, *More Than a Symbol*. For reasons that will be apparent from my argument throughout this book, I regard this approach as a road to nowhere.

30. Blumhardt, *Gospel of God's Reign*, 21.

31. The term, "public use of reason," is taken from Immanuel Kant's 1784 essay, "What is Enlightenment?" Kant explained that, "By the public use of one's reason I understand the use which a person makes of it as a scholar before the reading public." Kant contrasted this with "private use of reason," by which he means, "that which one may make of it in a particular civil post or office which is entrusted to him." See Reiss,

tians claim to know what the "Word of God" is, but we often seem incapable of expressing it in the material reality of our lives and working in solidarity with society and the wider church. Protestant churches, in thrall to Christendom, have often exhibited an unhealthy preoccupation with the religious abstractions to the detriment of solving evident and concrete problems. As a result, evangelical Protestants generally know all too well what the "I" is, but do not know the "we." Despite our theoretical commitment to the doctrine of the Trinity and the communal context of individual salvation, our prayer and worship often reflect the me-and-Jesus spirituality that replicates much more the imported ideology of western individualism than it expresses the true values of the gospel.

Some theologians, swept up on a rising tide of modernity and secularization, have sought to preserve a distinctive ecclesial identity for Christianity by appealing to the self-sufficiency of the church and Christian tradition. Such endeavors have even resorted to assertions concerning the alleged primacy of Christendom. One such example is a movement known as Radical Orthodoxy, which posits the self-sufficiency of Christian tradition over and against the claims of secular reason and envisages "a recovery of the essentially sacramental, embodied nature of authentic Christian presence."[32] Theologians associated with Radical Orthodoxy define its aims in terms of reclaiming the world "by situating its concerns within a theological framework" that includes "the Trinity, Christology, the Church and the Eucharist."[33] Underlying the Radical Orthodoxy project is a suspicion— reminiscent of Karl Barth—of Enlightenment rationalism and a resistance towards the use of language derived from non-theological sources in order to defend the truth claims of Christianity. Within the discourse of Radical Orthodoxy, the world is degenerate and in the thrall of idols, whereas the church is idealized as the light on the hill, the Noah's Ark of redemption within a sea of sin and decadence.

Despite the laudable aspiration to be radical, the impulse of the movement is essentially bourgeois. Its thinkers also exhibit the Christendom tendency towards ecclesiocentrism at the expense of the theology of God's coming Kingdom. The main problem with Radical Orthodoxy, as critics have noted, is that it tends towards the idealization of the church and the sacramental understanding of ministry. The church is regarded not as a concrete reality in the world, but as an idealized entity that is abstracted from

---

Kant, 55.

32. Graham, *Rock and a Hard Place*, 117.

33. Milbank, Pickstock and Ward, *Radical Orthodoxy*, 1; quoted in Graham, *Rock and a Hard Place*, 118.

the world.[34] Radical Orthodoxy thus becomes content with the symbolic and liturgical expression of the gospel within the church, rather than with the concrete embodiment of the gospel within the world. As Russel R. Reno puts it:

> Radical Orthodoxy cannot invent the flesh and blood of a Christian culture, and so must be satisfied with describing its theoretical gestalt, gesturing in postmodern fashion, toward that which might be . . . Christian faith and practice must be raised to a level of purified abstraction so that it can be saved from its own failure to make Christ present in the Church and in society.[35]

In other words, Radical Orthodoxy, in common with Christendom more generally, is content to symbolize the gospel in sacramental gestures within church subcultures, but falls short of infusing social reality with the transforming power of the gospel. A more constructive approach is proposed by Elaine Graham, who, drawing on Jeremiah's prophecy, maintains in opposition to Radical Orthodoxy, that public theology in post-Christendom "is concerned primarily with 'the welfare of the city where I have sent you into exile, and pray to the Lord on its behalf, for in its welfare you will find your welfare.'" She claims that such a theology is "something conducted in solidarity with the secular, and concerned above all with the common good beyond the confines of the institutional Church."[36]

This underlies one of the main problems with Christendom: namely, that although the Christendom church was able to express the Kingdom of God symbolically and liturgically, it was generally incapable of actualizing the Kingdom as a material reality within the world. The official Church of Christendom was content to symbolize and simulate the Kingdom in liturgical signs, whereas true faithfulness to the gospel would have required a more material realization of the gospel. Within Christendom, as Berdyaev put it, "symbolic sacralization has substituted itself for the realization of Gospel commands."[37] Christian values of honesty, dignity, freedom, justice and compassion need to be inculturated and embedded not just in explicit church activities, but in the mundane realities that govern social and personal relations in the nation as a whole.[38] As the Russian reformer, Alexander Herzen (1812–1870), averred, "There will be no freedom in the

---

34. Graham, *Rock and a Hard Place*, 119.

35. Reno, quoted in ibid., 135.

36. Ibid., 213.

37. Berdyaev, quoted in Lowrie, *Christian Existentialism*, 269.

38. Searle, J., *Church without Walls*, 36.

world until what is religious and political are turned into what is human and simple."[39] The global Christian community of post-Christendom must therefore be content with nothing less than the enactment and actualization of the Kingdom of God as a tangible reality in the world, not in liturgy, dogma, and sacraments, but in the concrete realities of life. The same principle also applies to academic theology and theological formation, which must be concerned not with the formulation of concepts, but with the transformation of life.

Academic Theology and the Renewal of Theological Education

Education reform is crucial if the next generation of Christians is to be equipped for ministry and mission within post-Christendom. In light of the challenges confronting Christians in the post-Christendom transition, it seems necessary to give a new definition to the term, "theological education." One means towards the elucidation of the word, "education," is to consider how it can be translated from and into other languages. The English word, "educate," is derived from the Latin verb "*educere*," which connotes the bringing forth or realization of innate abilities or potentialities.[40] The less-common English word, "to educe" (to draw out or to extract something latent), shares the same etymological root. This notion of "drawing out" latent knowledge derives from Plato's influential theory of education as a process of recollection.[41] The knowledge acquired through education, according to Plato, was gained by matching conscious perception to latent memories.[42] Applied to human intellectual and moral formation, the term, "education," implies the flourishing of human beings through the careful nurture of the mind's latent abilities.

By contrast, the German term, *Bildung*, which is usually translated from the English "education," could also be translated as "formation." Other possible translations from the English, "education," include *Erziehung* (upbringing) and *Ausbildung* (instruction, training). Post-Christendom theology, which aims for the spiritual transformation of the character into Christlikeness, regards education in terms of *Bildung*. *Bildung*, according to one definition, refers to "the process through which a human being acquires the proper form of his or her humanity, as well as the product or the result

39. Herzen, quoted in Berdyaev, *Slavery and Freedom*, 190.
40. Mayes, *Spirituality in Ministerial Formation*, 64.
41. Scolnicov, *Plato's Metaphysics of Education*, 67–68.
42. Plato, *Meno*, 80d–81a.

of this formative process."[43] *Bildung* occupies an expansive semantic field within which other related concepts take root. According to the eminent German educationalist, Wolfgang Klafki (1927–2016), *Bildung* encompasses the Enlightenment notions of self-determination, freedom, emancipation, autonomy, objectivity, as well as the social values of solidarity and humanity.[44]

Similarly, the Russian word, *obrazovanie*, translated from the English "education" and the German *Bildung*, is derived from the word, *obraz*, meaning "form" or "image." Given that Russian theories of education in the twentieth century were dominated by Marxist ideology, the term, *obrazovanie*, tended to refer to the formation of consciousness and was regarded as a tool for building a communist society. Marxist educators were particularly cognizant of the ways in which social relations form people's consciousness.[45] As well as placing a premium on the reform of education (*Bildung* or *obrazovanie*) as the dominant priority in the anticipated new world of communist utopia,[46] Marx famously remarked that, "philosophers have only interpreted the world; but the real task is to change it."[47]

Accordingly, Marxist educationalists regarded education from a comprehensive perspective, as a social tool that "extends far beyond the classroom and the workshop into society, and indeed into the ways of thinking and perceiving human relationships of every kind."[48] For example in 1959, the Soviet Minister of Higher Education, Vyacheslav Yelyutin (1907–1993), wrote that "the role of Soviet education is to assist in the building up of a communist society; in shaping the materialist world outlook of the students; equipping them with a good grounding in the different fields of knowledge; and preparing them for socially useful work."[49] In view of their aim to transform the deep structures of consciousness according to communist principles of social engineering, Soviet Marxist theorists tended to substitute the older Russian words for education, *prosveshchenie* ("enlightenment") and *vospitanie* ("upbringing"), with the more ideologically-loaded term *obrazovanie* ("formation").[50] The methodologies pursued by Soviet pedagogues

43. Tongeren, "Measure and *Bildung*," 97.

44. Heide von Felden, *Bildung und Geschlecht*, 26–27.

45. Suchodolski, *Grundlagen der Marxistischen Erziehungstheorie*, 408–9.

46. Marx and Engels, *Manifest der Kommunistischen Partei*, 28.

47. Marx, *Theses on Feuerbach*, 123.

48. King, "The Concept of Ideology in Communist Education," in *Communist Education*, 1–2.

49. Yelyutin, *Higher Education in the USSR*, 41.

50. These distinctions in Russian higher education can be traced back to Catherine the Great, who ruled Russia between 1762 and 1796, as Anna Kuxhausen explains in

were remarkably effective in so far as they were directed towards people's material practices. Although the secular, atheistic, materialistic ideology of Marx-Leninism was shown to be fatally flawed, Christian educationalists might nevertheless be able to adapt some of the Soviet pedagogical principles in order to understand the importance not only of changing students' worldviews, but of transforming their material practices in ways that serve the building of the Kingdom of God, rather than the moribund idols of communism.

Understanding education in terms of *Bildung* and *obrazovanie* might also offer a much-needed corrective to the overemphasis on the concept of "worldview" in many Christendom-oriented models of theological education. Under the influence of North American approaches, many conservative evangelicals have posited the goal of Christian education in terms of "worldview transformation."[51] According to this interpretation, the aim of theological education is to change students' beliefs about the world. However, in light of our discussion concerning the priority of character formation over propositional belief, post-Christendom theology should be directed towards the transformation of students' pre-critical "convictions"[52] in a way that effects a comprehensive transformation of their material interaction with the world. Christianity, as Brian McLaren put it, should be thought of as "a way of believing," rather than as "a system of belief."[53]

The basic problem with an educational approach which has as its primary goal the induction of students into a Christian worldview, is that it is possible for learners to obtain intellectual cognition of Christian concepts in a way that does not shape their pre-critical orientation to life as embodied beings in the real world. Theology, maintains Sobrino, "has to do not only with *concepts*—philosophical, political, theological, biblical, or systematic—but with *realities*."[54] An over-reliance on "worldview" can lead to a reductive presentation of Christian faith as a system of propositional truth claims, rather than as a comprehensive mode of being that radically alters one's material participation in the world.[55] Theological education must be concerned not only with the "life of the mind,"[56] but also with the formation

---

her book, *From the Womb to the Body Politic*, 14–15.

51. Beckwith et al., *To Everyone an Answer*; Moreland and Craig, *Philosophical Foundations*; cf. Searle, J., "From Christian Worldview to Kingdom Formation," 104–15.

52. McClendon and Smith, *Convictions*; cf. McClendon, *Ethics*, 1–21.

53. McLaren, *New Kind of Christianity*, 8.

54. Sobrino, *Witnesses to the Kingdom*, 102.

55. Rollins refers to Christianity as "a radical transformation that alters one's mode of being in the world." See Rollins, *Fidelity of Betrayal*, 95.

56. Smith, *Desiring the Kingdom*, 18.

of hopes and passions. Theological formation involves the transfiguration of the imagination in ways that correspond to the Kingdom values of the gospel and which "evoke a radically transformed life of loving enemies, giving away worldly goods, and standing up against injustice."[57]

These reflections lead us to a definition of theological education that prioritizes holistic transformation of character over the impartation of certain skills and competencies. As Robert Banks rightly maintains, as well as offering "professional development," and "academic excellence," theological education is concerned most fundamentally with "spiritual formation."[58] Theological education is a spiritual process that leads to growth in grace and knowledge of Christ. It should aim, in the words of Whitehead to "suffuse knowledge with imagination."[59] Its goal is the comprehensive transformation of the character into the likeness of Christ. Students are formed to "put on Christ" (Rom 13:14; Gal 3:27). Students are novices or—to use Dallas Willard's terminology—"apprentices" in Christ's "master class of life."[60] As apprentices, students are learning about what it means to experience holistic transformation of their characters into the likeness of Christ. The emphasis is on spiritual formation, rather than intellectual comprehension or professional training. John Sullivan explains this key difference in these terms: "Formation is something much more all-enveloping than training; it involves simultaneously a way of believing, a way of behaving, a way of belonging and a way of worshipping."[61] To this helpful definition we can add that, most fundamentally, formation involves a new way of living.

The envisioning of theological education primarily in terms of character formation has even brought some theologians to the conclusion that the terms "education" and "moral formation" are practically synonymous. This is the approach of Stanley Hauerwas, who contends that, "all education, whether acknowledged or not, is moral formation."[62] This is a commendable insight, but it must also be emphasized that *theological* education both encompasses and transcends moral formation. Theological education is formation into the likeness of Christ in loving response to the promptings of the Holy Spirit, who brings people to rebirth and to a new revelation of the aesthetic and spiritual, as well as the moral dimension of life. Robert Banks rightly bewails the "failure to give the Spirit a central pedagogical role

---

57. Rollins, *Fidelity of Betrayal*, 100.

58. Banks, *Reenvisioning Theological Education*, 9.

59. Whitehead, *Modes of Thought*, 68.

60. Moon, *Eternal Living*, 26.

61. Sullivan, "Reading Habits," 222.

62. Hauerwas, *State of the University*, 46.

in theological education."[63] In post-Christendom there is a new recognition that theological education is primarily a pneumatological enterprise in so far as it is initiated, sustained and guided by the Holy Spirit.

Pedagogical wisdom begins with the recognition that all education, to the extent that it forms the human character, is a spiritual process. It is now widely recognized that, "Learning is not only about the acquisition of skills or knowledge; it is also about the formation and transformation of persons."[64] Authentic and enduring transformation requires a deep work of the Holy Spirit, assisted by appropriate spiritual disciplines that train the heart and mind in the virtues of compassion, gentleness, humility and grace that characterize life in the Kingdom of God. The transformation of the deep structures of consciousness is not just a pragmatic or technical issue concerning teaching methods or even the content of a curriculum; it also involves a spiritual transfiguration of the entire person into a "new creation" (2 Cor 5:17).

Such transformation involves not a programmatic conveying of facts or information, but the long and difficult work of the entire learning community working in solidarity towards the formation of students in the spiritual values of humanity, integrity, tolerance, courtesy and, above all, compassion. Witnessing this kind of transformation in one's students is the crowning glory of the teacher's endeavors. As a teacher of theology and philosophy, I have discovered that there is no greater privilege of teaching than seeing students thriving and flourishing and being transformed by their encounters with the truth as they are led to a depth of insight and awareness that changes the whole course of their lives and ministries, which in turn has a positive leavening effect on the wider society.

Christian Theology in the Academy

The basic aim of theology in the post-Christendom, post-secular West must be the spiritual regeneration of humankind through the realization of the Kingdom of God "on earth as in heaven." Such a regeneration depends on the recovery of a vision of unity that encompasses every aspect of life within an inclusive metaphysic of human existence. Post-Christendom theology asks the question about what it means to be human in terms of the postmodern emphases on authenticity, tolerance and respect for diversity. Such an emphasis on diversity is tempered by the quest for wholeness and

---

63. Banks, *Reenvisioning Theological Education*, 63.
64. Rae, "Learning the Truth," 101.

integrity which overcomes the divisive fragmentation and disunity of human life in the world today.

The trends of secularization and modernity have led to a fragmentation of intellectual life in contemporary post-Christendom. Science, philosophy, and theology have not only diverged, but have even been regarded as being in opposition to each other. The signs of our postmodern times indicate a renewed desire for integration between theology and philosophy. The fragmentation of human existence into polarized spheres (such as the spiritual and the social, the sacred and the secular, the religious and the political, etc.) must be overcome by a reorientation of the elements of life within a vision of the unity of all things. Post-Christendom theology should aim for what Solovyev called "a universal synthesis of science, philosophy and religion," leading to "the restoration of the inner unity of the intellectual world."[65]

The postmodern shift entails a transition "from a world-view premised on objective, pure reason to one of reflexivity and contextuality."[66] It has been argued that the emerging postmodern condition offers an opportunity to reconnect theology with science and philosophy, because these spheres of knowledge have in common a basic concern with the "discovery, understanding, and interpretation" of convictions.[67] Postmodernism has deconstructed the outwardly formidable but structurally vulnerable edifices of scientific materialism and has facilitated a new general awareness of mystery, spirituality and transcendence. Theology and philosophy are no longer hypnotized by the spell of omnicompetent science. Neither theologians nor scientists can appeal naively to objectivity, but must be sensitive to the ways in which knowledge depends on one's convictional perspective. McClendon thus proposes the notion of "convictions" as a new starting point for theological method. "Convictions," McClendon explains, are not the same as mere opinions or beliefs in so far as convictions "are less readily expressed but more tenaciously held. It may take me a long time to discover my own convictions, but when I do, I have discovered myself. My convictions are the gutsy beliefs that I live out—or in failing to live them out, I betray myself."[68] Convictions are a matter of habit-induced, conscience-forming, inarticulate and pre-critical assumptions concerning the deepest issues of life, faith and meaning. McClendon explains, "A conviction is a persistent belief such that if X (a person or community) has a conviction, it will not be easily aban-

65. Solovyev, quoted in Copleston, *Philosophy in Russia*, 214.

66. Graham, *Rock and Hard Place*, 106.

67. McClendon, *Ethics*, 23.

68. Ibid., 22.

doned and it cannot be abandoned without X making a significantly different person or community than before."[69] On the basis of this understanding
of convictions, McClendon offers the following definition of theology: "It
is the discovery, understanding or interpretation, the transformation of a
convictional community, including the discovery and critical revision of
their relation to one another and to whatever else there is."[70]

By taking convictions as its point of departure, this theological method
seeks to overcome the subject-object dualism that has characterized western
philosophy, theology, and science since at least the time of René Descartes
(1596–1640). Convictional perspectivism, as articulated by James McClendon, Nancey Murphy and others, attempts to dissolve the dualism between
the thinking subject and the passive object, by arguing that all understanding involves interpretation,[71] which is always and necessarily determined
by the personal commitment of the enquirer. This approach corresponds
with the hermeneutical theory of H. G. Gadamer (1900–2002), who located
understanding at the point of the interpretive fusion between the horizon of
the reader and the horizon of the text.[72]

Before theologians engage in any cognitive activity, they are immersed
in the depth of existence and embodied in narrative-formed traditions
which govern their precritical orientation towards the world. In the words of
the philosopher and mathematician, Blaise Pascal (1623–1662), "The heart
has its reasons that reason does not know."[73] Berdyaev expresses this idea lucidly when he contends that knowledge "is a spiritual act which involves not
only intellection, but also the concentration of the totality of man's spiritual
forces, of both his voluntary and sentient being . . . Intellection is an act and
not a passive reception of things; it endows the object with meaning, and
establishes a similitude, a common measure between the knowing subject
and the known object."[74] Theology is not a detached experimental method,
but is a passionate quest for transformative knowledge which pursues the
truth not in the domain of pure reason, but in the freedom of the spirit.

69. Ibid., 22.

70. McClendon, *Ethics*, 23.

71. Gadamer, *Gesammelte Werke: Volume 1*, 305–12.

72. Gadamer writes, "understanding is always the fusion of these horizons supposedly existing by themselves . . . In a tradition this process of fusion is continually going
on, for the old and new are always combining into something of living value, without
either being explicitly foregrounded from the other." See Gadamer, *Truth and Method*,
306.

73. "*Le cœur a ses raisons que la raison ne connaît point*"– Pascal, *Pensées*, 204.

74. Berdyaev, *Solitude and Society*, 11.

Theology thus aims at the transformation of material reality. The theologian should not be satisfied merely to understand and interpret the world, but should desire to transform, rejuvenate and regenerate it in the power of the spirit-inspired imagination.[75] Theology thus, in the words of McClendon, "represents something deeply self-involving for its adherents."[76] To this extent, theology has in common with science a pursuit of truth that depends on the passionate commitments of the inquirer. Nicholas Wolterstorff explains that,

> the practice of science is not some purely and generically human enterprise, nor some autonomous self-governing and self-sustaining enterprise; but an eminently concrete social-historical enterprise incorporating goals and standards and intuitions and values that people bring to it and that emerge from their interaction with each other after their induction into the practice.[77]

Twentieth-century philosophy, under the influence of the "postmodern condition,"[78] has problematized the assumption of neutrality and objectivity of all scientific knowledge. All knowledge relies upon a framework of implicit, *a priori* assumptions, which leading philosophers have variously described as "forms of life,"[79] "webs of belief,"[80] "fiduciary frameworks,"[81] "hermeneutical horizons,"[82] and "regimes of truth."[83] Sociologists have formulated these pre-critical assumptions in terms of "plausibility structures,"[84] whereas theologians have used the lexicon of "convictional perspectives,"[85] or "hermeneutic pre-understanding."[86] Whatever terminology is employed, theology in post-Christendom should be directed towards the transformation of these implicit assumptions and turning these towards the humanization of the world and the socialization of the gospel.

The theological academy should stand on the frontline in the cultural conflicts of our time and theology must be able to contribute to the

75. Marx, *Theses on Feuerbach*, 123.

76. McClendon, *Ethics*, 22.

77. Wolterstorff, quoted in Higton, *Theology of Higher Education*, 115.

78. Lyotard, *La Condition Postmoderne*.

79. Wittgenstein, *Philosophical Investigations*.

80. Van Orman Quine and Ullian, *Web of Belief*.

81. Polanyi, *Personal Knowledge*, 34–35.

82. Gadamer, *Wahrheit und Methode*.

83. Foucault, *Power/Knowledge*, 131.

84. Berger and Luckmann, *Social Construction of Reality*, 174.

85. McClendon and Smith, *Convictions*, 184.

86. Thiselton, *Hermeneutics of Doctrine*, 441.

renewal of contemporary society by bringing to light the "transcendent purposes" to which culture seeks to give expression.[87] Theology unmasks the self-contradictions and nihilism of secular materialism and gives lucid expression to the anastatic aspirations of the human condition. Theology in post-Christendom cannot make any presumptions about its right to be heard. "Religious voices," notes Elaine Graham, "have no automatic right to speak, given the nature of the secular pluralist realm. Public theology speaks into an increasingly contested and fragmented context."[88] Theologians must not appeal to authority, but will need to express their convictions in the language of debate and mutual respect.

In other words, theologians in post-Christendom must "be prepared to give an answer to everyone who asks you to give the reason for the hope that you have. But do this with gentleness and respect" (1 Pet 3:15). Likewise, when we talk to academic colleagues from other disciplines who have not yet come to know about the new life and hope in Christ, we should follow the advice of Paul, who encouraged us to "be wise in the way we act towards outsiders, making the most of every opportunity. Let your conversation be always full of grace, seasoned with salt, so that you may know how to answer everyone" (Col 4:5–6).

This kind of gentle persuasiveness recalls the example of Dallas Willard, who sought to present the truth of Christ to the gospel's cultural despisers through what he termed, "the allure of gentleness."[89] I learned from Dallas Willard (1935–2013), whom I was blessed to know personally, that to live in the reality of God's kingdom meant to exhibit a profound awareness of the world as a place pulsating with the mysterious presence and subtle activity of God. The Scriptures set out a vision of the world as a grand theatre in which God is living and active in redeeming the world through subtle—but deeply subversive and transformative—initiatives of divine compassion.[90] Willard helped me to grasp what Paul meant when he referred to Christ as the one "in whom are hidden all the treasures of wisdom and knowledge" (Col 2:3). Jesus, Willard reminded me, "is not just nice. He is brilliant. He is the smartest man who ever lived."[91]

Moreover, Willard as a formidable scholar and Christian philosopher, teaches us the crucial difference—often overlooked in many theology

---

87. Neuhaus, quoted in Stott, *Issues Facing Christians Today*, 42.

88. Graham, *Rock and a Hard Place*, 211.

89. Willard, *Allure of Gentleness*.

90. Willard referred to this as God's "cosmic conspiracy to overcome evil with good." See Willard, *Divine Conspiracy*, 103.

91. Willard, *Divine Conspiracy*, 109.

departments—between genuine knowledge on the one hand, and the academic ferment that is produced under the guise of "research," on the other. Describing the postmodern shift and its effect on the research goals of theology and philosophy faculties today, Willard observed that, "The process [of the loss of the Bible as a source of knowledge] historically culminates in a condition—*truly* the postmodern condition—where we do not have knowledge of knowledge, there is no acceptable truth about truth, and methodology is, with little exception, a matter of modish practice with no point of reference above the surrounding social flow."[92] What passes as research in this postmodern situation, is often determined by commercial forces and is directed not towards the discovery of knowledge, but is concerned merely to experiment with various interpretations and theories.[93] Willard called upon Christian theologians in the postmodern and post-Christendom West to rediscover the vocation of the university as a source of transformative knowledge that would translate into "practical wisdom." He envisaged the university as a scholarly community that aims "to find in knowledge a solid basis for action."[94] I am persuaded that Willard's call for the reformation of the theological academy needs to be heeded more than ever in this emerging post-Christendom era.

The Case for Public Theology in Post-Christendom

Within post-Christendom, Christian theology must be able to express itself publicly in non-violent and non-dogmatic forms. Christianity must find expression in creative, winsome, provocative and radical demonstrations of love that convey the gospel of life and hope to a culture of death and despair. Despite the seemingly inexorable decline of the institutional church in the West, the late twentieth and early twenty-first centuries have exhibited a strong remnant of religious belief within post-Christendom culture. This phenomenon has been described over the past twenty years in terms of "believing without belonging"[95] and "religion beyond the churches."[96] Other commentators have referred to "the present religious impulse,"[97] the

---

92. Willard, "Bible, the University and the God Who Hides," 30.

93. Ibid., 28.

94. Ibid., 17.

95. Davie, *Religion in Britain since 1945*.

96. Bruce, *Religion in Modern Britain*, 46.

97. Robinson, *Faith of the Unbeliever*, 69–73.

"desecularization of the world,"[98] and even the "spiritual revolution"[99] to describe the resurgence of interest in spirituality in Western society at the beginning of the twenty-first century. The resurgence of spirituality as a major transformative force in the public sphere has led notable philosophers, such as Jürgen Habermas and Charles Taylor, to speculate that the western world is entering a new "post-secular age."[100] Consequently, public space is no longer considered necessarily secular. Elaine Graham traces how "the emergence of post-secular society signals that the conventional demarcations of 'public' and 'private,' 'secular' and 'religious' are dissolving."[101] This means that for the church, the door is open. The current time of transition may be a particularly auspicious time for the church to engage with society.

The notion of public theology is based on the fundamental conviction that there is no sphere of human activity that is beyond the reach of the kingdom of God; the transforming power of the gospel penetrates the whole world with its redeeming light. For the Holy Spirit there are no "no-go" areas. One is just as likely to encounter God on the street, in the park, in the hospital, in the youth offenders' institution, in the orphanage, and in the care home, etc., as one is to meet Him in a church. God is active in the world for which He cares and provides.

This conviction that God cares for the whole world, rather than merely the Christian portion of it, underlies the Christian commitment to "seek the welfare of the city" (Jer 29:7). This may involve identifying points of synergy between the gospel and social and political movements that can be channeled towards the fulfilment of gospel imperatives, such as the establishment of righteousness and justice and the welfare and flourishing of all people, regardless of religious adherence or ethnic identity. To seek the welfare of the city means to bless the work of those social actors who are somehow involved in fulfilling God's purposes on earth. It may be the case that many of those who undertake such tasks do so anonymously without even realizing that they are participating in the *missio Dei*. Yet God delights in their work and they belong to Him, whether they are aware of this or not.

---

98. Berger, "The Desecularization of the World: A Global Overview," in Berger, *Desecularization of the World*, 1–18.

99. Heelas and Woodhead, *Spiritual Revolution*.

100. See, for example, the contributions of Taylor and Habermas in Mendieta and Vanantwerpen, *Power of Religion in the Public Sphere*.

101. Graham, *Between and Rock and a Hard Place*, 69.

8

Church without Walls

Post-Christendom Theology and the Renewal of Community

What is the Church?[1]

Post-Christendom creates opportunities for the reaffirmation of the gospel as public truth. Post-Christendom does not mean post-Christian or post-spiritual. In this new spiritual age, the church that will thrive and exert a leavening effect on the wider society will not be the institutional church of Christendom, but the church without walls of post-Christendom. This vision of church without walls is practically synonymous with the Kingdom of God, as depicted in the previous chapter.

The post-Christendom shift requires that Christians address with new urgency the question: "What is the church?" The English word, "church," is translated from the Greek, *ekklesia*, which contains two primary significations. The first part, *ek*, indicates "out from" or "out to," and the second part, *kaleo*, signifies "to call." In a strictly linguistic sense, therefore, the church is that which is "called out from or to" something. In Christian tradition, the term *ekklesia* has had two primary connotations: firstly, the church is the local community of believers gathered for the sake of worship and witness in a particular place; secondly, the church is the mystical body of Christ that constitutes the fulfillment of God's eternal plan of creation, redemption and glorification. Boff neatly summarizes that, "the Church is the encounter of

1. Much of this section is based on my reflections on the nature of the church in Searle and Cherenkov, *Future and a Hope*, 91–99.

the community of the faithful, an encounter prompted by Christ and the Spirit to celebrate, deepen faith, and to discuss the questions of the community in light of the Gospel."[2] It is significant that nowhere in the Gospels is there is any reference to the church as an organization or as a building.[3]

The church is both a visible and an invisible reality. The definitive expression of the meaning and nature of the church is to be found in the book of Revelation. The New Jerusalem of Revelation 21 represents a transfigured world and the fusion of the entire human community into a spiritual fellowship without barriers or dividing walls of any kind.[4] The church is a radical eschatological community: the church, as the people of God, constitutes "a spiritual house, a holy priesthood . . . a chosen generation, a royal priesthood, a holy nation, a peculiar people" (2 Pet 2:9). A universal priesthood requires a church without walls. If the Bible depicts the church against the backdrop of a "new heavens and a new earth" in which all barriers and separations have been abolished, why, then, is the reality of our contemporary church life at such variance to this biblical standard?

In post-Christendom, churches need a generous and inclusive vision that is focused on Christ and the teaching of Scripture, rather than on denominations and the philosophies and traditions that are based on devotion to sinful organizations or individuals. The focus should be on the biblical teaching of the redeemed humanity, particularly as depicted in the Gospels and elaborated in Revelation 21 and 22. A renewed focus on the eschatological vision of hope can serve as the theological point of departure for the church in post-Christendom.

One of the promises of the eschatological vision of the church without walls is that we will one day be able to perceive things as they really are (1 John 3:2). Walls are those barriers that prevent us from seeing things as they truly are. There are physical walls that block our view as well as walls of prejudice that close our minds and obstruct our worldviews, leading to sectarianism and dogmatism. The only cure for these ecclesial pathologies is the creation of communities of grace under the leading of the Holy Spirit. The vision of church without walls helps us to see that the central characteristics of the Holy Spirit are not signs, wonders, miracles or other spectacular manifestations of God's activity. These are important, but they are manifestations, rather than the presence or essence of the Holy Spirit. The crucial hallmark of the Holy Spirit is God's people living together peaceably in a community (κοινωνία) of mutual love (ἀγάπη).

---

2. Boff, *Church*, 155.

3. Bulgakov, *Bride of the Lamb*, 255.

4. Ibid., xvii.

In the accounts of Jesus's life in the Gospels, nowhere do we read that Jesus established a religious institution. In fact, quite the opposite is the case. Far from founding a religious institution based on order and hierarchy, He built a community in which the values of love, acceptance and hospitality were lived out in the context of a new order of existence made possible by the Kingdom of God. In fact, Jesus even explicitly discouraged this kind of hierarchical order and power relations that governed the "kings of the Gentiles" (i.e., the authorities that enforce the power systems of the world—see Luke 22:24–26). The Holy Spirit is active in the world, creating egalitarian communities of grace in which the Kingdom of God is manifested, not symbolically in dogma or rituals, but incarnationally in the material reality of everyday life. God—as Father, Son and Holy Spirit—has ordained community as His chosen means to build His Kingdom on earth.

In the first few centuries of its existence, the pre-Constantinian Christian church had a terrible reputation; it was hated, despised and even brutally persecuted by the rich and powerful in society. Under Christendom respectability was one of the walls that prevented the churches from fulfilling their vocation to make the gospel a visible reality in the world. A respectable church is a compromised church. Now that the western world is transitioning into post-Christendom, it is time that churches once again had a bad reputation, and for churches to become "communities of discernment and resistance," taking a stand against dominant cultural trends that impede the realization of God's Kingdom.

Radical witness for the sake of the Kingdom of God will inevitably incur the wrath of the ruling social powers, as Jesus himself warned (John 16:1–4). In witnessing faithfully to its calling in post-Christendom, the church without walls would follow the radical example of Jesus, who always valued relationships more than reputation to the point of being stigmatized by His religious and political enemies with the sneering sobriquet, "friend of sinners" (Luke 7:34). Jesus was not concerned about His reputation and neither should His church without walls today. Above all, the church without walls is a church that builds community and thus becomes the answer to Jesus's prayer that, "thy Kingdom come, thy will be done, on earth as it is in heaven" (Matt 6:10).

An Example of Church without Walls in Post-Christendom: The Northumbria Community

An illustration of what this church without walls looks like in practice is offered by new monastic communities, such as the Northumbria Community.

These communities welcome the advent of post-Christendom as an era of spiritual awakening. They recognize that Christians in post-Christendom are exiles in a foreign land. They are searching for an authentic expression of Christian living that will communicate the hope of the gospel in ways that are credible and compelling. New monastic expressions of Christian renewal embrace the monastic (from the Greek word, *monos*, "the one thing necessary"—Luke 10:42) call "to seek God, to sing His song in a strange land, and to ask how we might live as believers in a changing church and emerging culture."[5] Through its *Rule of Life*, which draws on the monastic and Celtic Christian traditions, the Northumbria Community seeks to pioneer an "uncompromising allegiance to the Sermon on the Mount"[6] that can serve as a paradigm of initiation into an alternative way of living, rooted in radical obedience to Christ. This alternative lifestyle aims self-consciously to engage with people who are disillusioned by the prevailing cultural alternatives of materialism and consumerism. This expression of Christian faith also has a growing appeal among burnt-out and disillusioned Christians who feel alienated from traditional expressions of church.

The Northumbria Community is an example of post-Christendom-incarnational theology in action. The Northumbria Community has sought to rediscover a "new type of monasticism" that would address three fundamental questions: "Who is it that you seek?," "How then shall we live?," and "How shall we sing the Lord's song in a strange land?" These questions informed the *Rule of the Northumbria Community*, which encompassed the values of "Availability" and "Vulnerability." Within the semantic field of the *Rule*, availability means simply "to be available to God" and "to be available to others in a call to exercise hospitality."[7] To embrace the vow of vulnerability involved, among other things, "speaking out when necessary or asking awkward questions that will often upset the status quo."[8]

The Public Theology of the Northumbria Community

The values and ethos of the *Rule* emerged organically out of the lived experience of the Community's origins and development. The Northumbria

---

5. Searle, J., "Northumbria Community in an age of cultural change and the decline of Christendom." Available online: http://www.northumbriacommunity.org/articles/northumbria-community-in-an-age-of-cultural-change-and-the-decline-of-christendom/.

6. Bonhoeffer, *Testament to Freedom*, 424.

7. Northumbria Community, *Way for Living*, 4.

8. Ibid., 5.

Community originated in the 1970s and grew rapidly throughout the 1980s and 1990s. The Community thus began to emerge at a critical point of intersection between two socio-cultural processes: the one, a widespread feeling among the British people of disillusionment with institutional expressions of church; and the other, a related process, which led to the rediscovery of neo-pagan spiritual practices connected with the emergence of the New Age movement.[9] These two processes took place against the backdrop of a significant cultural shift which has been traced throughout this book: namely, the transition from Christendom to Post-Christendom.

Moreover, the foundation of the Northumbria Community, which emphasised the saving power of the gospel and understood Christ as "the Way, the Truth and the Life" (John 14:6), coincided with the onset of a postmodern culture which inclined towards moral relativism and was suspicious of any tradition which purported to lay exclusive claims on the truth. Although the Northumbria Community was careful to guard its orthodox, trinitarian identity, its leaders sought to move beyond divisive doctrinal issues towards the unconditional welcome and hospitality, regardless of denominational affiliation or socio-cultural or religious background. Two of the Community's founder leaders, Roy Searle and John Skinner, explained that, "The Northumbria Community came into existence to provide companionship, coherence and community for those believers who have felt isolated by this crisis of faith; who, while honestly addressing their doubts and fears, still retain that fearful hope for human life in society, nurtured by their allegiance to Christ. Community development has been a direct response to this quest."[10]

The Community has always embraced a position of uncertainty and paradox; it aims to present a self-consciously counter-cultural challenge to the prevailing social attitudes and values, whilst simultaneously seeking to subvert those assumptions where they perceive a conflict with the peaceable and life-giving vision of God's Kingdom. One of the founders explains that, "We were seeking a spirituality that was firmly based in Christ but which provided a frame of reference to take us through the inner and outer changes happening all around."[11]

9. The New Age in this period was not a single homogeneous phenomenon, but a miscellany of various brands of paganism and unorthodox, alternative or occult spiritualities. Moreover, many adherents of New Age religions were, in the words of one commentator, "militantly anti-Christian." See Robinson, *Faith of the Unbeliever*, 73. Bainbridge describes the New Age movement as "a cultural fog bank" surrounding traditional religion. See Bainbridge, *Sociology of Social Movements*, 390.

10. Searle and Skinner, letter dated 30th January 1997, entitled, *Application to the London Bible House Research Fund*.

11. Miller, "Notes for an Official History of the Northumbria Community," 7.

Deriving inspiration from the ancient Celtic saints, most notably Aidan (d.651) and Cuthbert (c.634–687), who first evangelized the British Isles, the Community sought not merely to reform the church, but to transform the society according to their vision of God's Kingdom. The missional objectives of the Northumbria Community were formulated in the following statement: "Covenanted together in the love of Jesus, we are a group of Christian friends who share a common vision and concern to see God's Kingdom extended in the regions that are covered by the ancient Kingdom of Northumbria, from the Forth to the Humber."[12] Other mission statements expressed the need to communicate the Christian message to a spiritually confused society in terms of "carrying the torch of the gospel wherever the Father leads."[13]

This commitment to the public truth of the gospel set the Community on a collision course with a culture that exhibited the traits of scepticism and indifference towards the truth claims of the gospel. Rejecting the notion that all truth claims are relative, the Community sought to establish and affirm the continuing relevance and explanatory power of Christian faith within a religiously plural culture. The Midday Prayer of the Community which was integrated into the Community's Daily Prayer routine, includes a simple and forthright assertion of trinitarian orthodoxy:

> We believe and trust in God the Father almighty,
>
> We believe and trust in Jesus Christ His Son,
>
> We believe and trust in the Holy Spirit,
>
> We believe and trust in the Three in One.[14]

The prayer, however, did not end with this emphatic statement of faith, for the next section, based on Psalm 90, included an appeal to God for wisdom and guidance in the midst of the trivial round of each individual's common daily tasks:

> Teach us dear Lord, to number our days that we may apply our hearts unto wisdom . . . And let the beauty of the Lord our God be upon us and establish Thou the work of our hands, dear Lord.[15]

---

12. Searle, R., "Northumbria Ministries Charter."

13. Searle, R., "Northumbria Community Prayer Guide, November-December 1994."

14. Midday Prayer of the Northumbria Community. See, *Celtic Daily Prayer*, 20.

15. *Celtic Daily Prayer*, 21.

In their efforts to remain faithful to their Christian convictions, Companions and Friends[16] of the Community also aimed to respond sensitively and compassionately to the wider society. The Community did not seek to relate Christian truth claims to the wider culture in a static or dogmatic way, but aimed, instead, to discover a way of life which would be sufficiently flexible to allow spiritual seekers to find their own way of living in a religiously plural culture whilst remaining faithful to the first call of God on their lives. The leaders of the Community helped to pioneer a way of life which would enable people to respond to the wider culture without compromising on the central tenets of the Christian faith or the freedom of the gospel. The leaders of the Community stated that, "We want to emphasize that our rule does not prescribe; it provokes." The *Rule of Life*, accordingly, was created to be "deliberately flexible and adaptable, so that it does not prescribe uniformly, but provokes individually."[17]

The Northumbria Community's Incarnational Theology of Hope and Renewal

The Community self-consciously aimed to confer hope, meaning and hospitality in a society of despair, nihilism and indifference. This required a realistic assessment of the predicament of the Christian faith in an increasingly pluralistic society in which "Christianity is no longer taken for granted, or is a frame of reference."[18] One of the early leaders of the Community, Trevor Miller, observed that, "modern society is steeped in pluralism: everything is relative and anything may be considered acceptable . . . we have to recognise that what we call 'Biblical Christianity' is now perceived to be just another choice in today's world."[19] After discussing the rediscovery of transcendence and spirituality in contemporary society, Miller stated that, "the institutional Church, with its external trappings and traditional

16. Up until 1998, the Community operated a three-tier membership structure of Members, Companions and Friends. Concerns were raised, however, that the term, "Member," carried misleading connotations of membership of a club, the exclusivity of which was thought to contradict the ethos of the Community's commitment to Availability. The category of Member was therefore dropped and the levels of involvement were reduced to Companions and Friends, which remains the case at the time of writing. For a full account of the reasons behind the change, see Searle and Miller, *Northumbria Community Newsletter*, 1.

17. Northumbria Community, *Way for Living*, 8.

18. Skinner, document entitled, "The Post Christian Era and the Birth of a New Age," 2.

19. Miller, *Heretical Imperative*, 9–10.

expressions of Christianity, is often charged with playing a major role in the central problem associated with this spiritual search."[20]

Recognizing the unique challenges of postmodernism and post-Christendom, the Northumbria Community in the late 1990s began to explore the possibility of working in partnership with other Christian organizations which aimed to connect the gospel with society. In 1997, the Community partnered with the British and Foreign Bible Society in a project entitled, "Rediscovering the Johannine Tradition for a Postmodern Age." The Gospel of John, with its incarnational emphasis, was a constant source of inspiration as the Community continued to ask the fundamental question: "How then shall we live?" Explaining the motivation behind the initiative Roy Searle and John Skinner stated that that the Community was "seeking a language that can be heard, understood, intuited and appreciated in the reconstruction of society in the postmodern world. While we have been helped by the Desert/Celtic Traditions towards this goal, they have pointed us to another source from which they would claim their inspiration—the Tradition of St. John the Beloved. It is the rediscovery of this tradition that we believe will enable us to not only live hopefully but to speak clearly to a postmodern age."[21] The leaders of the Northumbria Community were aware of the need to articulate a cultural lexicon that would allow them to present an authentic Christian witness to the wider society whilst remaining faithful to the truth of the gospel.

The cultural lexicon adopted by the Community was determined not primarily by the demands and expectations of the wider culture, but by the intrinsic life of the Northumbria Community itself. The Community used terms which reflected its own vision of new monasticism. Such symbols of the early Celtic monastic tradition as "cell" and "coracle"[22] and "mission" and "monastery," were used by the Northumbria Community as metaphors for its witness to the world in the present age.[23] The "cell," or place of prayer, symbolized "aloneness before God," and life in the cell was used as a metaphor for a life of contemplation and attention to the inner life, known in Celtic tradition as the "landscape of the heart." This inward

---

20. Ibid., 5.

21. Searle and Skinner, letter addressed to The London Bible House Research Fund, entitled, "Rediscovering the Johannine Tradition for a Postmodern Age," dated 30th January 1997.

22. A coracle was a small round boat made of wickerwood and propelled with a paddle. The coracle, which was difficult to control and liable to be blown off course by an adverse wind, was a quite deliberate representation of the vulnerability of the believer in a state of complete abandonment to God.

23. Miller, "Some Metaphors Used in Our History."

aspect was counter-balanced by the symbol of the "coracle," which signified a preparedness, as one Community document put it, "to wander for the love of Christ."[24] The double emphasis on the cell and the coracle was reflected in the metaphors of "mission" and "monastery," which comprised the two fundamental components of the ethos and spirituality of the Northumbria Community.

Narrative Theology and Story-Formed Communities in Post-Christendom

The Community never sought to be a church or to provide an alternative to more mainstream expressions of church. Roy Searle wrote that, "The Northumbria Community which had its origins in the 1970s . . . is not an alternative church but a new monastic community that is part of and committed to the Church."[25] The Community therefore had a rather ambivalent relationship with both the church and the wider society insofar as it refused to be identified with either, but was nevertheless committed to the wellbeing of both.

Notwithstanding its renunciation of the label, "church," the Community did share some of the characteristics which one might typically associate with churches. Like most Christian monastic communities, the Northumbria Community understood the importance of ritual and symbol as a means of conferring a sense of common identity among its Friends and Companions. This was largely a response to the cultural context within which the Community found itself in the 1980s and 1990s. Jean-Francois Lyotard (1924–1998) famously claimed that one of the defining characteristics of the emerging postmodern condition was "incredulity toward metanarratives."[26] Attentive to the destruction of grand systems—such as the Judeo-Christian tradition, which had formerly supplied an interpretive framework within which to make sense of their experiences—that had taken place in this period, the leaders of the Community responded by exploring the possibilities of narrative theology. The leaders of the Northumbria Community recognized the potential of story as mediated through ritual, as a way of giving to their members a metanarrative which would confer meaning and identity within a Christian framework.

24. Searle, R., Untitled document (Northumbria Community Archive, 1994).

25. Searle, R., quoted in, Miller, "Official History," 59.

26. Lyotard, Postmodern Condition, xxiv. See also Browning, Lyotard and the End of the Grand Narratives.

This principle of narrative-formed meaning is apparent in the Northumbria Community's *Rule of Life*. The *Rule* states that, "The human spirit requires ritual. The stories we tell, the myths that shape us and give us meaning need to be acted out."[27] An indication of how seriously the Northumbria Community took the importance of story is the fact that in 1998, the Community set up a task-specific storytelling body, known as "The Telling Place." This initiative was launched by the Community in partnership with the British and Foreign Bible Society. Its first director was Roy Searle, a Baptist minister and one of the founders of the Northumbria Community. The aim of The Telling Place was to proclaim the "enduring story" of the gospel amid and in defiance of all the "endearing myths" of a postmodern society.[28]

The prophetic mandate of the Northumbria Community found expression in it story-telling ministry. In a sermon delivered in 2004 Searle further revealed his understanding of the importance of story: "People often ask me what I do for a living and I find it very difficult to say. I often feel like saying, Well, I tell stories and hear people's stories."[29] Another founder leader, John Skinner, in a sermon on "The New Age" delivered at a Mainstream conference in January 1994, defined the art of prophecy simply as "story-busting."[30] The emphasis on narrative was reflected in the activities and ethos of the Northumbria Community. Roy Searle remarked that, "What is imperative is that those of us who are called to this Way of Life . . . retain the story, keep telling it and living the life."[31]

For the Northumbria Community, theology is not an abstract concept, but is expressed in the life of Friends and Companions, not only in their church activities, but in the mundane activities of their everyday lives. This embodied and narrative-formed theology is expressed "by seeking to live out the story God has laid upon our hearts in the ordinariness and every day experiences of life, by offering the shattered fragments of our own brokenness and weakness to be used by God in speaking a word of hope in a fractured and changing world."[32] This focus on narrative is a constant theme of the Community's internal communications: "Let's live what we believe and

27. Raine, *Way for Living*, 9.

28. Searle, R., cited in Fancourt, *Brand New Church*, 48.

29. Searle, R., "Address at Holy Trinity Church Conference, Hothorpe Hall."

30. Skinner, "The New Age" (audiotape).

31. Searle, R., "Musings from the Garden," 4. *Caim* 10 (Summer 1999). *Caim* is the Northumbria Community newsletter. In the words of its former editor, *Caim* is "an in-house publication specifically addressed to Companions and Friends and those folk beginning to take an interest in the vision and vocation of the Northumbria Community." See Miller, "Editorial," *Caim* 9, p. 2.

32. Searle, R., "Covenanted Together within the Love of Christ," 5.

in living out the story that God has given, capture hope for our own hearts, for the church and for culture—all of whom cry out for transformation."[33]

The *Rule* of the Northumbria Community is embodied in a narrative; it is a story to live by. The *Rule* is clear that in order to become meaningful to people, this story needs to be "acted out"[34] in ordinary life; it is not enough simply to express the story in liturgical or sacramental form. The *Rule,* in the words of Andy Raine, another founder leader of the Northumbria Community, "has become our story. It is a story that needs to be lived out, not just talked about. The *Rule* continues to challenge our hearts and lives, as it is immediately relevant to real living."[35] The lived experience of the Northumbria Community offers an example of how narrative can be directed towards the renewal of Christian community amid the challenges and opportunities of the post-Christendom transition.

The narrative understanding of the Community's experience gives a perspective that is informed by the past, rooted in the present and hopeful about the future. Trevor Miller explains that, "The meaning and importance of our collective Memory and Story is highlighted as we recall and remember the covenant times of past years. These times are to be celebrated with thankfulness. They support us, re-energise us and encourage hope within us for our ongoing faith journey to see the kingdom extended in our hearts and in Northumbria and wherever the Father leads."[36] The "collective Memory and Story" of the Community gives rise to the promise that God will continue to bless their efforts in the future as He has done in the past. Speaking of the Northumbria Community's development and expansion, Miller notes that, "It never ceases to amaze us that God has taken such a diverse, struggling group of very ordinary people with nothing to offer but Availability and Vulnerability, and because of their deep desire to seek after God and be obedient to Him, has used them to bless so many lives. Why is this? Perhaps it's because we are pioneering a new way to live that has mirrored the heart's desire of many, sick of materialism and consumerism, for a different way to express the gospel."[37]

The Community has been successful in connecting with people because of the way in which it embodies a radical vision of life in God's

33. Searle, R., "Jottings From A Ferry Over to Ireland," 2.

34. Northumbria Community, *Way for Living,* 9.

35. Raine, quoted in Searle, *"Northumbria Community in an age of cultural change and the decline of Christendom."* Available online: https://www.northumbriacommunity.org/articles/northumbria-community-in-an-age-of-cultural-change-and-the-decline-of-christendom.

36. Miller, "Easter Workshop 2005," 3.

37. Miller, "Editorial," 2.

Kingdom which engages with people who are disillusioned by the prevailing cultural alternatives of materialism and consumerism. The *Rule of Life* presents a vision of an alternative way for living that gives perspective on the present and hope for the future. By setting out its convictions in a clear and resolute, though non-dogmatic, manner, the Northumbria Community enables people in the midst of a relativistic, anxiety-ridden culture to respond with the defiant and hope-filled proclamation: "The Lord is my light, my salvation; whom shall I fear?" (Ps 27:1).[38]

Narrative Theology and Covenant Communities

New monastic movements, such as the Northumbria Community, correspond to what Alasdair MacIntyre referred to as those "new forms of community within which the moral life could be sustained so that both morality and civility might survive the coming ages of barbarism and darkness."[39] MacIntyre concludes his influential study, *After Virtue*, with an appeal to rediscovery of the true meaning of moral and spiritual communion:

> What matters at this stage is the construction of local forms of community within which civility and the intellectual and moral life can be sustained through the new dark ages which are already upon us. And if the tradition of the virtues was able to survive the horrors of the last dark ages, we are not entirely without grounds for hope. This time however the barbarians are not waiting beyond the frontiers; they have already been governing us for quite some time. And it is our lack of consciousness of this that constitutes part of our predicament. We are waiting not for a Godot, but for another—doubtless very different—St. Benedict.[40]

MacIntyre has argued persuasively that in an age of moral fragmentation there is a great need to rediscover the concepts of virtue, tradition, and community. Stanley Hauerwas, James McClendon and Nancey Murphy and many others have made extensive use of MacIntyre's concept of virtue ethics and applied it to the life of the contemporary Christian faith community. MacIntyre maintains that, "The story of my life is always embedded in the story of those communities from which I derive my identity."[41] Hauerwas

38. This phrase is taken from the Evening Prayer of the Northumbria Community and is based on Psalm 27. See *Celtic Daily Prayer*, 24.

39. MacIntyre, *After Virtue*, 263.

40. Ibid., 264.

41. Ibid., 221.

concurs that community is important because "we become who we are through the embodiment of the story in the communities in which we are born."[42] The story of our communities helps us "to locate ourselves in relation to others, our society, and the universe."[43] The Northumbria Community, whose members cohere around a common tradition-formed identity and participate in shared practices of prayer and the exercise of hospitality according to the moral expectations that are laid out in its *Rule of Life*, could be said to constitute an example of a "form of community within which the moral life could be sustained," as described by MacIntyre.[44]

What, therefore, is the meaning of community from the perspective of new monastic communities like the Northumbria Community? It is a free and intentional association of Friends and Companions, whose common life aspires to embody the values of God's Kingdom and to pass on a living tradition that extends from one generation to the next. During a crucial time of transition, one of the founder leaders of the Community wrote that, "We are now handing down the story God has given us to a new generation of people who weren't part of the Community's early days but who have nevertheless been called by God to share in the same vocation and journey with us."[45]

Out of the sense of shared vocation and the inter-generational continuity of the vision, a distinct communal identity emerges. In the same way that Hauerwas and others have argued that community is essential to one's theological identity, the Northumbria Community likewise gives its members an identity as people are initiated through a "novitiate process" as Friends and Companions. The sense of belonging to the community is expressed in a shared commitment to *the Rule* of Availability and Vulnerability, out of which arises a community of people "covenanted together within the love of Christ."[46] One of its founders thus defined the Northumbria Community as "a story of people whom God has brought together . . . journeying together in the heart, forming covenant relationships."[47]

42. Hauerwas, *Community of Character*, 148–9.

43. Hauerwas, quoted in Aku, *Redefining Community*, 215.

44. MacIntyre, *After Virtue*, 264.

45. Searle, R., "Musings from the Garden," 4.

46. These words form part of the original charter of a community called Northumbria Ministries, which later joined with another community called the Nether Springs Trust to become what is now known today as the Northumbria Community. See, Searle, R., "Northumbria Ministries Charter" (Northumbria Community Archive, 1989).

47. Searle, R., document entitled, "Exploring a Way for Living" (Northumbria Community Archive, 1999), 1.

For the Northumbria Community the notion of community is important not merely as the carrier of a certain social identity or as the locus of moral growth; it is also an expression of the hope that the Community can be a foretaste of the fullness of life in the Kingdom of God, which is the anticipated culmination of the divine grand narrative in which they participate. There is a recognition that this story is unfinished, but the anticipation of the end of the story enables Companions and Friends to look to the future with hope. Since it is based on a future anticipation of God's people united and redeemed by the love of Christ, the meaning of community in the context of Northumbria could be described as the embodiment of a hopeful narrative that is passed down through the generations as a living tradition.

The Northumbria Community is just one of many new monastic expressions emerging across Europe and North America. The Northumbria Community seeks to embody the light and hope of the gospel in the midst of a changing culture through a disciplined and radical appropriation of monastic practices that are aimed not only at the renewal of the church, but also the transformation of society. The Northumbria Community's experience of living as a pilgrim people in cultural exile amid a rapidly changing society reminds us that the integrity of our witness to the Kingdom of God requires a full integration of life, community and mission.

There are signs that even the established churches are beginning to perceive the value of new monastic renewal movements, such as the Northumbria Community. The Rt. Rev. John Pritchard, former Bishop of Oxford, who has observed the Community over many years, has noted that, "The Northumbria Community occupies an interesting "Third Space," which is not the long established denominations and their traditional monastic communities . . . One of the gifts of the Northumbria Community to the body of Christ today is that it is rooted through its thirty years of exploration, and yet at the same time it is also still seen to be experimental and prophetic." I am persuaded that the new monastic movement will make a decisive contribution to the preservation of the gospel values of civility and compassion. Although they were generally marginalized by Christendom, the advent of post-Christendom presages the dawn of a new era in which prophetic communities of grace will bring transformation and renewal. The new monastic vision of the Christian life will become increasingly relevant and transformative as western society descends further into destructive spirals of dehumanization and fragmentation.

Conclusion

Looking to the Future with Hope

The key differences between Christendom and post-Christendom theology can be expressed in the following way: theology during Christendom was concerned with articulating a true way of believing in accordance with a doctrinally correct understanding of God; theology in post-Christendom is concerned with embodying the truth of God by living in accordance with the vision inspired by the world-changing events of incarnation, crucifixion and resurrection.[1] Theology in post-Christendom is charged with the task of awakening what Boff calls "the dangerous yet powerful memory of the life, death and resurrection of Jesus Christ."[2] The truth of this "dangerous memory" to which theology testifies must be embodied, rather than simply articulated.[3] This memory should spark the imagination towards the creative discovery of a true vision of humanity in a post-Christendom society. Theology in a post-Christendom key should be directed towards the elucidation of what it means to be human in the world today. In the current consumer-driven world in which everything from spirituality to sex is turned into a commodity and human beings are reduced to units of production, there is a new desire for authenticity and depth and a vision of human personhood that is rooted in compassion.

Given these profound issues of dignity, justice and compassion (which are clear biblical imperatives), the post-Christendom world needs a prophetic theology that can raise its voice against social trends that obstruct the coming of God's Kingdom. Christian spirituality is necessarily an embodied spirituality that transforms material reality. A new theology is needed which recognizes that social responsibility, justice, truth, freedom, solidarity, and working for the transformation of society are not merely social justice

1. Rollins, *Insurrection*.
2. Boff, *Church*, 48.
3. Banks, *Reenvisioning Theological Education*, 172.

issues, but are also gospel and spiritual issues. Such a reenvisioning of theology can ensure that our current post-Christendom era does not descend into a non-Christian era.

These are indeed momentous times. A great and dark shadow is descending over the world. The lights of compassion and kindness are going out in all corners of the earth. The forces of evil are re-energized and the "powers and principalities" (Eph 6:12) are unleashed in all their destructive fury. Humanity is experiencing a collective dark night of the soul, which expresses itself in a "crisis of compassion." This is perhaps inevitable, for before the joy of Easter, the world must pass through the pain and desolation of Good Friday. It may even seem that the world is passing through its twilight period and entering the darkness of a universal night. But amid the prevailing darkness, the everlasting light still shines, summoning God's people to repentance and onto faith and courage. Inspired by this hope, we must persevere amid the adversity of the great spiritual struggle of our times. The global Christian movement must continue to search for compassionate and creative solutions to the great issues of our times.

We must persist in these endeavors, because the alternative is too fearsome even to contemplate. If no resolution can be found, if Christianity cannot become the new humanizing locus of contemporary culture, if no means can be found to nurture compassion, solidarity and love over the elemental impulses of hatred and aggression, then the likely result will be a war on a truly global scale, the destructive consequences of which will exceed even the most devastating genocidal episodes in all human history.

These momentous times call for the raising up of a new generation of prophets, of women and men of God who can address the crisis of compassion through creative and subversive acts of courageous love. The prophet whose heart burns with compassion will be heard; the systematic theologian whose brain is full of high-minded theories about "sound doctrine" and "Christian worldviews" will be ignored. The visionary prophet whose passion is kindled by the suffering of her fellow human beings will bring transformation and healing to the world; the theologian-bureaucrat who is preoccupied with sustaining a church institution will collude in the spiritual decline and degradation of the world.

The question thus arises: Why is all this important? Knowing about these challenges, why should we move forward? The answer is simple: because we need to transform our Christianity. Christianity stands in need, not only of renewal and restoration but of resurrection and transfiguration. Christendom has died and our hope now rests on the resurrection of Christianity as a spiritual movement for the transformation of the world. The Christendom project has failed. The ignominious demise of institutional

Christianity heralds the birth of a new movement of the Holy Spirit, unshackled from the deadweight of pseudo-Christian tribalism and dogmatism. In the same way that the seed cannot produce new life unless it falls into the ground and dies, so it is that the old order of Christendom must perish in order to generate a new Christian movement of universal compassion and solidarity that transforms the world in the power of the Holy Spirit. Berdyaev said with great truth that, "Death must occur in order for new life to arise. The world and humankind are being crucified. But the last word will belong to the Resurrection."[4]

Today, the light of Christ's gospel flickers like the flame of a candle in a musty old church, but it does not set the world on fire with the all-consuming love of God. Christendom has entombed Christ within church structures. The fire of the gospel has turned to stone, petrified into moribund forms that quench the Holy Spirit. Christendom is on its way out. The period of transition is already upon us. The apparent "glory days" of Christendom are gone and they will not return. We must set our gaze on the future. We cannot afford to look back nostalgically to the past. We cannot consider our present situation and pretend that all is well. Let us not be deceived by the false prophet who cries, "peace, peace," when there is no peace (Jer 6:14; Ezek 13:10). The world is changing and Christendom is dying. All that has remained is a dismal legacy of nominal religiosity that has divided the church into competing tribes of conflicting doctrines and institutional identities.

Albert Einstein (1879–1955) is credited with having said that, "insanity is doing the same thing over and over again and expecting different results." We need radical solutions to solve deeply entrenched problems. In the same way that it is impossible to change the flow of a river by throwing pebbles into it, so is it futile to assume that simply reading the Bible more diligently or praying more fervently will change the spiritual course of the world. We need not larger pebbles, but the creative and skillful creation of new canals, diverting the current into life-giving channels that will redirect the spiritual course of the world towards the living waters of Christ and His gospel of grace.

A day is coming when Christians will finally realize that they are sent by God not to serve and sustain the church, but to redeem the world in the power of Christ's compassion. In the coming years, we will witness a flowering of solidarity among diverse Christians as the walls of denominationalism and sectarianism come crashing down. Tribal identities will evaporate like the morning dew in the light of God's glorious new order in which all

---

4. Berdyaev, *Ekzistentsialnaya Dialektika*, 509.

who follow Jesus will come to see that they are one in Christ. Instead of institutionalized religion, there will be a gospel movement of compassion that expresses itself in a new vision of church without walls. And God will delight in this.

In the end, our hope depends on not on our own efforts, but on the faithfulness of God and His promise to give us a future and a hope. We can plant and water as best we can, but it is God who must give the increase (1 Cor 3:16). As theologians we are just playing our part. We may have the privilege to be partners or "co-workers" (1 Cor 3:9) with God in His great plan of redeeming the world, but we will always be the junior partners. When all has been said and done, we should expect no reward, but should simply say: "we are unprofitable servants: we have done only that which was our duty to do" (Luke 17:10). As we take a leap of faith into the new world of post-Christendom, we should have full confidence in our God, "who is able to do immeasurably more than all we ask or imagine, according to His power that is at work within us" (Eph 3:20).

Bibliography

Abel, Günter. *Nietzsche: die Dynamik der Willen zur Macht und die ewige Wiederkehr.* Berlin: de Gruyter, 1998.

Adams, Nicholas. *Eclipse of Grace: Divine and Human Action in Hegel.* Oxford: Wiley-Blackwell, 2013.

Aguilar, Mario I. *Religion, Torture and the Liberation of God.* London: Routledge, 2015.

Aku, Edmund. *Redefining Community: A Discourse on Community and the Pluralism of Today's World with Personalist Underpinnings.* Berlin: Peter Lang, 2000.

Alison, J. *Living in the End Times: The Last Things Re-Imagined.* London: SPCK, 1997.

Anglican House of Bishops. *The Eucharist: Sacrament of Unity.* London: Church House, 2001.

Archbishops' Council and the Trustees for Methodist Church Purposes, *Fresh Expressions in the Mission of the Church.* London: Church House, 2012.

Aristotle. *Metaphysics.* Translated by H. Lawson-Tancred. London: Penguin, 1998.

Attwater, D., *Modern Christian Revolutionaries: Kierkegaard, Eric Gill, G. K. Chesterton, C. F. Andrews and Berdyaev.* New York: Devin-Adair, 1947.

Augustine. *The City of God.* Translated by M. Dods. New York: Random House, 1950.

Austin, John L. *How to Do Things with Words.* Oxford: Oxford University Press, 1975.

Bainbridge, William S. *The Sociology of Social Movements.* New York: Routledge, 1997.

Ball, Les. *Transforming Theology: Student Experience and Transformative Learning in Undergraduate Theological Education.* Eugene, OR: Wipf and Stock, 2012.

Balthasar, Hans Urs von. *Gottbereites Leben: Der Laie und der Rätestand: Nachfolge Christi in der heutigen Welt.* Einsiedeln: Johannes Verlag, 1993.

Balthasar, Hans Urs. *Man in History: A Theological Study.* Translated by W. G. Doepel. London: Sheed and Ward, 1982.

Banks, Robert. *Reenvisioning Theological Education: Exploring a Missional Alternative to Current Models.* Grand Rapids: Eerdmans, 1999.

Barrow, John D. *Impossibility: The Limits of Science and the Science of Limits.* Oxford: Oxford University Press, 1998.

Barth, Karl. *Evangelical Theology: An Introduction.* Grand Rapids: Eerdmans, 1979.

———. *The Faith of the Church: A Commentary on the Apostles' Creed According to Calvin's Catechism.* Eugene, OR: Wipf and Stock, 2006.

Bauman, Zygmunt. *Modernity and the Holocaust.* Cambridge: Polity, 1989.

Bauman, Zygmunt, and Leonidas Donskis. *Moral Blindness: The Loss of Sensitivity in Liquid Modernity.* Cambridge: Polity, 2013.

Beckwith, Francis, et al. *To Everyone an Answer: A Case for the Christian Worldview.* Downers Grove, IL: InterVarsity, 2004.

Berdyaev, Nikolai. *Christian Existentialism: A Berdyaev Anthology,* edited by D. A. Lowrie, London: Allen and Unwin, 1965.

———. *Ekzistentsialnaya Dialektika Bozhestvennogo i Chelovecheskogo.* Moscow: Astrel, 2011.

———. *The Destiny of Man.* Translated by N. Duddington. London: G. Bles, 1959.

———. *The Divine and the Human.* London: G. Bles, 1947.

———. *Dream and Reality: An Essay in Autobiography.* London: G. Bles, 1950.

———. *Dukh i Realnost.* Minsk: Izdatelstvo Belorusskogo Ekzarkhata, 2011.

———. *The End of Our Time.* Translated by D. Attwater. New York: Semantron, 2009.

———. *The Fate of Man in the Modern World.* Translated by D. A. Lowrie. Ann Arbor, MI: Michigan University Press, 1961.

———. *Istoki i Smysl Russkogo Kommunizma.* St. Petersburg: Azbuka, 2016.

———. *O Rabstve i Svobode Cheloveka.* Paris: YMCA, 1939.

———. *Russkaya Ideya.* Moscow: Astrel, 2002.

———. *Samopoznanie: Opit Filosofskoi Avtobiografii.* Moscow: Mir Knigi, 2010.

———. *Self-Knowledge: An Essay in Autobiography.* Translated by Katharine Lampert. San Francisco: Semantron, 2009.

———. *Slavery and Freedom.* Translated by R. M. French. London: G. Bles, 1944.

———. *Smysl Tvorchestva.* Moscow: Astrel, 2011.

———. *Solitude and Society.* Translated by G. Reavey. London: G. Bles, 1938.

———. *Tsarstvo Dukha i Tsarstvo Kesarya.* Moscow: Respublika, 1995.

Berger, Peter. "The Desecularization of the World: A Global Overview." In *The Desecularization of the World: Resurgent Religion and World Politics,* edited by P. Berger, 1–18. Grand Rapids: Eerdmans, 1999.

Berger, Peter, and Thomas Luckmann. *The Social Construction of Reality.* New York: Doubleday, 1966.

Bergson, Henri. *Creative Evolution.* New York: Henry Holt. 1911.

Berlin, Isaiah. *Against the Current: Essays in the History of Ideas.* Princeton, NJ: Princeton University Press, 2013.

Berman, Morris. *The Reenchantment of the World.* Ithaca, NY: Cornell University Press, 1981.

Bevans, S. B., and R. P. Schroeder. *Constants in Context: A Theology of Mission for Today.* Maryknoll, NY: Orbis, 2004.

Blankertz, Stefan. *Die Katastrophe der Befreiung: Faschismus und Demokratie.* Berlin: BoD, 2015.

Blumhardt, C. F. *Everyone Belongs to God.* Robertsbridge: Plough, 2015.

———. *The Gospel of God's Reign: Living for the Kingdom of God,* Translated by P. Rutherford et al. Eugene: Wipf and Stock, 2014.

Boda, Mark J. and Gordon T. Smith, eds. *Repentance in Christian Theology.* Collegeville, NY: Liturgical Press, 2006.

Boesak, Allan A. *Comfort and Protest: The Apocalypse of John from a South African Perspective.* Eugene: Wipf and Stock, 2015.

Boff, Leonardo. *Christianity in a Nutshell.* Maryknoll, NY: Orbis, 2013.

———. *Church: Charism and Power.* New York: Crossroad, 1988.

———. *Die Wahrheit ist größer: Der Weg eines unbequemen Theologen.* Regensburg: Topos, 2016.

———. *Essential Care: An Ethics of Human Nature*. Translated by A. Guilherme. London: SPCK, 2007.

———. *Fundamentalism, Terrorism and the Future of Humanity*. Translated by A. Guilherme. London: SPCK, 2006.

———. *Global Civilization: Challenges to Christianity and Society*. London: Equinox, 2003.

Bolger, Ryan K., ed. *The Gospel after Christendom: New Voices, New Cultures, New Expressions*. Grand Rapids: Baker, 2012.

Bonhoeffer, Dietrich. *The Cost of Discipleship*. Translate by R. H. Fuller and I. Booth. London: SCM, 1959.

———. *Ethics*. Translated by N. H. Smith. London: SCM, 1995.

———. *Letters and Papers from Prison*. London: SCM, 1967.

———. *A Testament to Freedom: The Essential Writings of Dietrich Bonhoeffer*. Edited by G. B. Kelly and F. B. Nelson. New York: HarperOne, 1995.

Borg, Marcus J. *Convictions: A Manifesto for Progressive Christians*. London: SPCK, 2014.

Bosch, *Transforming Mission: Paradigm Shifts in Theology of Mission*. Maryknoll, NY: Orbis, 1991.

Brackley, Dean. "Theology and Solidarity: Learning from Sobrino's Method." In *Hope and Solidarity: Jon Sobrino's Challenge to Christian Theology*, edited by Stephen J. Pope, 3–15. Maryknoll, NY: Orbis, 2008.

Braidotti, Rosi. *The Posthuman*. Cambridge: Polity, 2013.

Brown, Dan. *The Da Vinci Code*. London: Bantam, 2003.

Browning, *Lyotard and the End of the Grand Narratives*. Cardiff: University of Wales Press, 2000.

Bruce, Steve. *Religion in Modern Britain*. Oxford: Oxford University Press, 1995.

Brueggemann, Walter. *The Prophetic Imagination*. Louisville, KY: Fortress, 2001.

Buber, Martin. *I and Thou*. Translated by W. Kaufmann. New York: Scribner, 1970.

Bulgakov, Sergius. *The Bride of the Lamb*. Translated by Boris Jakim. Grand Rapids: Eerdmans, 2002.

———. *The Lamb of God*. Translated by Boris Jakim. Grand Rapids: Eerdmans, 2007.

Cage, John. *X: Writings '79–'82*. Hanover, NH: University Press of New England, 1983.

Calvin, John. *Institutes of the Christian Religion*, edited by J. T. McNeill. Louisville, KY: Westminster John Knox, 1960.

Caputo, John D. *The Prayers and Tears of Jacques Derrida*. Bloomington, IN: Indiana University Press, 1997.

———. *What Would Jesus Deconstruct?: The Good News of Postmodernism for the Church*. Grand Rapids: Baker, 2007.

Carpenter, Joel A. "The Mission of Christian Scholarship in the New Millennium." In *Faithful Learning and the Christian Scholarly Vocation*, edited by Douglas V. Henry and Rob R. Agee, 62–74. Grand Rapids. Eerdmans, 2003.

Carroll, James. *Constantine's Sword: The Church and the Jews*. New York: Mariner, 2002.

Carter, Craig A. *Rethinking Christ and Culture: A Post-Christendom Perspective*. Grand Rapids: Brazos, 2006.

Cavanaugh, William T. *Torture and Eucharist: Theology, Politics and the Body of Christ*. Oxford: Blackwell, 1998.

Chawla, Navin. *Mother Teresa: The Centenary Edition*. London: Penguin, 1998.

Chesterton, G. K. *The Collected Works of G. K. Chesterton,* Vol. 2. San Francisco: Ignatius, 1986.

Cobb, John and David Ray Griffin. *Process Theology: Introductory Exposition.* Louisville, KY: Westminster John Knox, 1976.

Cone, James. *A Black Theology of Liberation.* Philadelphia, PA: J. B. Lippincott, 1970.

Copleston, Frederick C. *Philosophy in Russia: From Herzen to Lenin and Berdyaev.* Wellwood: Search, 1986.

Corduan, Winfried. *Mysticism: An Evangelical Option?* Eugene, OR: Wipf and Stock, 2009.

Cox, Harvey. *The Future of Faith.* New York: HaperCollins, 2011.

———. *The Secular City: Secularization and Urbanization in Theological Perspective.* Princeton, NJ: Princeton University Press, 2013.

Cox, Harvey, and Daisaku Ikeda. *The Persistence of Religion: Comparative Perspectives on Modern Spirituality.* London: Tauris, 2009.

Critchley, Simon. *The Ethics of Deconstruction: Derrida and Levinas.* Edinburgh: Edinburgh University Press, 2014.

Crowley, Paul G. "Theology in the Light of Human Suffering: A Note on Taking the Crucified Down from the Cross." In *Hope and Solidarity: Jon Sobrino's Challenge to Christian Theology,* edited by Stephen J. Pope, 16–30. Maryknoll, NY: Orbis, 2008.

Davie, Grace. *Religion in Britain since 1945: Believing Without Belonging.* Oxford: Blackwell, 1994.

Davies, O. *Theology of Transformation: Faith, Freedom and the Christian Act.* Oxford: Oxford University Press, 2013.

Davy, M. M. *Nicolas Berdyaev: Man of the Eighth Day.* London: G. Bles, 1967.

D'Costa, Gavin. *Theology in the Public Square: Church, Academy and Nation.* Oxford: Blackwell, 2005.

Deane, Jennifer Kolpacoff. *A History of Medieval Heresy and Inquisition.* Plymouth: Rowman & Littlefield, 2011.

De Gruchy, Steve. "Theological Education and Missional Practice: A Vital Dialogue." In *Handbook of Theological Education in World Christianity,* edited by D. Werner et al., 42–50. Oxford: Regnum, 2010.

De Lubac, Henri. *Paradoxes of Faith.* Paris: Livre Français, 1946.

———. *The Church: Paradox and Mystery.* Translated by J. R. Dunne. New York: Alba House, 1969.

De Luca, Vincent Artur. *Words of Eternity: Blake and the Poetics of the Sublime.* Princeton, NJ: Princeton University Press, 1991.

Dixon, Patricia. *Nietzsche and Jung: Quest for Wholeness.* Bern: Peter Lang, 1999.

Dostoevsky, Fyodor. *Bratya Karamazovy.* Moscow: Bertelsmann Media, 2011.

———. *The Brothers Karamazov.* Translated by C. Garnett. Ware: Wordsworth Classics, 2007.

Dubrovskij, A. "Fundamentalizm kak tormozjashhij faktor v razvitii evangelskih tserkvej postsovetskogo perioda." *Forum* 20 (2011) 27–45.

Duraisingh, Christopher. "Toward a Postcolonial Re-visioning of the Church's Faith, Witness, and Communion." In *Beyond Colonial Anglicanism: The Anglican Communion in the Twenty-First Century,* edited by Kwok Pui-Lan, Ian T. Douglas, 337–67. New York: Church Publishing, 2001.

Eagleton, Terry. *Culture and the Death of God.* New Haven, CT: Yale University Press, 2014.

Eliot, T. S. "Burnt Norton." In *The Complete Poems and Plays*. London: Faber and Faber, 2004.

Ellacuría, Ignacio. "The Crucified People." In *Mysterium Liberationis: Fundamental Concepts of Liberation Theology*, edited by I. Ellacuria and J. Sobrino, 580–603. Maryknoll, NY: Orbis, 1993.

———. "Discernir los signos de los tiempos," *Diakonía* 17 (1981).

———. *El Pueblo Crucificado: Ensayo de Soteriología Histórica*. Mexico: CRT, 1978.

Estep, James R. "The Role of Developmental Theories in Christian Formation." In *Christian Formation: Integrating Theology & Human Development*, edited by Estep et al. Kindle ebook. Nashville, TN: B & H Academic, 2010.

Eusebius, *The History of the Church from Christ to Constantine*. Translated by G.A. Williamson. London: Penguin, 1965.

Faber, Roland. *The Divine Manifold*. Lanham, MD: Rowman and Littlefield, 2006.

Faith and Order. *The Church: Towards a Common Vision*. Geneva: WCC, 2013.

Fancourt, *Brand New Church: The Church and the Postmodern Condition*. London: SPCK, 2013.

Farley, Edward. *Theologia: The Fragmentation and Unity of Theological Education*. Philadelphia: Fortress, 1983.

Fiddes, Paul S. *The Creative Suffering of God*. Oxford: Clarendon, 1992.

———. *The Promised End: Eschatology in Theology and Literature*. Oxford: Blackwell, 2000.

Fiorenza, Schüssler. "Thinking Theologically about Theological Education." In *Theological Perspectives on Christian Formation: A Reader on Theology and Christian Education*, edited by J. Astley, L. Francis and C. Crowder, 98–119. Grand Rapids: Eerdmans, 1996.

Flett, John G. *The Witness of God: The Trinity, Missio Dei, Karl Barth, and the Nature of Christian Community*. Grand Rapids: Eerdmans, 2010.

Ford, Michael. *Spiritual Masters for All Seasons*. Mahwah, NJ: Paulist, 2009.

Foster, Richard J. *Celebration of Discipline: The Path To Spiritual* Growth. San Francisco: HarperCollins, 1978.

———. "Salvation is for Life." In *Theology Today* 61 (2004) 297–308.

Foucault, Michel. *Power/Knowledge: Selected Interviews and Other Writings, 1972–1977*. Edited by Colin Gordon. New York: Pantheon, 1980.

Fowler, Stanley K. *More Than a Symbol: The British Baptist Recovery of Baptismal Sacramentalism*. Carlisle: Paternoster, 2002.

Franke, John R. and Stanley J. Grenz. *Beyond Foundationalism: Shaping Theology in a Postmodern Context*. Louisville, KY: Westminster John Knox, 2007.

Frick, Peter. "The Imitatio Christi of Thomas à Kempis and Dietrich Bonhoeffer." In *Bonhoeffer's Intellectual Formation: Theology and Philosophy in His Thought*, P. edited by P. Frick, 31–52. Tübingen: Mohr Siebeck, 2008.

Freeman, Charles. *The Closing of the Western Mind: The Rise of Faith and the Fall of Reason*. London: Pimlico, 2003.

Frost, Michael. *Exiles: Living Missionally in a Post-Christian Culture*. Peabody, MA: Hendrickson, 2006.

Gadamer, H. G. *Gesammelte Werke: Volume 1*. Tübingen: Mohr, 1990.

———. *Truth and Method*. Translated by J. Weinsheimer and D. G. Marshall. New York: Continuum, 2003.

———. *Wahrheit und Methode: Grundzüge einer philosophischen Hermeneutik.* Tübingen: Mohr, 1975.

Gaillardetz, R. R., and C. E. Clifford. *Keys to the Council: Unlocking the Teaching of Vatican II.* Collegeville, MN: Liturgical Press, 2012.

Gajdenko, P. P. *Vladimir Solovyev i Filosofiya Serebryanogo Veka.* Moscow: Progress, 2001.

Gasset, José Ortega. *Mission of the University.* London: Kegan, 1946.

Gay, Peter. *The Enlightenment: The Science of Freedom.* London: Norton, 1996.

Geddes, Jenny. "Protestants: Different Views on Ukraine." In *Keston Newsletter* 22 (2015) 26–30.

Gibbon, Edward. *The Decline and Fall of the Roman Empire.* Ware: Wordsworth Classics, 1998.

Girardet, Klaus M, ed. *Der Kaiser und sein Gott. Das Christentum im Denken und in der Religionspolitik Konstantins des Großen.* Berlin: de Gruyter, 2010.

Gleick, James. *Chaos: Making a New Science.* London: Vintage, 1997.

Godsey, John D. *The Theology of Dietrich Bonhoeffer.* Eugene, OR: Wipf and Stock, 2015.

Goodhew, David, ed. *Church Growth in Britain, 1980 to the Present Day.* Aldershot: Ashgate, 2012.

Gottlieb, Christian. *Dilemmas of Reaction in Leninist Russia: The Christian Response to the Revolution in the Works of N. A. Berdyaev, 1917–1924.* Odense: University Press of Southern Denmark, 2003.

Graham, Elaine. *Between and Rock and a Hard Place: Public Theology in a Post-Secular Age.* London: SCM, 2013.

Graham, Elaine, Heather Walton and Frances Ward, *Theological Reflection: Methods.* London: SCM, 2005.

Greene, Colin, and Martin Robinson. *Metavista: Bible, Church and Mission in an Age of Imagination.* Milton Keynes: Paternoster, 2008.

Green, Laurie. *Let's Do Theology: Resources for Contextual Theology.* London: Mowbray, 1990.

Grenz, Stanley J. "Conversing in Christian Style: Towards a Baptist Theological Method for the Post-Modern Context." In *Baptist History and Heritage* 35 (2000) 82–103.

Grenz, Stanley J., and John R. Franke. *Beyond Foundationalism: Shaping Theology in a Postmodern Context.* Louisville, KY: Westminster John Knox, 2001.

Grenz, Stanley J., and Roger Olson. *Who Needs Theology? An Invitation to the Study of God.* Downers Grove, IL: InterVarsity, 1996.

Grudem, Wayne. *Systematic Theology: An Introduction to Biblical Doctrine.* Grand Rapids: Zondervan, 1994.

Guder, Darrell L. "Theological Formation for Missional Faithfulness After Christendom: A Response to Steve de Gruchy." In *Handbook of Theological Education in World Christianity: Theological Perspectives, Ecumenical Trends, Regional Surveys,* edited by D. Werner et al, 51–55. Oxford: Regnum, 2010.

Guthrie Jr., Shirley C. *Christian Doctrine.* Louisville, KY: Westminster John Knox, 1994.

Gutierrez, Gustavo. *The Power of the Poor in History.* Translated by R. R. Barr. Eugene, OR: Wipf and Stock, 2004.

Habermas, Jürgen. "Secularism's Crisis of Faith: Notes on a Post-Secular Society." In *New Perspectives Quarterly* 25 (Fall 2008) 17–25.

Haile, H. G. *Luther: An Experiment in Biography.* Princeton, NJ: Princeton University Press, 1980.

Hall, Douglas John. *The End of Christendom and the Future of Christianity*. Valley Forge, PA: Trinity, 1997.

Harle, Wilfried. *Outline of Christian Doctrine: An Evangelical Dogmatics*, Translated by Nicholas Sagovsky. Grand Rapids: Eerdmans, 2015.

Hart, Trevor, *Faith Thinking: The Dynamics of Christian Theology*. London: SPCK, 1995.

Hauerwas, Stanley. *After Christendom: How the Church Is to Behave If Freedom, Justice, and a Christian Nation are Bad Ideas*. Nashville: Abingdon, 1996.

———. *The State of the University: Academic Knowledge of God*. Oxford: Blackwell, 2007.

Hauerwas, Stanley, and L. Gregory Jones, eds. *Why Narrative?: Readings in Narrative Theology*. Eugene, OR: Wipf and Stock, 1997.

Hayes, Dennis, and Robin Wynyard, eds. *The McDonaldization of Higher Education*. London: Bergin and Garvey, 2002.

Hazard, Paul. *La Crise de la Conscience Européenne, 1680–1715*. Paris: Boivin & Cie, 1935.

Heelas, Paul, and Linda Woodhead. *The Spiritual Revolution: Why Religion is Giving Way to Spirituality*. Oxford: Blackwell, 2005.

Heidegger, Martin. *Being and Time*. Translated by John Macquarrie and Edward Robinson. Oxford: Blackwell, 1962.

———. *The Essence of Human Freedom: An Introduction to Philosophy*. Translated by T. Sadler. London: Continuum, 2005.

Alfred T. Hennelly, ed. *Liberation Theology: A Documentary History*. Maryknoll, NY: Orbis, 1990.

Henry, Douglas V. and Bob R. Agee, eds. *Faithful Learning and Christian Scholarly Vocation*. Grand Rapids: Eerdmans, 2003.

Hertog, Katrien. *The Complex Reality of Religious Peacebuilding: Conceptual Contributions and Critical Analysis*. Plymouth: Lexington, 2010.

Higgins, Cathy. *Churches in Exile: Alternative Models of Church for Ireland in the 21st Century*. Dublin: Columba, 2013.

Higton, Mike. *A Theology of Higher Education*. Oxford: Oxford University Press, 2015.

Hobbes, Thomas. *Leviathan*. Mineola, NY: Dover, 2006.

Hogg, M. A., and K. D. Williams. "From I to We: Social Identity and the Collective Self." In *Group Dynamics: Theory, Research, and Practice* 4 (2000) 81–97.

Hovey, Craig. *Nietzsche and Theology*. London: T. & T. Clark, 2008.

Howard, Thomas Albert. *Protestant Theology and the Making of the Modern German University*. Oxford: Oxford University Press, 2006.

Huntington, Samuel P. *The Clash of Civilizations and the Remaking of World Order*. London: Penguin, 1996.

Hume, David. *An Enquiry concerning Human Understanding*, edited by Peter Millican. Oxford: Oxford University Press, 2007.

Hvidt, Niels Christian. *Christian Prophecy: The Post-Biblical Tradition*. Oxford: Oxford University Press, 2007.

Ingham, M. E. "John Duns Scotus: An Integrated Vision." In *The History of Franciscan Theology*, edited by Kenan B. Osborne, 185–230. St. Bonaventure: Franciscan Institute Publications, 1994.

Jones, K. G. "Eucharistic Liturgy." In *A Dictionary of European Baptist Life and Thought*, edited by J. H. Y. Briggs, et al., 175. Milton Keynes: Paternoster, 2009.

Jürgenbehring, Heinrich. *Christus für uns heute: Dietrich Bonhoeffer lesen, interpretieren, weiterdenken*. Aachen: Fischer, 2009.

Kähler, Martin. *Schriften zur Christologie und Mission*. München: Kaiser, 1971.

Kant, Immanuel. *Critique of Practical Reason*. Translated by L. W. Beck. New York: Liberal Arts Press, 1956.

Karpova, G. L. "Martin Luther and Philipp Melanchthon in Russian Pedagogical Literature." In *Luther and Melanchthon in the Educational Thought of Central and Eastern Europe*, edited by Reinhard Golz and Wolfgang Mayrhofer, 189–193. Muenster: LIT, 1997.

Kearney, Richard. *Navigations: Collected Irish Essays, 1976–2006*. Syracuse, NY: Syracuse University Press, 2006.

Keller, Catherine. *On the Mystery: Discerning Divinity in Process*. Minneapolis, MN: Fortress, 2007.

Kershaw, Ian. *Hitler 1889–1936: Hubris, Vol 1*. London: Penguin, 2001.

Kierkegaard, Søren. *Attack upon Christendom, 1854–1855*. Translated by W. Lowrie. Princeton, NJ: Princeton University Press, 1968.

———. *Concluding Unscientific Postscript*. Edited by Alastair Hannay. Cambridge: Cambridge University Press, 2009.

———. *Concluding Unscientific Postscript*. Translated by D. F. Swenson. Princeton, NJ: Princeton University Press, 1941.

———. *Kierkegaard's Journals and Papers*. Edited and translated by H. V. Hong and E. H. Hong. Bloomington: Indiana University Press, 1975.

———. *The Diary of Søren Kierkegaard*. Edited by P. P. Rohde. London: Peter Owen, 1960.

———. *The Journals of Søren Kierkegaard*. Edited by A. Dru. Oxford: Oxford University Press, 1938.

Kim, Kirsteen, and Andrew Anderson, eds. *Edinburgh 2010: Mission Today and Tomorrow*. Oxford: Regnum, 2011.

King, Edmund, "The Concept of Ideology in Communist Education," in *Communist Education*, edited by Edmund King, 1–27. London: Routledge, 2012.

King, Martin Luther, Jr. *Strength to Love*. New York: Harper and Row, 1963.

Kirkpatrick, Matthew D. *Attacks on Christendom in a World Come of Age: Kierkegaard, Bonhoeffer, and the Question of Religionless Christianity*. Eugene, OR: Pickwick Publications, 2011.

Kleffmann, Thomas. *Nietzsches Begriff des Lebens und die evangelische Theologie*. Tübingen: Mohr Siebeck, 2003.

Kreitzer, Larry. *The Gospel According to John*. Oxford: Regent's Park College, 1990.

Kuhn, Thomas S. *The Structure of Scientific Revolutions*, 50th Anniversary Edition. Chicago, IL: Chicago University Press, 2012.

Küng, Hans. *On Being a Christian*. Translated by Edward Quinn. London: Collins, 1977.

———. *My Struggle for Freedom: Memoirs*. Translated by J. Bowden. London: Continuum, 2003.

Kuxhausen, Anna. *From the Womb to the Body Politic: Raising the Nation in Enlightenment Russia*. Madison, WI: University of Wisconsin Press, 2013.

Laing, R. D. *The Divided Self: An Existential Study in Sanity and Madness*. London: Routledge, 2001.

Leinsle, Ulrich G. *Einführung in die scholastische Theologie*. Paderborn: Verlag Ferdinand Schöningh, 1995.

Leithart, Peter J. *Defending Constantine: The Twilight of an Empire and the Dawn of Christendom*. Downers Grove, IL: InterVarsity, 2010.

Lincoln, Andrew. *Spiritual History: A Reading of William Blake's Vala, or The Four Zoas*. Oxford: Clarendon, 1995.

Locke, Hubert G. *Learning from History: A Black Christian's Perspective on the Holocaust*. London: Greenwood, 2000.

Lloyd, Genevieve. *Routledge Philosophy Guidebook to Spinoza and the Ethics*. London: Routledge, 1996.

Lossky, Vladimir. *The Vision of God*. Clayton, WI: Faith, 1963.

Lowrie, D. A. *Christian Existentialism: A Berdyaev Anthology*. London: Allen and Unwin, 1965.

———. *Rebellious Prophet: A Life of Nicolai Berdyaev*. London: Gollancz, 1960.

Lowrie, Walter. *Kierkegaard*. Oxford: Oxford University Press, 1938.

Löwith, Karl. *Nietzsches Philosophie der ewigen Wiederkehr des Gleichen*. Munich: Felix Meiner, 1956.

Löwith, *Von Hegel zu Nietzsche: Der revolutionäre Bruch im Denken des 19. Jahrhunderts*. Hamburg: Felix Meiner 1995, 138.

Luther, Martin. "Disputation against Scholastic Theology." In *Martin Luther's Basic Theological Writings*, edited by Timothy F. Lull, 13–20. Minneapolis, MN: Fortress, 1989.

Lyotard, Jean-Francois. *La Condition Postmoderne: Rapport sur le Savoir*. Paris: Minuit, 1979.

Mackintosh, D. C. *Theology as an Empirical Science*. London: Macmillan, 1919.

MacIntyre, Alasdair. *After Virtue: A Study in Moral Theory*. Notre Dame: University of Notre Dame Press, 1981.

Macquarrie, John. *An Existentialist Theology*. London: SCM, 1960.

———. *In Search of Humanity: A Philosophical and Theological Approach*. London: SCM, 1982.

Manganiello, Dominic. *Joyce's Politics*. London: Routledge, 2016.

Mann, Thomas. *The Magic Mountain*. Translated by H. T. Lowe-Porter. London: Vintage, 1999.

Marsden, George. *Understanding Fundamentalism and Evangelicalism*. Grand Rapids: Eerdmans, 1991.

Marx, Karl. *Capital: A Critique of Political Economy: Volume 1*. Translated by B. Fowkes. London: Penguin, 2004.

———. *Theses on Feuerbach*. London: Lawrence and Wishart, 1970.

Marx, Karl, and Friedrich Engels. *Manifest der Kommunistischen Partei: Grundsätze des Kommunismus*. Stuttgart: Phillip Reclam, 1999.

Mayes, Andrew. *Spirituality in Ministerial Formation: The Dynamic of Prayer in Learning*. Cardiff: University of Wales Press, 2009.

McClendon, James Wm., Jr. *Biography as Theology: How Life Stories Can Remake Today's Theology*. Eugene, OR: Wipf and Stock, 2002.

———. *Systematic Theology: Volume One: Ethics*. Nashville: Abingdon, 2002.

———. *Systematic Theology: Volume Two: Doctrine*. Nashville: Abingdon, 1994.

———. *Systematic Theology: Volume Three: Witness*. Nashville: Abingdon, 2002.

McClendon, James Wm., Jr., and James M. Smith, *Convictions: Defusing Religious Relativism*. Eugene, OR: Wipf and Stock, 2002.

McGrath, Alister E. *The Future of Christianity*. Oxford: Blackwell, 2002.

———. *Christianity: An Introduction*. Oxford: Blackwell, 2006.

McGuckin, J. A. "The Trinity in the Greek Fathers." In *The Cambridge Companion to the Trinity*, edited by Peter C. Phan, 50–69. Cambridge: Cambridge University Press, 2001.

McKnight, Scot, and Joseph B. Modica. *Jesus Is Lord, Caesar Is Not: Evaluating Empire in New Testament Studies*. Downers Grove, IL: InterVarsity, 2013.

McLaren, Brian D. *The Secret Message of Jesus: Uncovering the Truth that Could Change Everything*. Nashville: Nelson, 2006.

———. *A Generous Orthodoxy*. Grand Rapids: Zondervan, 2004.

———. *A New Kind of Christianity*. London: Hodder and Stoughton, 2011.

McLean, Monica. *Pedagogy and the University: Critical Theory and Practice*. London: Continuum, 2006.

McLeod, Hugh. *The Religious Crisis of the 1960s*. Oxford: Oxford University Press, 2007.

Mendieta, E., and J. Vanantwerpen, eds. *The Power of Religion in the Public Sphere*. New York: Columbia University Press, 2011.

Metaxas, Eric. *Bonhoeffer: Pastor, Martyr, Prophet, Spy*. Nashville: Thomas Nelson, 2010.

Milbank, John, Catherine Pickstock, and Graham Ward, ed. *Radical Orthodoxy: A New Theology*. London: Routledge, 1999.

Middleton, Richard J., Brian J. Walsh. *Truth Is Stranger Than It Used to Be: Biblical Faith in a Postmodern Age*. Downers Grove, IL: InterVarsity, 1995.

Migliore, Daniel L. *Faith Seeking Understanding: An Introduction to Christian Theology*. Grand Rapids: Eerdmans, 2004.

Miller, Trevor. *Heretical Imperative*. Hetton Hall, UK: Cloisters, 2003.

Min, Kyongsuk. *The Solidarity of Others in a Divided World: A Postmodern Theology after Postmodernism*. London: T. & T. Clark, 2004.

Moltmann, Jürgen. *God in Creation: An Ecological Doctrine of Creation*. Translated by M. Kohl. London: SCM, 1985.

———. *God in Creation: An Ecological Doctrine of Creation*. London: SCM, 2005.

———. *The Crucified God*. Translated by R. A. Wilson and J. Bowden. London: SCM, 1974.

———. *Theologie der Hoffnung*. München: Kaiser, 1964.

Moon, Gary W. *Eternal Living: Reflections on Dallas Willard's Teaching on Faith and Formation*. Downers Grove, IL: InterVarsity, 2015.

Moreland, J. P., and W. L. Craig. *Philosophical Foundations for a Christian Worldview*. Downers Grove, IL: InterVarsity, 2003.

Morgan, David. *Protestants and Pictures: Religion, Visual Culture, and the Age of American Mass Production*. New York: Oxford University Press, 1999.

Muers, Rachel. *Keeping God's Silence: Towards a Theological Ethics of Communication*. Oxford: Blackwell, 2004.

Murphy, Nancey C. *Beyond Liberalism and Fundamentalism: How Modern and Postmodern Philosophy Set the Theological Agenda*. New York: Continuum, 1996.

———. *Theology in the Age of Scientific Reasoning*. Ithaca, NY: Cornell University Press, 1990.

Murray, Stuart. *A Vast Minority: Church and Mission in a Plural Culture*. Milton Keynes: Paternoster, 2015.

———. *Church After Christendom*. Carlisle: Authentic, 2005.

———. *Post-Christendom: Church and Mission in a Strange New World*. Milton Keynes: Paternoster, 2004.

Newbigin, Lesslie. *The Gospel in a Pluralist Society.* Grand Rapids: Eerdmans, 1989.

———. *Truth to Tell: The Gospel as Public Truth.* Grand Rapids: Eerdmans, 1991.

Nicolaus, Georg. *C. G. Jung and Nikolai Berdyaev, Individuation and the Person: A Critical Comparison.* London: Routledge, 2011.

Nichols, Aidan. *The Shape of Catholic Theology.* Edinburgh: T. & T. Clark, 1991.

Nicholson, Ernest, ed. *A Century of Theological and Religious Studies in Britain.* Oxford: Oxford University Press, 2003.

Nietzsche, Friedrich. *Also Sprach Zarathustra: Ein Buch Für Alle Und Keinen,* 1883–1885. Berlin: de Gruyter, 1968.

———. *Thus Spake Zarathustra: A Book for All and None.* Translated by T. Common. Mineola, NY: Dover, 1999.

———. Nietzsche, Friedrich. *Thus Spoke Zarathustra: A Book for All and None.* Translated by R. Pippin. Cambridge University Press, 2006.

———. *On the Genealogy of Morals: A Polemic.* Translated by Douglas Smith. Oxford: Oxford University Press, 1996.

———. *The Birth of Tragedy Out of the Spirit of Music.* Translated by S. Whiteside. London: Penguin, 2004.

Noll, Mark A. *The Scandal of the Evangelical Mind.* Grand Rapids: Eerdmans, 1994.

Northumbria Community. *Celtic Daily Prayer: Prayers and Readings from the Northumbria Community.* San Francisco: HarperOne, 2002.

———. *Way for Living.* Hetton Hall, UK: Cloisters, 2002.

Nynas, Peter, Mika Lassander and Terhi Utriainen, eds. *Post-Secular Society.* New Brunswick: Transaction, 2015.

O'Donohue, John. *Anam Cara: A Book of Celtic Wisdom.* New York: HarperCollins,1997.

———. *Anam Cara: Spiritual Wisdom from the Celtic World.* London: Bantam, 1997.

———. *Eternal Echoes: Exploring our Hunger to Belong.* London: Bantam, 2000.

O'Farrell, Clare. *Michel Foucault.* London: Sage, 2005.

O'Hagan, Timothy. *Rousseau.* London: Routledge, 1999.

Ojara, Pius. *Tragic Humanity and Hope: Understanding Our Struggle to be Scientific, Sapiential and Moral.* Eugene, OR: Wipf and Stock, 2007.

Olafson, Frederick A. *Heidegger and the Ground of Ethics: A Study of Mitsein.* Cambridge: Cambridge University Press, 1998.

Oliver-Dee, Sean. *God's Unwelcome Recovery: Why the New Establishment Wants to Proclaim the Death of Faith.* Oxford: Monarch, 2015.

Olson, Mancur. *The Rise and Decline of Nations: Economic Growth, Stagflation, and Social Rigidities.* New Haven: Yale University Press, 1984.

Oman, John. *Grace and Personality.* Cambridge: Cambridge University Press, 1917.

Orenstein, A. *W. V. O. Quine.* Princeton, NJ: Princeton University Press, 2002.

Oster, Stefan. "The Other and the Fruitfulness of Personal Acting." In *Love Alone Is Credible: Hans Urs von Balthasar as Interpreter of the Catholic Tradition,* edited by David L. Schindler, 303–17. Grand Rapids: Eerdmans, 2008.

Paeth, S. R., et al., eds. *Shaping Public Theology: Selections from the Writings of Max L. Stackhouse.* Grand Rapids: Eerdmans, 2014.

Pagden, Anthony. *The Enlightenment: And Why It Still Matters.* Oxford: Oxford University Press, 2013.

Palmer, Parker J. "Toward a Spirituality of Higher Education." In *Faithful Learning and the Christian Scholarly Vocation,* edited by D. V. Henry and Bob R. Agee, 75–84. Grand Rapids: Eerdmans, 2003.

Pascal, Blaise. *Pensées*. Paris: Hachette, 1904.

Pietersen, Lloyd. *Reading the Bible After Christendom*. Milton Keynes: Paternoster, 2011.

Placher, William C. *Essentials of Christian Theology*. Louisville, KY: Westminster John Knox, 2003.

Plato, *The Symposium*. Edited by M.C. Howatson and F. C. C. Sheffield. Cambridge: Cambridge University Press, 2008.

Plato. *Six Great Dialogues: Apology, Crito, Phaedo, Phaedrus, Symposium*. Translated by B. Jowett. Mineola, NY: Dover, 2007.

Polanyi, Michael. *Personal Knowledge Towards a Post-Critical Philosophy*. London: Routledge and Kegan, 1958.

Pope, Stephen J. "On Not Abandoning the Historical World to its Wretchedness: A Prophetic Voice Serving an Incarnational Vision." In *Hope and Solidarity: Jon Sobrino's Challenge to Christian Theology*, edited by Pope, 44–62. Maryknoll, NY: Orbis, 2008.

Pugh, Jeffrey C. *Religionless Christianity: Dietrich Bonhoeffer in Troubled Times*. London: Bloomsbury, 2008.

Quine, Willard Van Orman, and J. S. Ullian. *The Web of Belief*. New York: Random House, 1978.

Rae, Murray A. "Learning the Truth in a Christian University: Advice from Søren Kierkegaard." In *The Idea of a Christian University: Essays on Theology and Higher Education*, edited by J. Astley, et al., 98–112. Milton Keynes: Paternoster, 2004.

Rah, Soong-Chan. *Prophetic Lament: A Call for Justice in Troubled Times*. Downers Grove, IL: InterVarsity, 2015.

Rasmussen, Larry L. *Dietrich Bonhoeffer: Reality and Resistance*. Louisville, KY: Westminster John Knox, 2005.

———. "The Ethics of Responsible Action." In *The Cambridge Companion to Dietrich Bonhoeffer*, edited by John W. de Gruchy, 206–225. Cambridge: Cambridge University Press, 1999.

Reiss, H. S. *Kant: Political Writings*. Cambridge: Cambridge University Press, 2003.

Ritzer, George. *The McDonaldization of Society: 20th Anniversary Edition*. London: Sage, 2013.

Robinson, Martin. *The Faith of the Unbeliever*. Crowborough: Monarch Publications, 1994.

Rollins, Peter. *How (Not) to Speak of God: Marks of the Emerging Church*. London: SPCK, 2006.

———. *Insurrection: To Believe Is Human, To Doubt, Divine*. New York: Howard, 2011.

———. *The Divine Magician: The Disappearance of Religion and the Discovery of Faith*. New York: Howard, 2015.

———. *The Fidelity of Betrayal: Towards a Church Beyond Belief*. London: SPCK, 2008.

Roth, John D., ed. *Constantine Revisited: Leithart, Yoder and the Constantinian Debate*. Eugene, OR: Pickwick, 2013.

Rousseau, J. J. *Emile, or On Education*. Mineola, NY: Dover, 2013.

Rowan, Stephen C. *Nicene Creed: Poetic Words for a Prosaic World*. Mystic, CN: Twenty-Third Publications, 1991.

Rowland, Christopher. *The Open Heaven: A Study of Apocalyptic in Judaism and Early Christianity*. New York: Crossroad, 1982.

Rozanov, Vasily. *Dostoevsky and the Legend of the Grand Inquisitor*. Translated by S. Roberts. Ithaca, NY: Cornell University Press, 1972.

Sartre, Jean-Paul. *Being and Nothingness: An Essay on Philosophical Ontology*. Translated by H. Barnes. New York: Philosophical Library, 1956.

Schacht, Richard. *Classical Modern Philosophers: Descartes to Kant*. London: Routledge, 1994.

Scheler, Max. *Zur Phänomenologie und Theorie der Sympathiegefühle und von Liebe und Hass*. Halle: Niemeyer, 1913.

Schleiermacher, Friedrich, Über die Religion: Reden an die Gebildeten unter ihren Verächter. Berlin, 1799.

Schleiermacher, Friedrich. *The Christian Faith*. Edited by H. R. Mackintosh and J. S. Stewart. New York: Harper and Row, 1963.

Schweitzer, Albert. "The Philosophy of Civilization." In *Reverence for Life: The Ethics of Albert Schweitzer for the Twenty-first Century*, edited by Marvin W. Meyer, Kurt Bergel, 70–90. Syracuse, NY: Syracuse University Press, 2002.

Scolnicov, Samuel. *Plato's Metaphysics of Education*. Abingdon: Routledge, 2013.

Searle, John R. *Making the Social World: The Structure of Human Civilization*. Oxford: Oxford University Press, 2010.

Searle, Joshua T. *Church Without Walls: Post-Soviet Baptists after the Ukrainian Revolution*. Oxford: Whitley, 2016.

———. *The Scarlet Woman and the Red Hand: Apocalyptic Belief in the Northern Ireland Troubles*. Eugene, OR: Pickwick, 2014.

———. "From Christian Worldview to Kingdom Formation: Theological Education as Mission in the Former Soviet Union." In *European Journal of Theology* 23 (Autumn, 2014) 104–15.

———. "Ideology, Convictions and Eschatology: Towards a Theological Critique of Ideology from an Eschatological Perspective." *Baptistic Theologies* 3 (Spring, 2011) 99–115.

———. "The Future of Millennial Studies and the Hermeneutics of Hope: A Theological Reflection." In *Beyond the End: The Future of Millennial Studies; Bible in the Modern World Series*, edited by Joshua T. Searle and Kenneth G. C. Newport, 131–147. Sheffield: Sheffield Phoenix, 2012.

Searle, Joshua T. and Mykhailo N. Cherenkov. *A Future and a Hope: Mission, Theological Education and the Transformation of Post-Soviet Society*. Eugene, OR: Wipf and Stock, 2015.

Searle, Joshua, and Roy Searle, "Monastic Practices and the Missio Dei: Towards a Socially-Transformative Understanding of Missional Practice from the Perspective of the Northumbria Community." In *Journal of Missional Practice*. Online journal (Autumn 2013) http://journalofmissionalpractice.com/monastic-practices-and-the-missio-dei-towards-a-socially-transformative-understanding-of-missional-practice-from-the-perspective-of-the-northumbria-community.

Seaver, George. *Nicolas Berdyaev: An Introduction to His Thought*. London: J. Clarke, 1950.

Shaw, Perry. *Transforming Theological Education: A Practical Handbook for Integrative Learning*. Carlisle: Langham, 2014.

Sherl, Gregory. *The Future for Curious People*. London: Pan, 2014.

Shillington, George V. "Engaging with the Parables." In *Jesus and his Parables: Interpreting the Parables of Jesus Today*, edited by V. George Shillington, 1–20. Edinburgh: T. & T. Clark, 1999.

Short, Edward. *Newman and His Contemporaries*. London: T. & T. Clark, 2011.

Siller, A., *Kirche für die Welt: Karl Barths Lehre vom prophetischen Amt Jesu Christi*. Zurich: TVZ, 2009.

Simonson, Harold Peter. *Radical Discontinuities: American Romanticism and Christian Consciousness*. London: Associated University Presses, 1983.

Smith, James K. A. *Desiring the Kingdom: Worship, Worldview, and Cultural Formation*. Grand Rapids: Baker, 2009.

———. *Imagining the Kingdom: How Worship Works*. Grand Rapids: Baker, 2013.

———. *Who's Afraid of Postmodernism? Taking Derrida, Lyotard, and Foucault to Church*. Grand Rapids: Baker, 2006.

Snoek, J. C. *Medieval Piety from Relics to the Eucharist: A Process of Mutual Interaction*. New York: Brill, 1995.

Snyder, Howard A., and Joel Scandrett, *Salvation Means Creation Healed: The Ecology of Sin and Grace: Overcoming the Divorce between Earth and Heaven*. Eugene, OR: Cascade, 2011.

Sobrino, Jon. *The Principle of Mercy: Taking the Crucified People from the Cross*. Maryknoll, NY: Orbis, 2015.

———. *Witnesses to the Kingdom: The Martyrs of El Salvador and the Crucified Peoples*. Maryknoll, NY: Orbis, 2003.

Sölle, Dorothee. *Thinking About God: An Introduction to Theology*. Translated by J. Bowden. London: SCM, 1990.

Solovyev, Vladimir. *Chteniya o Bogochelovechestve*. St. Petersburg: Azbuka, 2000.

Solzhenitsyn, A. I. *The Gulag Archipelago: An Experiment in Literary Investigation*. Translated by Thomas P. Whitney. San Francisco: Harper and Row, 1975.

Spicer, Kevin P. *Antisemitism, Christian Ambivalence, and the Holocaust*. Bloomington: Indiana University Press, 2007.

Stackhouse, John G. *Making the Best of It: Following Christ in the Real World*. Oxford: Oxford University Press, 2008.

Stamoolis, J. J. *Eastern Orthodox Mission Theology Today*. Eugene, OR: Wipf and Stock, 2001.

Stassen, Glen H. and David P. Gushee. *Kingdom Ethics: Following Jesus in Contemporary Context*. Downers Grove, IL: InterVarsity, 2003.

Stead, Christopher. *Philosophy in Christian Antiquity*. Cambridge: Cambridge University Press, 1994.

Steiner, George. *Grammars of Creation*. London: Faber and Faber, 2001.

Stern, Robert. *Kantian Ethics: Value, Agency, and Obligation*. Oxford: Oxford University Press, 2015.

Storkey, Alan. "Post-Modernism Is Consumption." In *Christ and Consumerism: Critical Reflections on the Spirit of Our Age*, edited by Craig G. Bartholomew and Thorsten Moritz, 100–17. Carlisle: Paternoster, 2000.

Stott, John R. W. *Issues Facing Christians Today*, 4th edition. Grand Rapids: Zondervan, 2006.

Stratton, S. Brian. *Coherence, Consonance, and Conversation: The Quest of Theology, Philosophy, and Natural Science for a Unified Worldview*. Lanham: University Press of America, 2000.

Suchodolski, Bogdan. *Grundlagen der Marxistischen Erziehungstheorie.* Warsaw: Deutscher Verlag der Wissenschaften, 1961.

Sullivan, John. "Reading Habits, Scripture and the University." In *The Bible and the University,* edited by David Lyle Jeffrey and C. Stephen Evans, 216–39. Milton Keynes: Paternoster, 2007.

Sunshine, Glenn. "Protestant Missions in the Sixteenth Century." In *The Great Commission: Evangelicals and the History of World Missions,* edited by Martin Klauber and Scott Manetsch, 12–22. Nashville: Broadman & Holman, 2008.

Sutherland, Stewart, "Philosophy of Religion in the Twentieth Century." In *A Century of Theological and Religious Studies in Britain,* edited by Ernest Nicholson, 253–70. Oxford: Oxford University Press, 2003.

Sweet, *Post-Modern Pilgrims: First Century Passion for the 21st Century* World. Nashville: B & H, 2000.

Taylor, Charles. *A Secular Age.* Cambridge: Harvard University Press, 2007.

Tennent, Timothy C. *Invitation to World Missions: A Trinitarian Missiology for the Twenty-First Century.* Grand Rapids: Kregel, 2010.

Tilley, Terrence W. *Postmodern Theologies: The Challenge of Religious Diversity.* Maryknoll, NY: Orbis, 1995.

Tillich, Paul. *A History of Christian Thought, from Its Judaic and Hellenistic Origins to Existentialism.* New York: Simon and Schuster, 1968.

———. *Systematic Theology Volume 1.* London: Nisbet, 1963.

———. *The Courage to Be.* Third Edition. New Haven, CT: Yale University Press, 2014.

———. *Theology of Culture.* Oxford: Oxford University Press, 1964.

Thiselton, Anthony C. *The Hermeneutics of Doctrine.* Grand Rapids: Eerdmans, 2007.

Thoreau, Henry D. *The Essays of Henry David Thoreau.* Albany, NY: Whitston, 1990.

Tongeren, Paul van. "Measure and Bildung." In *Nietzsche, Culture and Education,* edited by Thomas E. Hart, 97–112. Farnham: Ashgate, 2009.

Toulmin, Stephen. *Cosmopolis: The Hidden Agenda of Modernity.* New York: Free Press, 1990.

Tozer, A. W. *Evenings with Tozer: Daily Devotional Readings.* Edited by G. B. Smith. Chicago: Moody, 2015.

———. *Man the Dwelling Place of God: What it Means to Have Christ Living in You.* London: Kingsway, 1966.

———. *Voice of a Prophet: Who Speaks for God?* Edited by J. L. Snyder. Minneapolis, MN: Bethany House, 2014.

Tracy, David. *The Analogical Imagination: Christian Theology and the Culture of Pluralism.* London: SCM, 1981.

Vanhoozer, Kevin J. *The Drama of Doctrine: A Canonical-Linguistic Approach to Christian Theology.* Louisville, KY: Westminster John Knox, 2005.

Valiente, O. Ernesto. *Liberation Through Reconciliation: Jon Sobrino's Christological Spirituality.* New York: Fordham, 2016.

Volf, Miroslav. *Exclusion & Embrace: A Theological Exploration of Identity, Otherness, and Reconciliation.* Nashville: Abingdon, 1996.

Von Felden, Heide. *Bildung und Geschlecht zwischen Moderne und Postmoderne: Zur Verknüpfung von Bildungs-, Biographie- und Genderforschung.* Opladen: Lesker and Budrich, 2003.

Wake, Peter. *Tragedy in Hegel's Early Theological Writings.* Bloomington: Indiana University Press, 2014.

Walton, Roger. *The Reflective Disciple: Learning to Live as Faithful Followers of Jesus in the Twenty First Century*. London: Epworth, 2009.

Ward, Graham. *Barth, Derrida and the Language of Theology*. Cambridge: Cambridge University Press, 1995.

Ware, Kallistos. *The Orthodox Way*. Crestwood, NY: St Vladimir's Seminary Press, 1979.

Weaver, Denny. *The Nonviolent God*. Grand Rapids: Eerdmans, 2013.

Weber, Max. *Die protestantische Ethik und der Geist des Kapitalismus*. Mohr: Tübingen, 1934.

Whitehead, Alfred North. *Modes of Thought*. New York: Free Press, 1966.

———. *Process and Reality*. New York: Free Press, 1978.

Willard, Dallas. *The Spirit of the Disciplines: Understanding How God Changes Lives*. London: Hodder and Stoughton, 1996.

———. *The Divine Conspiracy: Rediscovering our Hidden Life in God*. London: HarperCollins, 1998.

———. "Living A Transformed Life Adequate To Our Calling." Online article (2005) www.dwillard.org/articles/artview.asp?artID=119.

———. "The Bible, the University and the God who Hides." In *The Bible and the University* edited by David Lyle Jeffrey and C. Stephen Evans, 17–39. Milton Keynes: Paternoster, 2007.

———. *Living in Christ's Presence: Final Words on Heaven and the Kingdom of God*. Downers Grove, IL: InterVarsity, 2014.

———. *The Allure of Gentleness: Defending the Faith in the Manner of Jesus*. San Francisco: HarperOne, 2015.

Willard, Dallas, and Don Simpson. *Revolution of Character: Discovering Christ's Pattern for Spiritual Transformation*. Nottingham: InterVarsity, 2006.

Williams, Reggie L. *Bonhoeffer's Black Jesus: Harlem Renaissance Theology and an Ethic of Resistance*. Waco, TX: Baylor University Press, 2014.

Williams, Rowan. "Theology in the Twentieth Century." In *A Century of Theological and Religious Studies in Britain*, edited by Ernest Nicholson, 237–52. Oxford: Oxford University Press, 2003.

Wink, Walter. *Engaging the Powers: Discernment and Resistance in a World of Domination*. Minneapolis, MN: Fortress, 1992.

———. *Naming the Powers: The Language of Power in the New Testament*. Minneapolis, MN: Fortress, 1984.

———. *Unmasking the Powers: The Invisible Forces that Determine Human Existence*. Minneapolis, MN: Fortress, 1986.

Wilhoit, James C. *Spiritual Formation as if the Church Mattered Growing in Christ through Community*. Grand Rapids: Baker Academic, 2008.

Witte, John, and Frank S. Alexander, eds. *The Teachings of Modern Orthodox Christianity on Law, Politics, and Human Nature*. New York: Columbia University Press, 2007.

Wittgenstein, Ludwig. *Philosophical Investigations*. Edited and translated by G. E. M. Anscombe. Oxford: Blackwell, 2001.

Wright, Christopher J. H. *The Message of Jeremiah*. Downers Grove, IL: InterVarsity, 2014.

———. *The Mission of God: Unlocking the Bible's Grand Narrative*. Nottingham: InterVarsity, 2006.

Wright, Nigel G. *Disavowing Constantine: Mission, Church and the Social Order in the Theologies of Yoder and Moltmann*. Carlisle: Authentic, 2002.

———. *Free Church, Free State: The Positive Baptist Vision.* Milton Keynes: Paternoster, 2005.

Wright, N. T. *Scripture and the Authority of God.* London: SPCK, 2005.

———. *Simply Christian: Why Christianity Makes Sense.* San Francisco: HarperCollins, 2009.

———. *Simply Good News: Why the Gospel is News and What Makes it Good.* London: SPCK, 2015.

Yelyutin, Vyacheslav. *Higher Education in the USSR.* London: Soviet Press, 1959.

Yoder, John Howard. "The Constantinian Sources of Western Social Ethics." In *The Priestly Kingdom: Social Ethics as Gospel,* by John Howard Yoder, 135–45. Notre Dame: University of Notre Dame Press, 1984.

Žižek, Slavoj. *First as Tragedy, Then as Farce.* London: Verso, 2009.

———. *Less Than Nothing: Hegel and the Shadow of Dialectical Materialism.* London: Verso, 2012.

———. *Living in the End Times.* London: Verso, 2012.

Primary Sources from the Northumbria Community Archive (NCA)

Miller, Trevor. "Easter Workshop 2005," Caim 32 (Spring, 2005), 3.

———. "Editorial." Caim 9 (Spring, 1999), 2.

———. "Notes for an Official History of the Northumbria Community." NCA, 1994.

———. "Some Metaphors Used in Our History." NCA, 2002.

Searle, Roy. "Address at Holy Trinity Church Conference, Hothorpe Hall," September 2001 (audiotape). NCA, 2001.

———. "Covenanted together within the love of Christ," Caim 14 (Autumn, 2000), 5.

———. "Exploring a Way for Living." NCA, 1999.

———. "Jottings From A Ferry Over to Ireland," Caim 29 (Summer, 2004), 2.

———. "Musings from the Garden," Caim 10 (Summer, 1999), 4.

———. "Northumbria Ministries Charter." NCA, 1989.

———. "Northumbria Community Prayer Guide." NCA, 1994.

———. Untitled Document. NCA,1994.

Searle, Roy and Miller, Trevor. *Northumbria Community Newsletter* (September 1998). NCA, 1998.

Searle, Roy, and Skinner, John. "Rediscovering the Johannine Tradition for a Postmodern Age." NCA, 1997.

———. "Application to the London Bible House Research Fund." NCA, 1997.

Skinner, John. "The Post Christian Era and the Birth of a New Age." NCA, 1994.

Lightning Source UK Ltd.
Milton Keynes UK
UKOW01f0017280218
318608UK00001B/73/P